Improving the Quality
of Schooling

Education Policy Perspectives

General Editor: Professor Ivor Goodson, Faculty of Education
University of Western Ontario, London,
Canada N6G 1G7

Education policy analysis has long been a neglected area in the United Kingdom and to an extent in the USA and Australia. The result has been a profound gap between the study of education and the formulation of education policy. For practitioners such a lack of analysis of the new policy initiatives has worrying implications particularly at such a time of policy flux and change. Education policy has, in recent years, been a matter of intense political debate — the political and public interest in the working of the system has come at the same time as the consensus on educational policy has been broken by the advent of the 'New Right'. As never before the political parties and pressure groups differ in their articulated policies and prescriptions for the education sector. Critical thinking about these developments is clearly necessary.

All those working within the system also need information on policy making, policy implementation and effective day-to-day operation. Pressures on schools from government, education authorities and parents have generated an enormous need for knowledge amongst those on the receiving end of educational policies.

This series aims to fill the academic gap, to reflect the politicalization of education, and to provide practitioners with the analysis for informed implementation of policies that they need. It will offer studies in broad areas of policy studies. Besides the general section it will offer a particular focus in the following areas: School organization and improvement (David Reynolds, *University College, Cardiff, UK*); Critical social analysis (Professor Philip Wexler, *University of Rochester, USA*); Policy studies and evaluation (Professor Ernest House, *University of Colorado-Boulder, USA*); and Education and training (Dr Peter Cuttance, *University of Edinburgh, UK*).

Improving the Quality of Schooling

Lessons from the OECD International School Improvement Project

Edited by
David Hopkins

The Falmer Press

(A member of the Taylor & Francis Group)
London, New York and Philadelphia

UK The Falmer Press, Falmer House, Barcombe, Lewes, East Sussex, BN8 5DL

USA The Falmer Press, Taylor & Francis Inc., 242 Cherry Street, Philadelphia, PA 19106-1906

First published 1987

Library of Congress Cataloging in Publication Data

Improving the quality of schooling.

(Education policy perspectives)
Based on a conference held at Nene College, Northampton, in April 1986, organized by the United Kingdom ISIP Steering Group.
"Publications from the International School Improvement Project": p.
Bibliography: p.
Includes Index.
1. School improvement programs—Congresses. 2. OECD International School Improvement Project—Congresses.
3. Comparative education—Congresses. I. Hopkins, David.
II. OECD International School Improvement Project.
III. United Kingdom ISIP Steering Group. IV. Series.
LB2822.8.149 1987 379.1'54 87-13419
ISBN 1-85000-190-1
ISBN 1-85000-191-X (pbk.)

Jacket design by Caroline Archer

Typeset in 10/12 Bembo by
Imago Publishing Ltd, Thame, Oxon

Printed in Great Britain by Taylor & Francis (Printers) Ltd, Basingstoke

Contents

Preface and Acknowledgements

The Organization for Economic Cooperation and Development (OECD) through its Centre for Educational Research and Innovation (CERI) has, since 1982, been sponsoring an International School Improvement Project (ISIP). ISIP is a decentralized project which involves some 150 people from fourteen countries. The project is divided into five areas that represent the major aspects of school improvement: school-based review; the role of school leaders; external support; research and evaluation; and policy development and implementation. Each area is composed of a working group which has an international membership and is concerned to examine current provision and to develop strategies for school improvement policy and practice.

In April 1986, the United Kingdom ISIP Steering Group, convinced of the importance of this work, organized a conference on 'Improving the Quality of Schooling: The Lessons of the International School Improvement Project', which was held at Nene College, Northampton. This book has evolved out of the presentations and discussion at that conference. Although the conference (and indeed this book) was billed as pertaining to the United Kingdom, strictly speaking much of the discussion relates to schooling in England and Wales. Having said this, the principles discussed — if not the detail — apply equally to schools throughout the United Kingdom and, of course, elsewhere.

I am most grateful to the members of the UK Steering Group, in particular, Michael Henley (Chairperson), Ray Bolam, Phil Clift, Ron Glatter and Keith McWilliams, for the opportunity to edit this book and for the support they have given me in so doing. I also wish to thank a number of others who have helped me with this task. My colleague, Peter Holly, took on the role of conference rapporteur and produced a synthesis of the conference discussions. Cyrilyn Fletcher, also a colleague at Cambridge, has typed the various drafts of the manuscript with the skill that characterizes all of her work. My sister, Mary Schofield, helped with proof reading and saved me (and others) from a number of infelicities in style. Pierre Laderriere of the OECD/CERI, Robert Bollen of the ISIP Foundation, Malcolm Clarkson of

Falmer Press, and Ros Micklem of Northamptonshire LEA, all provided valuable assistance at various stages during the production of the book. And *ad hoc* group of ISIP experts, including all those who contributed to the book, took time at the final ISIP meeting in Toronto to comment thoughtfully and constructively on the penultimate draft. It was Marloes Hopkins de Groot though, who once again provided the shelter conditions under which the manuscript was produced, with a minimum of tension and the maximum of support.

Finally, I must also acknowledge the OECD and ACCO (the ISIP publishers) for permission to reproduce material that was originally commissioned or copyrighted by them. It goes without saying that the views expressed here are individual opinions: they do not commit my colleagues, the OECD or any national authority. Nor do they commit myself, although as editor I accept responsibility for the form, if not the content, of what follows.

David Hopkins
March, 1987
Cambridge

Foreword: School Improvement in a Broader Context

George Papadopoulos

The educational programme of OECD, within which ISIP has been located, endeavours to respond to two major preoccupations that are common to the western industrialized democracies which contribute to the OECD membership:

(i) What role can education play in facilitating the process of structural adaptation, in all its social and economic facets, which OECD countries are currently undergoing?

(ii) How can the quality of education, particularly basic education, be sustained and reinforced as the essential prerequisite for the development of a flexible and dynamic population capable of confronting the uncertainties which the future holds for our societies?

School improvement remains crucial to both of these challenges. This has always been so, but the context within which it arises has changed. In the past, when educational systems were growing and public resources were more easily available to maintain this growth, the impetus for change came largely from above. Grass root initiatives, backed by political commitment at the top, found their proper place in a more generalized educational reform movement, and in a search for consensus about objectives and direction for change.

Under the changed circumstances which prevail today, particularly limitations in the availability of public resources and sharpened conflicts about priorities, the locus of reform initiatives has become more diversified, with the schools themselves (together with their support structures and institutions) taking a leading role in the search for the means to maintain their vitality. One consequence of this has been a realignment of educational reform partnerships and the forging of new alliances, both within individual national contexts and at the international level. These alliances have been designed to release local creativity, tap new resources within the school and the community, and pool efforts to facilitate the development of new strategies for improving the quality of schooling.

It is against this background that the OECD International School Improvement Project (ISIP) has been conceived and implemented. The present volume provides the evidence on which the validity of its approach and the applicability of its results in a given national situation can be sustained.

1   Improving the Quality of Schooling

David Hopkins

Introduction

School improvement and quality of education are terms that have, as yet, not been assimilated into the common parlance of education in the United Kingdom. So a book which is not only devoted to discussing these ideas but is also intended to be read by school people needs some justification, and the terms some explanation. This introductory chapter therefore provides a guide to what follows. Various terms such as 'school improvement' and 'quality of schooling' are first defined and some ways in which they apply to schooling in this country discussed. A brief overview of the International School Improvement Project (ISIP) and the UK dissemination conference from which the book emanated is then given. Because of the complexity of the topic and the difficulties of translating the dynamics of a conference into such a static medium, the book is designed to be 'user friendly' and some advice is given on how best to use it. Finally the substance of the book — the presentations made at the conference — is briefly reviewed.

School Improvement[1]

School improvement is defined in ISIP as (van Velzen *et al*, 1985, p48):

> a systematic, sustained effort aimed at change in learning conditions and other related internal conditions in one or more schools, with the ultimate aim of accomplishing educational goals more effectively.

This definition is rather abstract and needs some explanation.

Much practical and research experience in the past decade has supported three main conclusions. First, achieving change is much more a matter of implementation of new practices at the school level than it is of simply deciding to adopt them. Second, school improvement is a carefully planned and managed process that takes place over a period of several years: change is a process, not an event. Third, it is very difficult to change education — even in a single classroom — without also changing the school organization; the cooperation of fellow teachers and the endorsement of the school leader are usually necessary too. These perspectives are pertinent to the following elaboration of the definition.

School improvement is more than just classroom change; it also presupposes attention to other 'related internal conditions' such as the curriculum, the school organizational structure, local policy, school climate, relations with parents and so on. If change is only aimed at the improvement of 'learning conditions' (*ie* the immediate activities students experience) in a particular classroom, it is not included in the definition nor is the isolated training of individual teachers. But when a school pays attention to the conditions necessary for improvement on both classroom and institutional levels, that is school improvement according to the definition. Thus, without ignoring the classroom there must be a 'classroom exceeding' perspective.

The phrase 'one or more schools' also points to the fact that many schools can in principle be involved; be it in a district, a LEA or even nationally. But even in large scale efforts, attention must always be paid to each school as a working organization. The definition does not prejudge where the initiation of the effort is located: it may have been started by the school itself; by the inspectorate; by the educational authorities (local or national); by support system persons or groups — or by any combination of these.

Change simply means any alteration of 'learning conditions', or 'related internal conditions' in the school. 'Learning conditions' refer to organized activities of the school, directed by teachers or others, aimed at accomplishing educational goals. 'Related internal conditions' refers to all aspects of the school that are connected in any way with learning conditions and to intended achievement of pupil goals. These conditions are inevitably related to learning conditions, some very closely (for example, curriculum materials), others more distantly (for example, staff recruitment) but they are not the same thing as the actual learning conditions — the immediate activities that students experience.

Generally speaking, educational goals are what a school is 'supposed' to accomplish for its students and for society. For students, such goals are an increase in knowledge, basic skills, social skills, self concept, vocational competence. These vary a great deal from country to country, and indeed from school to school. But there are also societal goals for schools, or distinct social functions of the educational system, such as equity, filling labour market needs, reducing delinquency, responsible citizenship and many others.

There are many definitions of the term 'effectiveness'. All that is meant here is that a school, to be called 'effective' within a certain cultural context, is (i) accomplishing the best possible pupil outcomes (defined in both individual and societal terms); with (ii) as little wastage of pupil talent as possible;

and with (iii) efficient use of means. Naturally, to achieve increased effectiveness, there will have to be changes in both learning conditions and related internal conditions, as well as improvement in what is called the school's organizational and pedagogical capacity.

Effective Schools

Much recent research on 'effective schools' in the UK (Rutter *et al*, 1979; Mortimore *et al*, 1986) and the USA (Purkey and Smith, 1983) has found that certain internal conditions are typical in schools that achieve higher levels of outcomes for their students. What is particularly interesting about these studies is not only the claim that schools can and do make a difference to pupils' achievement but that these differences in outcome are systematically related to variations in the schools' climate, culture or ethos and their 'quality' as social systems. The literature is also in agreement on two further issues. First, positive features of 'effective schools' are to do with 'process type' manifestations of schooling; and second, that all these features are systematically related to the schools' characteristics as human social systems and, as such, are amenable to alteration by concerted action on the part of the school staff. This is not an easy task. Nevertheless, the research suggests that teachers and schools have more control than they may have imagined over their ability to change their present direction and become efficient and effective agents of pupils' learning and development.

Not only does the 'effective schools' research conclude that schools do make a difference but there is also broad agreement on the factors that are responsible for that difference. The following eight factors are representative of the so-called organization factors that are characteristic of effective schools:

1 Curriculum-focussed school leadership
2 Supportive climate within the school
3 Emphasis on curriculum and teaching (for example, maximizing academic learning)
4 Clear goals and high expectations for students
5 A system for monitoring performance and achievement
6 Ongoing staff development and in-service
7 Parental involvement and support
8 LEA support

These factors do not, however, address the dynamics of schools as organizations. There appear to be four additional factors which infuse some meaning and life into the process of improvement within the school. The process factors have been described as follows (Fullan, 1985).

1 A feel for the process of leadership; this is difficult to characterize because the complexity of factors involved tends to deny rational

      planning, a useful analogy would be that organizations are to be sailed rather than driven.

2   A guiding value system; this refers to a consensus on high expectations, explicit goals, clear rules, a genuine caring about individuals *etc.*

3   Intense interaction and communication; this refers to simultaneous support and pressure at both horizontal and vertical levels within the school.

4   Collaborative planning and implementation; this needs to occur both within the school and externally, particularly in the local educational authority.

The process factors provide the means of achieving the organizational factors; they lubricate the system and 'fuel the dynamics of interaction.'

    There is, of course, a great deal of similarity between the notions of school improvement and effective schools (Clark *et al*, 1984). The school improvement studies, however, tend to be action and developmentally-oriented. They embody the long term goal of moving towards the vision of the 'problem solving' or 'thinking' or 'relatively autonomous' school and are committed to promoting and evaluating school improvement strategies. This approach is exemplified in the work of ISIP. The effective schools literature is more concerned to develop criteria that characterize the effective school; to provide a model for effective schooling (Kyle, 1985). It is important to bear in mind, however, that the emphasis on models is misleading. Schools do not change in a linear fashion; they are 'loosely coupled' (Weik, 1982), improve slowly and unpredictably and often change capriciously.

The Quality of Schooling

The most difficult place to effect educational change is at the level of the teaching-learning process in classrooms. Many of those charged with the management and development of educational systems are aware that equal quantitative inputs (money, personnel, facilities) into schools in similar neighbourhoods with similar structures and curricula do not lead to similar outcomes. What accounts for improved outcomes, as we have seen in the discussion on effective schools, is the quality of interaction between resources, individuals, societal norms and the culture or climate of the school. The problem is that determining school 'quality' (for example, learning climate, capacity for change, ability to achieve a wide range of goals) is difficult to measure; the tendency therefore is to rely on easily measurable outcomes such as competitive examinations and standardized tests.

    Taking examinations as a major outcome measure, however, limits the range of educational aims because they are only a part of the quality of education. Examinations usually measure only cognitive achievement; they do not assess personal qualities and character. Ironically, the over-emphasis on outcome measures like examinations may have the effect of reducing the quality of education because in order to increase examination results more emphasis is placed on instrumental forms of teaching.

When quality, however, is defined in terms of the teaching-learning process and what schools are actually doing with their resources in order to create the best possible learning conditions, then accountability can be defined more broadly. Accountability can then be seen as a means for schools to make their efforts at improving the quality of education more explicit rather than in terms of minimum outcomes or examination results. Within this framework, the definitions of quality and accountability used by policy makers will have to place more emphasis on the definition of goals, the content of the school curriculum, the organization of the teaching-learning process and teaching styles. It is in this sense that the term 'quality of schooling' is used in this book.

School Improvement in the United Kingdom

From what has already been said it should be becoming apparent that school improvement is to do with curriculum development, strengthening the school organization; changes in the teaching-learning process, and teaching styles. Its focus is the classroom and the school; it is content and process orientated. Within this concept of school improvement, the teacher is receiving more priority in the change process, but not at the expense of the school leader, the subject department or the faculty; therefore the collaboration among all school personnel becomes central. This approach also focuses attention on the process of strengthening the school's capacity to deal with change.

Those involved in ISIP (for example, van Velzen *et al*, 1985) do not expect profound structural changes in the school. The accent is on making the best of the school's staff and resources, increasing flexibility and the adaptation of the school to ensure students a good transition to an active life. Differential treatment of schools, and more school-focussed improvement efforts, will be the main characteristics of the improvement strategy. Improving the competencies of a school to manage itself, to analyze its problems and its needs and to develop and carry out a strategy of change, is a key approach for school improvement in the eighties and beyond.

If this is how ISIP envisages school improvement developing in the near future, how does this apply to the United Kingdom? Interestingly, recent developments in the UK educational system are much in line with the scenario just outlined. Innovations such as the Technical and Vocational Education Initiative (TVEI) tend to emphasize curriculum development, changes in teaching style and policy implementation at the school and local level. The focus of the new arrangements for INSET (Grant Related In-service Training — GRIST) are content orientated and also devolve more responsibility to the local level. The appraisal of teachers and the evaluation of schools are both issues that are receiving considerable attention at present. The management approach of the National Development Centre is developmental rather than instrumental, and so on.

The first chapter of *Better Schools* (DES, 1985) discusses a variety of weaknesses in our educational system and suggests that in order to tackle these weaknesses and to improve standards, action is necessary in four areas of policy *viz* curriculum, examinations, teachers and management, and parents. The language of *Better Schools* is, however, instrumental, its focus is on outcomes, on raising standards, and the tenor of the approach is somewhat different to the image of school improvement presented here. Despite this caveat I suggest that much of the current change in schooling in the UK at present falls within the broad ambit of school improvement as defined by ISIP and has a potential for enhancing the quality of schooling in this country. How far this will be achieved depends in part on how well the lessons from ISIP are disseminated and learnt. One thing is for sure; quality schooling is not achieved by instrumental means.

International School Improvement Project

The International School Improvement Project (ISIP) began its work in the autumn of 1982 and continues until the end of 1986. ISIP builds on previous OECD/CERI initiatives such as *The Creativity of the School*, (Nisbet, 1973) and the *INSET* (Bolam, 1982; Hopkins, 1986) projects. At a time when the educational system as a whole is facing not only retrenchment but also pressure for change, a project that focusses on school improvement — a change at the meso-level, at strategies for strengthening the school capacity for problem solving, at making the school more reflexive to change, as well as sustaining the quality of education — is both important and necessary.

ISIP is a decentralized project which means that its members are associated with different groups who meet regularly in different locations to pursue their collaborative work. Some 150 people are involved from fourteen countries, namely Australia, Belgium, Canada, Denmark, United Kingdom, Federal Republic of Germany, France, Italy, Japan, the Netherlands, Norway, United States of America, Sweden and Switzerland. The members of ISIP represent a variety of interests and positions in education in their respective countries. The working groups usually contain policy makers from the national and local level (for example, chief education officers), local school leaders (for example, heads), teacher representatives (for example, teacher centre wardens), members of the support systems and other external bodies (for example, HMI, LEA advisers and university or college lecturers). Since the start, ISIP has been committed to sharing and developing an understanding of what it takes to make school improvement work, at a level deeper than any group of individuals could manage in their own countries.

ISIP does its work through a series of cross-national 'area groups' each focussed on a specific topic:

Area 1: School-based review for self improvement.

Area 2: Principals and internal change agents in the school improve-ment process.

Area 3: The role of support in school improvement processes.

Area 4: Research and evaluation in school improvement.

Area 5: Development and implementation of school improvement policies by education authorities.

Area 6: Conceptual mapping of school improvement.

Each group has regular meetings. The members prepare and read papers; visit schools, support system organizations and ministries; offer mutual con-sultation and assistance and sometimes pair with other groups for codevelop-ment (shared work) projects. In some member countries there are also country specific ISIP groups working on area group topics. A newsletter, *ISIP News*, keeps everyone in contact. ISIP has already produced a number of tangible outcomes, for example: international collaboration on school improvement policy and practice; the development of school improvement strategies; a series of books published by ACCO (the Belgian publishing company) is listed on page 205.

The UK Dissemination Conference

A three-day conference on school improvement and the lessons of the Inter-national School Improvement Project was held at Nene College, North-ampton, on 8–10 April 1986. It was intended for chief education officers and their deputies, chief inspectors/advisers, heads, chairs of education commit-tees, teacher trainers and representatives of teachers' professional associations and the other organizations concerned with education in schools.

The aims of the dissemination conference were:

(i) to disseminate to key UK people the outcomes so far of the ISIP Project, as a whole and in each area of activity;

(ii) to relate these outcomes directly to current UK policy concerns;

(iii) to consider their implications for UK policy at national, regional, local and institutional levels;

(iv) to promote a continuing interchange between ISIP members, other conference members and OECD/CERI;

(v) to produce a UK book on the implications of ISIP.

The conference began with two introductory presentations on 'What is

ISIP?' and 'School Improvement in the UK' which provided a context for more detailed discussion of the four major themes that emanated from ISIP: namely, School-Based Review for School Improvement, the Role of Head-teachers and Internal Change Agents in School Improvement, the Role of External Support in School Improvement Processes, and the Development and Implementation of School Improvement Policies by Education Author-ities. The themes were explored and discussed by means of an invited presentation, an international and UK case study, a response from a member of the UK steering group and structured group discussion. Structured and unstructured group discussion and informal networking were, in fact, a major feature of the conference.

The Form of the Book

I mentioned earlier that the book is designed to be 'user friendly'. This aspiration is manifest in a number of ways.

First, this introductory chapter is intended to 'stake out the territory' by defining some of the terms, by discussing ISIP and the UK conference and in reviewing the contents of the book.

Second, there is a consistency of presentation in the chapters dealing with the major themes of the conference. Each of these chapters has four substantive sections. First is the invited ISIP presentation that relates to one of the major ISIP themes and this is followed by two case studies, one from abroad the other from the UK, that illuminate the theme. Finally the pre-sentation and the case studies are commented on from the UK perspective by a member of the UK steering group.

Third, each chapter is preceded by an editorial introduction that summa-rizes its contents. These introductions provide signposts for each chapter and enable the reader to identify what is of most relevance to them fairly quickly.

Fourth, the book has a number of appendices which give more informa-tion about school improvement. There is a select annotated bibliography on school improvement, a list of ISIP publications and the names and affiliation of those who attended the conference. It is hoped that the latter will assist in some form of networking for school improvement in this country. If you are interested in the ideas discussed in this book and want to do something about them in your school or LEA, then see if there is anyone that you know on that list. Networking is a powerful means for initiating and sustaining im-provement.

By structuring the book in this way it is hoped that the reader will find the contents more useful and accessible than is the case in most books of this type.

A word about the intended audience for the book. Books such as this often claim to be of use to teachers, heads and LEA officials but rarely are. This may not be true in this case. As should be evident from the discussion of school improvement so far, if its aspirations are to succeed then it is only because of teachers, heads and LEA officials working hard together in a collaborative and systematic fashion. The book will hopefully also be of interest and use to policy makers, researchers and evaluators those in the support system, and school governors. They all have an important part to play but it must be emphasized that school improvement is predicated essentially on the quality of interaction at the school and local level.

The Content of the Book

The book follows fairly closely the structure of the conference. The following chapter by Wim van Velzen discusses the background, scope, activities and achievements of ISIP and what the future without ISIP will look like. Chapter 3 is devoted to School-Based Review (SBR). This activity is better known as school self-evaluation within the UK. Reviewing what is going on in schools is a necessary precursor to action for improvement. Chapter 4 concerns the role of the headteacher and other internal change agents in school improvement. The pivotal role of the head in change is widely acknowledged and the various contributions in this chapter explore this theme. Chapter 5 examines the role of external support in school improvement. External support is another concept which may be unfamiliar to those in the UK; the contributions in this chapter provide a fairly comprehensive conceptualization of the topic. Chapter 6 is concerned with the development and implementation of school improvement policies. The whole area of policy formation is fraught with difficulty but is crucial to the success of school improvement efforts. Chapter 7 looks at the implications for national and local policy on school improvement in the UK. The four contributions in this chapter tackle the issue from very different perspectives: from the perspective of the DES, the public, the conference participants and from the lessons emanating from ISIP.

Taken together the contributions to the various chapters and the structure of the book itself present a fairly comprehensive review of the International School Improvement Project. The educational scene is changing rapidly in the United Kingdom at present and the signs are that the pressure for change will continue for some time. These developments contain great potential for positive improvement but only if they are presented in realistic policy terms and are successfully implemented at the local level. The International School Improvement Project contains many lessons for improving the quality of schooling. This book has been produced in the hope that these lessons may facilitate the contemporary pressure for change in achieving real quality in our educational system.

Note

1 This section is based on and elaborated in chapter 2 of *Making School Improvement Work* (van Velzen *et al*, 1985).

References

BOLAM, R (1982) *In-service Education and Training of Teachers*, Paris, OECD.

CLARK, D *et al* (1984) 'Effective schools and school improvement', *Educational Administration Quarterly*, 20, 3, Summer, pp41–68.

DES, (1985) *Better Schools* (Cmnd 9469), London, HMSO.

FULLAN, M (1985) 'Change processes and strategies at the local level', *Elementary School Journal*, 85, 3, pp391–421.

HOPKINS, D (1986) *In-service Training and Educational Development*, London, Croom Helm.

KYLE, R (1985) *Reaching for Excellence: An Effective Schools Sourcebook*, Washington, DC, US Government Printing Office.

MORTIMORE, P *et al* (1986) *The ILEA Junior School Project: Summary of the Main Report*, London, Research and Statistics Branch, ILEA.

NISBET, J (Ed) (1973) *The Creativity of the School*, Paris, OECD.

PURKEY, S and SMITH, M (1983) 'Effective schools: A review', *Elementary School Journal*, 83, pp427–52.

RUTTER, M *et al* (1979) *Fifteen Thousand Hours*, London, Open Books.

VAN VELZEN W *et al* (1985) *Making School Improvement Work*, Leuven, Belgium, ACCO.

WEIK, K (1982) 'Administering education in loosely coupled schools', *Phi Delta Kappan*, June, pp673–6.

2   The International School Improvement Project

Wim van Velzen

Introduction

The International School Improvement Project, as a strategy for educational change, is a child of its time. ISIP contrasts with previous efforts at school improvement because its objectives and working methods are peculiarly consistent with the wider educational and social milieu from which it emerged. The emphasis on strengthening the schools' capacity to deal with change, for example, reflects a socio political climate in which pressure for change is burgeoning, at a time when resources for education are declining, thus necessitating the school assuming increased responsibility for its own development. In this chapter Wim van Velzen describes the particular context of the project, its origins, objectives and working methods, the focus of the area groups' and the projects' substantive outcomes. As one of its principal instigators van Velzen is in a unique position to comment on the appositeness of ISIP as a strategy for school improvement in the eighties and beyond.

Origins of the Project

Previous work on change in schools occurred during a period of sustained economic and social development. Since the middle of the 1970s, however, the majority of Western school systems have faced demographic and economic contraction and the role and functions of their schools have been permanently challenged by new demands from individuals and groups as well as society at large. Whilst individuals and society were demanding greater equality of opportunity, schools were also asked to strengthen links with their surrounding community (for example, to ensure a better transition from school to work in a context of youth unemployment), to be more accountable and to take more advantage of new information technology. All this was occurring at a time when fewer young teachers were being recruited and less money was available for expanding or even sustaining facilities and incentives for change.

Towards the end of the 1970s the knowledge base on change in schools had two particular characteristics. On the one hand, there was evidence from a large number of national and international studies and research projects on effective innovation strategies. On the other hand, those outcomes had never been tested on a large scale or in a period of contraction. Moreover, it was generally agreed that the main problems in implementing educational policies were:

1 the difficulty of giving individual schools freedom of action in elaborating and implementing change;
2 the lack of an internal change capacity at school level related to internal functions and trained staff;
3 the difference in attitude between policy makers, practitioners and researchers over the design and implementation of policies; and the difficulty in bridging the differences in starting points, philosophies and needs between these three groups;
4 the availability of adequate external support structures and procedures.

Finally, it became obvious that the adaptation of schools to new societal and individual demands in the future had to be based on a sound and coherent school improvement policy which took into consideration the needs and limits of the school.

These conditions suggested that research and support agencies, faculties or schools of education, ministries of education and other educational bodies should engage in a collaborative effort to search for answers to similar questions. There was a conviction that, through international cooperation, we could learn from each other and that we could increase our knowledge and skills in the field of school improvement.

As indicated in chapter 1, fourteen countries, forty different institutions and about 150 people established and participated in the network called the International School Improvement Project (ISIP). It started officially in October 1982 in Palm Beach, USA, after a year-and-a-half of preparatory planning activities. In contrast to other international collaborative efforts ISIP was guided by the interests of its participants. ISIP had its roots and origins in the commitment of participating institutions and national bodies to use their own programmes and resources in an international endeavour for which they were strongly committed and from which they were convinced they could reciprocally benefit.

Objectives

The general aim of ISIP, as defined at the Palm Beach 1982 conference, was:

> to facilitate improved knowledge of and insights into the functioning of school improvement processes both on a small and a large scale and to contribute to the development of skills within various levels of educational administration, decision making and support.

ISIP's overall objective was to contribute to the development of knowledge, skills and materials through which schools, education authorities and consultants could improve their ability to implement school improvement activities. The accent of the work was on maximizing the useful knowledge about school improvement at local and system levels and on enhancing the skills of policy makers and external support personnel for conducting school improvement policies.

In 1982 the potential outcomes of ISIP, *ie* those that might be reasonably expected at the end of the project, were summarized as follows:

1 A better *understanding* of school improvement processes and their implementation on a small and large scale.
2 An improvement of *skills* in the management and planning of school improvement processes.
3 The development of new school improvement *instruments* such as evaluation procedures; school development techniques; and manuals for internal (within school) and external consultants.
4 The development of new *programmes* in the framework of school improvement: for example, training programmes for principals and internal consultants, support for schools, and policy programmes for carrying out school improvement activities on a large scale.
5 A series of *reports* on such subjects as:

   • The state of the art of school improvement in member countries.
   • Case studies of specific significant components in the school improvement process; for example, the role of teachers and headmasters, the role of a school district or local education authority.
   • Descriptions of school improvement processes in schools; for example, what headteachers' internal change agents and external consultants actually do.
   • Evaluation studies; for example, the factors hindering or promoting the implementation of school improvement programmes.
   • The analysis and development of a conceptual framework for school improvement.
   • Descriptions of school improvement policy efforts undertaken by educational authorities.

ISIP was different to most international projects. A number of ISIP's aspirations, if not unique, were certainly specific to it:

- The intention of reaching a wide range of target groups, for example decision makers, researchers, support system personnel, school leaders.
- The testing and refinement of outcomes through ongoing, cooperative (codevelopment) activities, which were connected to existing national school improvement efforts.
- A shared faith in cross role and cross cultural learning as the basic mode of work.
- A quasi-decentralized approach, which relied on the development of practical working networks that focussed on specific topics.
- The choice of a limited number of substantive topics; for example conceptual mapping of school improvement, school-based review, role and training of school leaders, the nature of support structures, research and evaluation, and policies and strategies developed by policy makers.
- A focus on the school as the unit of development.

ISIP in Action

The main working methods of ISIP were:

- development and discussion of case studies;
- field visits;
- targetted and in-depth analysis and discussion of one topic during a seminar;
- discussions about collaborative work;
- publications;
- mutual consultation and assistance.

Both the medium-term focus of ISIP and its working methods were conditions for its success.

At the beginning of the project, much energy was devoted to the development of a conceptual map wherein key ideas, definitions of school improvement, other major concepts and the relationships between factors that promote school improvement were situated. The need for a conceptual map relevant to most Western countries, which contain many differences in administrative context, educational system and culture, took a great deal of time. The developmental process included a large number of meetings and resulted in the book, *Making School Improvement Work*. The sub-title, *A Conceptual Guide to Practice*, emphasizes that the book aims to provide systematic ideas, concepts and theories that underlie practical success in school improvement. The major concern of *Making School Improvement Work* is with the strategies needed to bring about change for effective schooling, *ie*, with the process of school improvement.

In the meantime the area groups had started their work. As described in chapter 1, ISIP consisted of five area groups. Each area had its own programme but towards the end of the project the accent lay on further development and the integration of knowledge emerging from these areas.

Area 1 was concerned with School-Based Review (SBR) a topic better known in the United Kingdom as school self-evaluation. The group focussed on the development of a common concept and language with regard to school based review. They produced a series of national case studies, examined a variety of approaches to doing school-based review and made a number of field visits to observe good practice in member countries. Area 1 produced three books that summarized their work. The first *School-Based Review for School Improvement* is a preliminary 'State of the art' review that defines, reviews and conceptualizes the process of school based review. The second book *School-Based Review: Towards a Praxis* provides a conceptual framework for SBR, a series of ten national case studies, a critical analysis of issues and recommendations for practice. The third, *Doing School-Based Review* is a manual containing examples of SBR instruments and guidelines.

Area 2 dealt with two major topics — school leaders and the organization development of schools. Two publications relate to the first topic. The first is *The School Leader and School Improvement: Case Studies from Ten Countries*. The book analyzes case study data across national lines and then utilizes an international perspective to illuminate both what we already know and what we hope to learn about the school leader's role in school improvement. This book and the second, its more analytical partner, *The Role of School Leaders in School Improvement*, are discussed in more detail in chapter 4. With regards to the second topic a book is currently being prepared on *School Development: Organizational and Educational Models*. A crucial distinction is made in that book betweeen educational and organizational models and it documents attempts to design consistent combinations of these two kinds of approaches. The models have proved to be a useful aid in the analysis of problems in schools and in designing future developments.

Area 3 spent most of its time examining the role of external support in facilitating school improvement and the conditions under which it most successfully occurs. Their first publication *The External Support System Profile* describes an instrument which can analyze various support systems and facilitate communication about support systems in a country. Two other books will appear. The first deals with case studies on the role external support systems play in the different Western countries and includes discussion on policies, strategies, structures and design, practical problems and values. The second book raises the question of what role external support can play in the transfer of knowledge in order to facilitate local school improvement activities.

Area 4 is also responsible for a number of publications which includes amongst others, *Strategies for Large Scale Change in Education: Dilemmas and*

Solutions. The aim of that book is to make an analysis of the large scale approaches implicit in many school improvement projects and to discuss under what conditions large scale school improvement projects can be successfully executed. Another book, *Lasting School Improvement: Exploring the Process of Institutionalization*, focusses on the process of institutionalization. Many well intentioned, carefully planned school improvement efforts of the past decade have somehow failed to take root: lasting school improvement however, is not only adopted and implemented but is also embedded in the routine life of schools. The book demonstrates and encourages an analytical exploration of the institutionalization topic from different points of view.

Finally, *Area 5* had two major tasks; the first, was to help other areas with policy issues and the second, to assess the impact of policy making on school improvement. A major publication entitled *Key Issues in School Improvement Policy Making* describes four significant school improvement policies in Western countries, *ie*, basic education, junior secondary education, new information technology and transition from school to work. The book analyzes those policies from an ISIP perspective and recommends other approaches.

On the whole it is expected that between twelve and sixteen ISIP publications will appear.[1] That is a good success. ISIP's aspirations, however, encompass more than publications. There are at least four other, less tangible, but still significant outcomes of ISIP.

First, there is the development of common frameworks, concepts and language that can help bridge the different scientific and practical worlds across and within Western countries.

Second, the collaboration between policy makers, practitioners, researchers and external support persons have increased our body of knowledge.

Third, the ISIP publications have clearly demonstrated that, although there are many differences between countries, we can learn from each other. In particular we have gained a deeper insight into the process of school improvement. This understanding has occurred at the school level, at the level of external support, *ie*, how it can faciliate the process of improvement in schools and finally, how the work of policy makers can become more effective if they follow certain principles and strategies.

Fourth, it is the people who have participated in ISIP who have gained the most. They became aware of their own cultural limits and boundaries and how difficult it is to understand, or accept the reasons why another country is doing something different. They also became aware of the limits of their own solutions. The questioning of their solutions by other ISIP people was the beginning of deeper insights into the dynamics of their own situation. Sometimes, it resulted in a change of approach, theory or concept. It always resulted in an enrichment of our own experience. Consequently, it is the participants themselves who are the brightest jewels in the ISIP crown.

What Is Next?

ISIP has finished. The role of education, however, may well become even more important in the future as we strive to realize the potential of the new information society. It is, therefore, important to build the school for tomorrow. Preparing schools today to accomplish their tasks tomorrow is the major challenge for most countries. ISIP people and knowledge can facilitate the process of schools achieving their new role and tasks in the information society. Consequently, a number of ISIP activities will continue in the coming years. There are, for example, the dissemination conferences, such as the UK conference that provided the substance for this book. Other countries are organizing follow-up workshops, INSET activities, articles in teacher journals, where results from ISIP are being disseminated and so on. Most ISIP areas are keeping their network alive and intend to continue their flow of information albeit on a more *ad hoc* and less structured basis. ISIP members have also established a Foundation for International Collaboration on School Improvement to facilitate the publication and distribution of ISIP books as well as these other activities. The Foundation aspires to keep the ISIP spirit alive and to continue to stimulate publications and activities on school improvement in Western countries.

Note

1 The reports and books mentioned in this chapter are published by ACCO, the Belgian publishing company and are listed in full on page 205.

3   School-Based Review for School Improvement

Introduction

School-based review is more commonly known within the UK as school self-evaluation. School self-evaluation, as it is practised in England and Wales, is however, somewhat different to SBR as defined by ISIP. In particular, school self-evaluation has tended to assume accountability overtones and, in practice, is not usually systematically linked to school improvement. This is particularly true of LEA initiated schemes for school evaluation. A notable exception to this general trend are the GRIDS handbooks. Produced under the aegis of the Schools Council and the School Curriculum Development Committee (SCDC), these materials offer a school staff a specific and systematic process of review for developmental purposes which they can engage in on their own initiative. GRIDS represents the best example in the UK context of the ideal of SBR as it has become defined in ISIP.

Robert Bollen's paper begins by offering the ISIP definition of SBR and three perspectives on the phenomena of which SBR as a school improvement strategy in itself is the preferred mode. Viewing SBR in this way, however, vastly increases the complexity of the process and the different roles and functions that those involved can assume. Bollen illustrates this complexity by reference to a SBR matrix developed to assist in planning and conceptualizing the process. The complexity of the process is also reflected in the range of expectations those involved have for SBR. Bollen concludes his paper by pointing to the difficulty in, but the need for, linking review to development and by suggesting that a coherent action oriented SBR strategy at the school level, besides resulting in school improvement, may well also assist in the improvement of educational policy at the local, regional and national level.

The case study from Belgium is an example of SBR being used as a means to a specific end — the introduction of another innovation in this instance, the Renewed Primary School in Belgium. The nature of the SBR procedures used was strongly influenced by the UK GRIDS materials, which were introduced to Belgium as a result of mutual involvement in ISIP. The case study is in four parts. After a very brief introduction to the Belgian education system, the first part describes the Renewed Primary School project. This national primary school development project started in 1973 but SBR procedures were not included in it until ten years later. At that time, willingness to undertake SBR became a condition of membership of the RPS project. The second part of the case study details the very careful and systematic way in which SBR was introduced to the schools and the elaborate organizational structures which were set up to sustain it. Careful training was given to the participants, both before and during the process. Written contracts were made between the schools and the supporting agencies. Provision was made at several stages for whole school teams to renew their commitment to the project or to retire from it. Provision was also made for schools to be expelled from the project. In the third part of the case study, some early attempts to evaluate its use are discussed and in part 4 the authors reflect on their experience to date of SBR as a means to a specific end.

The case study of local education authority (LEA) initiated school-based review in England and Wales is in three parts. It begins with a brief overview of the provisions for the control and the monitoring of the quality of education. The reasons for the development of the LEA schemes are then briefly considered. In the second, major part of the case study, three such schemes are presented in turn: one in which involvement by schools is entirely voluntary, one in which it is mandatory and one in which mandatory involvement is followed by an 'audit'. These three were chosen because together they exemplify the variety of what has been developed in England and Wales. For each, the scheme itself and the intentions of its originators are first briefly introduced. These intentions are non-specific, being concerned with the general improvement of the quality of the education provided by schools. A report on research into the impact of each scheme on the schools in the LEA then follows. Finally, LEA initiated school-based review, as thus represented, is evaluated in terms of a matrix developed by members of ISIP Area 1. It is suggested that in none of these LEAs were the teachers adequately prepared technically and, as a consequence, their reviews were superficial. Such tangible school improvements which resulted were mainly in terms of increased resourcing from the LEA.

Philip Clift in his 'response' reiterates the main features of SBR and relates them to current practice in England and Wales. Clift suggests that GRIDS represents the most hopeful collusion of UK practice and ISIP ideals for SBR. In concluding he suggests that, to be effective, SBR presumes a highly professional teaching force with adequate resourcing and support free from contractual accountability.

School-Based Review (SBR) in the Context of Educational Policy

Robert Bollen

School-based review is not a new phenomenon. In the context of the International School Improvement Project, SBR is defined as 'a systematic inspection by a school, a sub-system or an individual of the actual functioning of the school'. If we describe SBR as school self-evaluation, it can be regarded as a normal function of a school, especially at the secondary and higher education level. It is difficult to run such complex organizations without some sort of ongoing evaluation process.

What is new about SBR, however, as defined in ISIP, is the systematic approach to the process. This implies that SBR has to be integrated into management procedures, that special instruments will be used and that the outcomes of the review are intended to be applied directly to the subsequent functioning of the school. Introducing SBR into school life as a systematic self inspection is only acceptable if the usefulness of the effort is clear to all persons involved. Otherwise, it will be regarded as only another trendy managerial innovation.

Certainly what also is new is the almost worldwide interest in the SBR phenomenon. In the OECD ISIP project, SBR was designated as area 1. This may have been accidental but nevertheless symbolizes the conviction of the area 1 group that in a process of school improvement, self-evaluation has to be introduced at an early stage to provide a firm and realistic base for further developments.

This general interest in SBR can, however, be as readily related to political issues as to professional views on the issue of school improvement. With increasing pressure on schools to account for the way in which they are spending public money and with widespread concerns about the quality of schooling, education authorities have also seen in SBR a tool that might enable them to obtain relevant information from schools and/or provide an impetus for schools to improve the quality of both their organization and the teaching learning processes.

This is where the confusion starts about what SBR really is about. As long as a school principal is merely monitoring the functioning of his/her school for personal managerial purposes, there are few implications for others. But conceptualizing SBR as a tool for the development of educational policy, as is done in ISIP, means that many more people are involved.

Those additionally involved may be divided first into people normally functioning in the environment of the school, including the education authorities and inspectorate, groups of parents with their great natural interest in the quality of their local school and all kinds of support agencies interested in strategies for school improvement. Second, if SBR is to lead to the improvement of a school, anyone who contributes to improving the curriculum and its implementation, to the improvement of attitudes toward pupils, to their assessment procedures or to the fulfilment of the general aims of the school, will also have to be included in the SBR process and each will have his/her own perspective. To illustrate this diversity I will describe three different perspectives on SBR.

First, SBR can be perceived as a technique. There is a job to be done — evaluating the system — and this is the tool. In this perspective, there is a strong emphasis on instruments like questionnaires and assessment schemes. Special computer programmes are being developed to tackle the problem of how to handle all the data. Data analysis techniques and interview skills have to be acquired and it is likely that some kind of external support will be needed. In this perspective, little attention is paid to the impact of the review on the school as a social system, or to the hidden values underlying its actual functioning.

Second, SBR can be seen as an inevitable phase in any process of innovation or improvement. The perception of SBR in this perspective is also very instrumental, but here a relationship is established between SBR and a specific strategy which means that the nature of the improvement strategy tends to dictate the nature of the SBR process. If an improvement policy embraces a 'top-down' implementation strategy, SBR must provide hard data strictly related to the aims and goals of the policy. Specific instruments will be needed and there will be little opportunity for people to gather data in their own favourite and particular ways. If, on the contrary, the improvement policy is based on an emphasis of more responsibility and creativity at the grass roots level, the SBR strategy will have to encourage that by providing guidelines and advice on how to tackle the problem of self-evaluation, using valid and reliable means. In this instance, the over prescription of tactics and instruments may be counter productive.

Third, SBR can be considered as a school improvement strategy in itself. There is a belief that introducing SBR into a school, not just at the managerial level but as a normal function of the school, will bring about structural and fundamental changes in the functioning of the school which can itself be perceived as school improvement. Success in this strategy will be evident in an increased self awareness of the school as an organization by those involved, of enhanced conditions for the teaching and learning processes, and in the triggering of a process of team building and long-term planning at the school level. In this perspective SBR is not just a tool, not even a phase in a process, but an end in itself. This means that, given the specific situation and environment of the school, we are looking at school-based improvement within the limitations set up by educational policies at the local, regional or national level. Those limitations are parameters for the process of SBR, which means that SBR will really be school-based, in technique as well as in strategy.

Having said all this, we should look at all the parties involved in the implementation of SBR in a more systematic way. In area 1 we developed a matrix (Bollen and Hopkins, 1987) for thinking about and planning for SBR. This is seen in table 1. One axis of this matrix consists of five phases that constitute an SBR process for school improvement. These phases are:

the Preparation (Readiness) Phase
the Review (Initial) Phase
the Review (Specific) Phase
the Development Phase
the Institutionalization Phase.

The other consists of the roles of those involved, who are:

subject to review
doing the review
managing the review
supporting the review
controlling the review
influencing the review.

It does not require much imagination to realize that some of these roles are potentially in conflict with others. If this matrix, generating over 150 cells in which people are acting and reacting, gives a notion of the real complexity of the SBR process, it will have contributed to a realistic discussion about the issue of SBR.

Assuming that the third perspective I have just described provides the richest concept of SBR, we can also see the difficulty of obtaining an overview of the dynamics of the SBR process. This is where international cooperation has proved so valuable. One is never able to see all those cells of the matrix in operaton in any one situation; this means that a profound understanding of the dynamics of SBR can only be obtained by reflection on several situations. International cooperation provides the basis for such a broad overview. The pattern of interaction between the cells of the matrix differs according to culture and conditions; thus one country displays quite clearly what is almost hidden in another.

Reflecting on the outcomes of our international comparisons, we have learned several important lessons about the hopes of people introducing SBR into school life, about the difficulties and constraints of such a strategy of school improvement and finally about the real benefits that SBR may offer.

Robert Bollen

Table 1: Process and Roles in School-Based Review: A Matrix

Process / Role	Subject to review	Doing the review	Managing the review	Supporting the review	Controlling the review	Influencing the review
Start Condition — Past Experience, History						
Preparation (Readiness) Phase: Initiation						
Negotiation over —						
* participation						
* control						
* training						
Decision to proceed						
Training for SBR						
Review (Initial) Phase: Planning for Review						
Decision on Instrumentation						
Data Gathering and Analysis						
Reporting and Discussion of Findings						
Decision to Proceed						
Review (Specific) Phase: Setting Priorities						
Planning for Review						
Mobilization of Resources/Expertise						
Training for the Review Process						
Gathering Information						
Validating Conclusions						
Feedback and Evaluation						
Decision to Proceed						
Development Phase: Establishing Policy						
Planning for Implementation						
Training (Inset) for Implementation						
Implementation of Policy with particular reference to:						
* school organization						
* materials						
* teaching style						
* knowledge utilization						
* acceptance of change						
Monitoring and Evaluation						
Institutionalization Phase: Monitoring of Action						
Utilization of SBR Process in other Areas of Curriculum and School Organization						
Development of Problem Solving Capacity as an Organizational Norm Within the School						

The hopes of people promoting SBR are manifold. Their most important hope is to initiate a process of school self-improvement by releasing the creative energies of those involved. We now know that SBR does not do that automatically: the institutional conditions have to be carefully prepared. The state of 'readiness' for SBR at the school level has many attributes: democratic leadership; the need for a climate or change; a tradition of constructive self-criticism; an openness in communication and capacity for problem solving.

There is also the hope that SBR will provide a monitoring function for the improvement process; thus ensuring that the improvement process will go on, if not for ever then at least until the moment that all parties involved are satisfied. We know, by looking at different cases, that monitoring a process of improvement presupposes a bundle of skills and concepts that often are not available inside the school system, which implies training and consultancy at different phases in the process.

Additionally, there is the hope that SBR will enable policy makers at all levels to manage the process of school improvement. In this case SBR will help with the attainment of given goals, formulated either inside or outside the school. SBR can be used as some sort of entrance procedure, estimating the state of readiness of a school for a given innovation project. It also enables the 'support structure' to give the correct input to the innovating or improving system.

Finally there is a more detached expectation of SBR. The other hopes concern change; that is, they are related to dynamic aspects of the system. But even without aiming at change *per se* it can be very useful to get a realistic view of what is really going on at the school level. There is a need for a valid insight into the life of schools to inform the process of educational policy making in the long-term. This activity should be carefully differentiated from the process of improvement at the school level, however. We know by looking at several cases that this gathering of information tends to induce a somewhat bureaucratic reaction at the school level. People do not like to invest too much energy in an enterprise that has not direct profit for themselves.

Looking at all these hopes and expectations it is clear that SBR is not a simple concept and there are a lot of tensions and constraints inherent in the SBR process. I will briefly mention just a few of them.

If SBR is addressed to the real needs of a given school, it also produces a clear picture of the weaknesses of that school. Looking critically at yourself is usually a painful experience and most people prefer to use the mirror in very private circumstances. Schools also, are reluctant to show their ugly faces in public. Schools are, and are not, professional organizations. The profitable use of SBR is more likely to occur in a school with a high standard of professional behaviour, rather than in a school with little or no common awareness of the importance of operating as a team or on working towards common goals.

Introducing SBR in schools often means introducing SBR instruments. Using such instruments without having a clear concept of SBR, its strategies and purposes can easily reduce the value of SBR to the level of just another set of handy tactics to be used by everybody for their own purpose. Since SBR is often introduced from the outside, conceptual differences amongst the different parties involved are likely to occur. These differences, especially between the school and its environment, can easily create different expectations with regard to outcomes, effects, need for resources, time management, process management and so forth. Those differences may frustrate the development of a climate in which SBR can make an effective contribution to school improvement.

If SBR is to be effective — and it has to be, given the energy that is demanded by the SBR process — the gap between reflection and action must somehow be bridged. SBR as such is not action. On the contrary, it postpones the action. It postpones it because it assumes that future action will be better prepared and better related to the specific needs and aims of the school by the gathering of relevant data and by reflection on them. We learned, by looking at several cases in different contexts, that moving from reflection into action is the crucial step which ultimately determines the value that people attach to the concept of SBR. This implies that SBR as a strategy should from the outset be action oriented. SBR flourishes best in a stimulating and supportive environment which possesses a reasonably clear concept of what a school should look like. That means, among other things, that SBR is a concept which is context bound.

This conclusion may encourage us to give up comparing case studies: but being context bound does not mean that the concept has no general application. To support this contention I will conclude this short introduction to the SBR concept by formulating a hypothesis on the possible use of an SBR strategy to solve a problem that seems to occur in all situations in which school improvement is promoted by external agencies.

At an ISIP conference on key issues in school improvement policy held recently in Paris, it became clear that the weak point of all policies is how to produce real improvement at the school level by means that are defined, structured and provided at the policy level. Somehow it appears that the concepts, knowledge, information, skills and all the other ingredients for a successful innovation strategy at the school level cannot be delivered at the right time and in the right combination to the right persons. Among other things this is caused by a mismatch between the needs of the schools on the one hand and the content, quality and flexibility of the offers made by the supporting systems on the other. Action-oriented SBR strategies at the school level, in the context of a clear educational policy, might contribute to the solution of this problem. We lose money, time and energy in efforts to stimulate school improvement without remarkable success. If schools are encouraged to define their problems, to articulate their real needs and to create by their own well prepared strategy motivation for improvement and a problem solving attitude, it may yet be possible to improve educational policy at the local, regional and national level.

Reference

BOLLEN, R and HOPKINS, D (1987) *School-Based Review: Towards a Praxis*, Leuven, Belgium, ACCO.

School Based Review as an Innovation Strategy: The Belgian Renewed Primary School[1]

Jan Depoortere, Marc de Soete and Johan Hellyn

Introduction

The National Context

Belgium, a small country of 10 million inhabitants, is divided by language into a Dutch speaking (Flanders) and a French speaking (Wallonie) part, each with a separate Ministry of Education. In both parts, education is organized by the state, the church and important municipalities. During the last ten years, there have been many differences between the two parts as far as the development of the educational system is concerned.

Culturally, there exists in Belgium a strong emphasis on 'freedom of education'. In general, the state, the church, the municipalities, and also groups of parents, have the right to organize education. On a more practical level, the norm of 'freedom of education' means that parents must have the opportunity to send their children to a school which represents their opinions (political, as well as religious).

The primary education authority structure is characterized by a relatively centralized organization. The three organizing bodies disseminate national curricula. The implementation of these curricula is, to some extent, controlled by a team of inspectors but the local schools and local boards have some power too. For instance, the national authorities cannot force a school to participate in a reform.

The Renewed Primary School Project (RPS)

The RPS project started in September 1973. It can be regarded as a large scale innovation project. Schools and teachers have to cope with a reform which is in fact a bundle of innovations. The main goals of the RPS are related to the following themes:

- enhanced integration and interdependence between the kindergarten (2.5 to 6 years) and the elementary school (6 to 12 years) and between the different grades of the primary school;
- attention to a well balanced and continuous education;
- attention to the individual pupil, with his/her own capacities, experiences and development;
- building up a school community in which the school exists for the community as well as for the school in the community.

The RPS Support Structure

In the context of the RPS a complex school support structure has been created. Figure 1 gives a general overview.

Figure 1

National Steering Committee

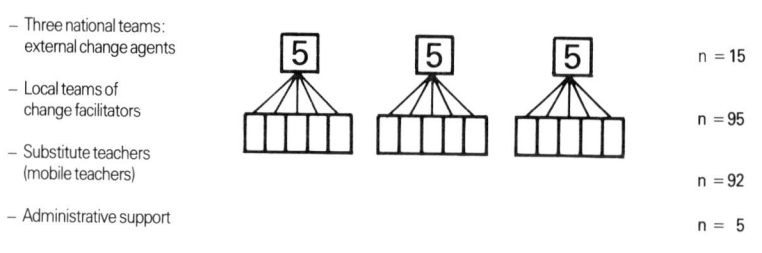

- Three national teams:
  external change agents   n = 15

- Local teams of
  change facilitators   n = 95

- Substitute teachers
  (mobile teachers)   n = 92

- Administrative support   n = 5

A National Steering Committee is responsible for the project and for its general development. That Committee is also responsible for a yearly evaluation report and for the formulation of advice to the Minister. The National Steering Committee consists of representatives from the major interest groups in elementary schools: the organizing bodies (state, church, municipalities), the inspectorate, the parent, the unions, the universities, the teacher training centres and the psycho-medical-social centres.

Three national teams of external change agents (related to the three organizing bodies) are responsible for the national coordination. They attend the monthly meetings of the National Steering Committee to discuss the general aims of the project, the in-service training of school principals and local change facilitators. They are also responsible for the production of a yearly evaluation report *etc.* During the first two years of the project, in cooperation with the staff of the nine schools involved and the other participants (parents, inspectors, psycho-medical-social centres), the change agents determined the future direction for the renewal of the primary school. This process-oriented democratic approach to educational change was rather un-usual for the Belgian situation.

Members of local teams (all of them former teachers) work with the teachers of three to four local schools. Mostly, they organize in-service training activities, have discussions with the principal about the way the general aims of the project can be implemented in the local school, *etc*. In other words, the local change facilitators try to organize a school-focussed implementation plan.

During the year, these local change facilitators organize at least three to four workshops for all the teachers of a local school. This means that the staff can get involved in discussions about the future of their school and about the activities which seem necessary for implementation of the ideas of the RPS. They can also evaluate past experiences. During such a workshop, pupils stay at school but the teachers are replaced by the so called 'mobile' teachers (substitute teachers). These teachers go from one school to another in order to give the regular teachers the opportunity to attend such in-service workshops.

Two university research teams are responsible for the external evaluation of the RPS project. The last two years (1983–85) of research were concerned with the mobilization process of the schools interested in entering the RPS project.

Participating Schools

Large-scale projects frequently use a dissemination strategy in which the underlying assumption is that material developed for, and partly by, these first generation schools can easily be transferred to a second and even a third generation. However, experience in the practice of educational change de-monstrates that although this strategy may lead to adoption, it may not lead to implementation. This was another reason for choosing to use a more school-based strategy.

Over the years of the RPS project, the number of schools taking part has grown as follows:

1973	9 schools
1976	21 schools
1977	59 schools
1980	275 schools
1983	start of the school-based review procedure

(The total number of primary schools in the Dutch speaking part of Belgium is approximately 2500.)

Because of the growing number of schools involved, and of the nature of the innovation process itself, it was decided that schools wishing to enter the RPS project should go through a programme of initiation and 'mobilization'.

For the schools which started in 1980, a specific mobilization process was set up. A general information campaign was organized, intended to inform all school communities about the content and the strategy of the RPS. After the information campaign, the schools were invited to discuss their local situation and to explore their own possibilities and limitations. They were also invited to express their willingness to enter the project. This approach to recruitment and selection (based on an information sheet 'School Image') was rather unsatisfactory. It was very difficult to assess the renewal capacity of the school and in many cases entry appeared to be a private initiative of the principal. These observations led to the conclusion that further expansion should be linked to more intense preparation. For this purpose a committee elaborated a new procedure, called school-based review (SBR).

School-Based Review as an Innovation Strategy

The Preparation Phase

School-based self-analysis is the process through which a complete school community thinks about the present functioning of the school. In general, SBR is a set of planned activities through which the whole school team makes an analysis of the existing situation. The staff looks for strengths and weaknesses. The teachers (and others) formulate priorities and objectives (related to the RPS project) and draft plans for the immediate future of their own school. The team analyzes what has been achieved previously, which goals are still to be achieved, what will be needed to achieve them, the way to proceed, who might be of any help, what kind of help one expects *etc*. In other words, the team checks whether they are willing and in a position to participate in a deliberate innovation in primary education.

It is important that this analysis takes place in the school itself. The school team analyzes itself and this is what counts. It cannot just be one person who decides whether the school will join RPS: the whole school community decides and this decision cannot be taken lightly. Past experience has shown that the renovation process was often supported by one person, or by a small group at the school. Conseqently, the results had remained only partial and temporary. In order to obtain visible and lasting results reaching to the level of the pupil in the classroom, it was necessary that all team members became involved in the renewal process.

The proposed SBR offered such a chance. In this analysis procedure, the emphasis is put on the activities of the school team rather than external change agents and proceeds in a relatively autonomous way. During the self-review process, the school is in a position to evaluate in a cautious way, all aspects, possibilities, doubts and expectations. The review consequently provides a good basis for the renewal process.

Initiation

All the schools were informed through a ministerial letter about the new strategy, based on the school-based review. It was assumed that the circular was read by all members involved. The letter also contained a review of the plan that would be used in the following school years.

This plan can be summarized as follows:

1982–83
1 Development of materials necessary for the training of the 'internal school coordinators'; the entire analysis procedure had to be worked out thoroughly (documents, guidelines, analysis techniques and instruments).
2 Presentation of the SBR procedure and the plan to other support structures (the inspectorate, the psycho–medico–social centres). Great attention was paid to this step because of the commitment to cooperation and support.

1983–84
1 Selection of the internal coordinators (or school coordinators/heads).
2 Training of the regional external coordinators (change facilitators).
3 Training of the internal coordinators.

1984–85
1 Operationalization of the school-based review.
2 At the end of the school year: decision whether or not to participate in the Renewed Primary School project.

1985–86
1 The RPS project starts in a number of schools.
2 After evaluation a new cycle of SBR starts for another group of internal coordinators.

The central educational authorities insisted on voluntary participation in this process and by so doing, they invited the school to demonstrate its autonomy. With regard to the further expansion of the RPS project, this approach included a risk: it might become a lingering process ...

Preparation of the Participants

The external support/the external coordinators

It is obvious that the proposed procedure was entirely new for some schools. For that reason, support was given and materials were provided. The support teams, the inspectorate and the psycho-medical-social centres were informed and were asked to support the schools during their self review process. The external coordinators were prepared for this new procedure. These persons were recruited from the national teams of external change agents (related to the three organizing bodies). As regards SBR itself, special attention was paid to the development of the required materials: analysis, instruments, guidelines for initial and specific review, documentation. A training programme for internal coordinators was also developed. In this programme, special attention was paid to the acquisition of skills and techniques: how to detect, analyze and solve problems; how to communicate within a team; how to organize a meeting; how to report objectively; how to collect data; how to organize a survey; how to analyze data; how to display data; how to make decisions about educational priorities *etc.*

Internal school coordinators

From what we have said it will be clear that the work to be accomplished within the school itself had to be understood by the entire school team. This implies that someone had to coordinate the work. This someone was usually the headmaster. In special cases, and with the agreement of the headmaster and the majority of the staff, a member of the staff could be appointed internal coordinator. He had to perform his duties, however, in agreement with the headmaster. From a total of 419 schools, only sixty-one persons who were not the headmaster acted as internal coordinator. The coordinators had to guide and support the process of self-review at the school level. They were to be trained to perform their tasks and to act as contact persons between the school team and the support teams. This preparation started during the school year 1983–84.

The tasks of the coordinator include:

- their own study of the procedure;
- participation in the preparation sessions organized by the RPS support team;
- evaluating those sessions;
- contact with other internal school coordinators; and
- development of an action plan for the school, possibly in coordination with RPS support team.

The option of starting the process of school-based review with only the support of the headmaster and then involving the members of the school team later was based on the following experiences and/or facts:

1 The evaluation of the innovation that started in 1979, emphasized the influential role of the headmaster — he invites, he stimulates and coordinates.

2 The organization of instruction in the primary school offers little opportunity for the external change facilitators to contact the teacher. Only the headmaster can be considered as a possible entry to the entire school team.

3 This choice confirmed the importance the government attached to the enlargement and support of the pedagogical task (versus the administrative task) of the headmaster.

4 Finally this gradualist approach, from the headmaster to the school team and then to other members of the school community takes care not to rush the process of school-based review.

In the circumstances, and taking into account the objective of using SBR as an innovation strategy, a step-by-step approach seemed entirely justified. In addition, it has to be noted that the involvement of parents as genuine members of the school community, was an even more delicate matter. In fact there is a large diversity in the extent to which parents participate in school life. For that reason it was good to deal with the question of involving parents in the SBR process, in an extremely cautious way.

Training During the Preparation Phase

The training the headmasters/internal coordinators participated in was built up around three central elements:

1 knowledge of and insight into the procedure of SBR:

- theoretical backgrounds;
- key principles;
- development of the procedure;
- essential instruments and documents;

2 requisite skills to carry out the procedure:

- general skills: to analyze, to diagnose *etc*;
- specific skills: to motivate, to stimulate, to inform, to report, to guide a meeting;

3 attitude-formation:

- innovation readiness;
- critical sense;
- sense of cooperation and delegation;
- willingness to study.

During the first year of the preparation phase, the training consisted of five training days. They became days of thinking and doing. Attention was paid to the acquisition of insight into the process, as well as to the specific school context. So, 'starting from headmasters' own experiences' and 'preparing every skill for use in school' were constant principles in the method used. By way of illustration, here is an outline of the content of these five seminar days.

1st Seminar:
1 Experiences concerning preliminary information, moments of decision and selection, reactions of the staff.
2 Information about the school-based review and its cyclic character.
3 The study in depth of the initial review, especially the components based on school life.
4 Emphases in the pre-arranging period are on:
   - working on the school climate;
   - conditions for the school-based initial review;
   - the skill to review;
   - the attitude to review.

2nd Seminar:
1 Experience of the schools.
2 From initial to specific review.
3 The technical side of the specific review.
4 The application of several skills for staff activities.

3rd Seminar:
1 Experience of the schools.
2 The use of a reference scheme for the specific review.
3 The RPS project as an element of the reference scheme.
4 The relation between RPS goals and RPS activities.
5 To provide and work out information in the staff meeting.

4th Seminar:
1 Experience of the schools.
2 Study in depth of the RPS project.
3 The fulfilment of the first guidance contract.
4 To the next moment of decision.

5th Seminar:
1 Preparation for the staff decision concerning the start of the initial and specific review.
2 Finalize the initial review phase:
   - the survey sheet;
   - the collection of the different opinions;
   - the survey for the assessment of priorities.
3 Preparation for the next steps.

Decision and Selection Procedure

Certain decisions are related to selection for RPS. Because of the importance of these decisions and their impact on the course and direction of the project, it was necessary to formulate a process whereby a school is assessed for its suitability for renewal. The selection procedure is based upon the following principles.

When?

Different stages are provided in the preparatory process. For each stage, a decision and selection moment can be built in. The provision of several decision and selection moments guarantees that the least motivated schools can leave the project. At each of these moments, the school has to consider whether to continue with the process or not. Each positive decision means a renewed engagement that has to be set down in a guidance contract.

Who?

Several authorities or individuals could be involved in the selection procedure. This depends on the nature and the content of the decision or the selection. According to the school-based principle of the procedure, the members of the school team are involved as much as possible in the different moments of decision.

On what basis?

When there are too many applicants, entry has to be restricted. This selection is done on the basis of objective criteria, including the motivation, the renewal capacities and the independence of the school.

Description of the Selection Process

During September of the school year 1983–84, a circular letter about the procedure was sent by the Minister of Education. In December 1983 a formal statement of intent to participate had to be made. It was assumed that collective consultation within the school had preceded the statement of intent. In January 1984, further information was provided for those who had committed themselves. After this, the school teams had to be consulted and they then had to decide whether their headmaster should follow the training for internal coordinators or not. After the confirmation that the headmaster would follow the training for internal coordinators, a training contract was made between the headmaster and the school committee on the one hand and the organizing bodies on the other.

Each internal coordinator was asked to deliver a report to the external coordinator. This had to contain the following:

1 a report of each of the five training days;
2 a description of the preparatory phase of the SBR procedure in the school;
3 the decision of the school team on their willingness to participate in the initial and specific review in their school; the decision of the school team is expressed in the signing of the guidance contract submitted to them for the school year 1984–1985; and
4 a 'design of planning' on the review procedure in the school.

The Contract 1983–1984
Contract concerning the training in 1983–1984 of the internal coordinator for the self-review procedure

Within this framework of the training of internal coordinators five preliminary meetings are planned.

The supporting team provides the following content for the training of the internal coordinator:

1 a profound discussion and step-by-step working out of the school-based self review process;
2 a training of the skills necessary to fulfil the school-based self-review.

The tasks of the internal coordinator are:

1 personal study of the school-based self-review procedure;
2 to participate in the organized seminars;
3 to work the information over again; personally and together with the staff;
4 to draw up a summary report describing the activities and experiences concerning the announcement and the training;
5 to prepare a proposal of planning to guide the self-review procedure in their own school, if necessary in cooperation with the supporting team;
6 to decide, at the end of the training period together with the school team, if they will start the self review.

The related school committee creates the conditions necessary for the internal coordinator to work.

the school committee	the regional and central supporting teams	the internal coordinator

name:
function:
signature:
date:

Results of the Decision and Selection Procedure

Number of schools which started (December 1983):	438
First moment of decision and selection (January 1984):	419
Second moment of decision and selection (September 1984):	279
Total number of schools that left the SBR procedure:	140

The 140 which quit comprised 100 that left the procedure of their own volition; forty that could not participate as a result of external selection. The relatively large number of 'drop-outs' was surprising. Yet it fitted the basic idea that the school should make its own decisions. Frequently cited reasons for contracting out were:

- the procedure requires too much time;
- the non-agreement of all the members of the team;
- the objectives of the RPS project were not clear.

The last cited reason concerned the external team because obviously the information about the objectives of the RPS project had not got across. Indeed, this was confirmed by the evaluation. Also, the external team had underestimated the obstacles a headmaster would encounter in reporting back to the school team. It also appeared that a lot of schools have been through the initial procedure without committing themselves. A lot of schools wanted information about the RPS project and the SBR procedure but were not motivated to start the project at the school level.

The Review Phase

Initial review

As a rounding-off of the training of the internal coordinators, the school team had to sign a guidance contract.

The following steps were foreseen:

1 introduction to the school team of the instruments for the initial review;
2 the filling in of the review list (initial review and priority indication);
3 analysis of the data;
4 discussion of the data in order to come to a consensus on the priority for further work.

This phase occurred during October–December 1984. At the end, a decision was made to do a further review (specific review) on the priorities.

The specific review

The main goals of the specific review were:

- a detailed review of the priority chosen in the initial review;
- to formulate recommendations to start improvement at the school or classroom level;
- to decide whether or not the school would enter the RPS project.

During this stage, the internal coordinator, together with a small working group, guided the process within the school. Their tasks involved the following steps:

1 an accurate description of the chosen priority area;
2 a description of the desired situation in relation to the goals of the RPS project;
3 a review of the actual situation with relation to the priority area;
4 an identification of conclusions and recommendations from the comparison between the desired and the actual situation.

In the meantime, the content of the action phase had to be made clear to the school. At the end of this stage, the school community had to decide whether it would agree the priority area. The next step consisted of the drawing up of an action plan in which school and external support describe their goals and their activities.

Support

The specific review was essentially an internal school event. External support was limited to the provision of background information on the conduct of SBR. However in certain cases it was necessary to draw the internal coordinators attention to the necessary basic information so that everybody would be able to work within the same content framework. Examples of this are: what is understood by 'school organization', 'professional relations between teachers', 'individualization'.

In the initial review as well as in the specific review, the internal coordinators engaged in a scenario like this:

- description of the steps;
- time investment;
- recommendations and examples;
- expected result at each phase.

Such a method gave clear support to the internal coordinator. It also gave the external coordinator the opportunity to control the process. Besides, the contract stipulated that the internal coordinator had to report on the process. Engaging in the right process rather than the final result of the initial review was the criterion for further selection.

Training During the Review Phase

Whilst the review process was continuing in the school, the seminars were now concentrating on the experiences of the school members/internal coordinator with the procedure. The contents of the second series of training days were stipulated by the members themselves. However, special attention was also paid to problems such as: how to use data to chart the 'desirable situation'; how to work with a sub-team; the magnitude of a set of priorities; how to inform other groups of the school community (for example parents); how to include the contribution of experts non-resident to the school.

Decision and Selection Procedure

The guidance contract for the school year 1984–85 was much more direct with the tasks of the external team being described more precisely. Besides instructions to internal coordinators, there was now much more demand to involve the school team in the SBR procedure.

The Contract 1984–1985
Guidance contract between the school team and the external support on the initial and specific review in the school year 1984–1985

The external support will provide the internal coordinator with the following training programme:

1 five days of study (seminars) which will examine the content of the initial and specific review process;
2 training in the skills necessary to fulfil the school-based self-review;
3 the drawing up and distribution of the necessary materials for the execution of the school-based review;
4 guidance concentrated on their own specific school situation by the carrying out of the initial and specific reviews.

The task of the internal coordinator includes:

1 further study of the process of school-based review;
2 to participate in the seminar;
3 to internalize the information;
4 to carry out the plan for the initial and specific review;
5 to draw up a summary report concerning the organization, the process and the results of the initial and specific review in the school;
6 to inform the staff, parents and the whole school community about the progress of the review;
7 to decide at the end of the specific review, whether to join the RPS project or not.

The task of the school team includes:

1 to take responsibility for the progress of the initial and specific review;
2 to take responsibility for the carrying out of the specific review;
3 to prepare for the decision to enter into the RPS project or not;
4 to take the decision to enter or not the RPS project;
5 to plan the developments for the coming period (of the school year 1985–1986).

The school committee:

1 informs itself about the development of the school-based self-review procedure in its school;
2 creates the conditions to enable the internal coordinator to take the training;
3 supports a positive climate for the initial and specific review.

Names of

the regional and central supporting team	the chairman of the school committee	the members of the school team (include the names and signatures)

During the school year 1984–85, external coordinators supported the process at the school level as requested by the internal coordinators: for example, they gave assistance at the initial review. There was also a new decision to be made on the following criteria:

1 attendance at the five training days;
2 a review of previous activities including:
   • experience of the initial and specific review at the school level;
   • the results of the initial review (choice of priority, consensus meeting);
   • results of the specific review, expressed in the form of an action plan;
   • a review on the initiatives taken towards others.

Information on these points was gathered from the reports on activities by the school and from the contacts of the external coordinators with the schools. At this stage, a completely worked out development plan was not required because further negotiations were necessary. Later, however, (September/October 1985) a detailed development plan, describing what would happen, how, when and where and who would be responsible, had to be worked out.

The school team and the school committee (and eventually other participants) were asked to decide whether they wanted to act upon the action plan within the whole of the RPS. If so, the school would attempt to implement the drafted action plan within the RPS concerns (goals). This means that the school sets up its action plan within the context of RPS goals. The area the school intends to improve is consequently located in the larger framework of the renewal of the primary school in accordance with RPS. By taking a decision to enter the RPS project, the school agrees to develop chosen priorities, in the direction of RPS concerns and in coordination with RPS guidance. This intention is clearly accepted by the school and should be the result of consultation between the participants involved.

Finally, proper school development requires the involvement of all those who are committed to the school. This shared responsibility takes shape in the formation of the so-called local Steering Committee which is, together with the headmaster, responsible for the improvement process in the school. A representative of the parents is a member of this local Steering Committee; together with representatives of the teacher group, of the psycho-medica-social centre, the headmaster and a representative of the organizing body.

Evaluation of the SBR Strategy

This school-based review strategy which presaged involvement in RPS is subject to both internal and external evaluation.

Internal Evaluation

Positive experiences of the internal coordinator (IC) in the use of the school-based self-review strategy include the following:

1   The IC has learned how to deal with written guidelines. This enhances the autonomy of the individual IC and has a considerable effect in improving the self supporting character of the innovation at the school level. It enhances the chance of mutual adaptation.
2   The IC looks for help from colleagues in a spontaneous way. This helps the creation of a network of contacts between ICs.
3   The IC non-headmaster contributes to the development of an innovation group within the school. More and more attention is paid to the specific qualities of the members of the team.
4   Because of the initial review, staff regard self-evaluation as an important thing to do.
5   The biennial SBR period creates the awareness that the extent of innovation one wishes to introduce and the amount of time one proposes to spend on the innovation have to be realistic.
6   Through contact or conflict, the IC learned to see the present

external school supporters as significant figures in the innovation process.

7   As a result of the process the IC realized how important and necessary support for SBR is.

8   The combination of the development of an action plan and the support contract led to a process oriented attitude by the IC.

9   Working with contracts gives both internal and external supporters and the school a clarity about their relationship and about SBR.

10   The ability of the headmaster/IC to analyze and give feedback is enhanced.

11   A perspective on the school as an organization is developed.

12   The IC realized the importance of making plans and managing them.

External Evaluation

The Catholic University of Leuven is currently undertaking an external evaluation of the use of the SBR strategy. At the moment three reports are ready:

1   The results of teacher interviews, from a sample taken at random of thirty-four schools (out of a total of 204) giving 201 teachers and thirty-four headmasters (July 1985, 78 pp.).

2   An investigation into the involvement of the IC and teachers (the same population was examined) (September 1985, 80 pp.).

3   The results of a configuration interview (the same population was examined) (December 1985, 156 pp.).

In 1979 the same research institute (KU Leuven) started an external evaluation of the RPS project. This led to the publication of a report on the analysis of the local innovation policy in relationship to the implementation of RPS goals (January 1985, 260 pp.). In it, it is emphasized how each school develops a local innovation and is characterized by it. The experiences of the SBR strategy illustrated that in order to achieve a local innovation policy, special attention in relation to the SBR procedure was paid to:

- setting up plans to obtain better coordination of the work to be done by the innovation;
- systematic and open discussion of the data and the structuring of information flow;
- making the action plans suited to each particular school;
- the enhancement of the professional ability of team members by a thorough analysis of the actual situation and the management of frames of reference in order to determine the desirable situation.

Conclusions on the Use of the SBR Strategy in the RPS Project

1 SBR creates a favourable climate for the development of RPS. Two points are important: a concern for the systematic development of the review process and the capacity of SBR to assist a school decide whether it is ready to enter the RPS project.

2 The headmaster/internal coordinator is a key actor in the process. The external team have to provide training for headmasters as internal change agents and the headmasters have to be prepared for their tasks as coordinators of the review and team builders.

3 SBR at the school level is increasingly considered as just one step in a long-term innovation process.

4 In the global context, it is important that policy structures as well as support structures subscribe to and support the review process.

5 The time investment required from the team members for the SBR procedure may be underestimated.

6 To prevent the process from being perceived as a top-down strategy (it is intended to be a bottom-up strategy), attention has to be paid to the linking of training sessions to the practical reality of the school situation. The experiences that headmasters bring to meetings are most important and need to be taken into account.

7 By strengthening the problem solving capacity of the school, the intention of SBR in the Belgian situation was to increase the relative autonomy of the school. The recent research on the RPS project, suggests that schools confronted with a large scale project (like RPS) develop different types of local policy making. Although SBR may be an effective means for the implementation of innovations in schools (by strengthening their problem solving capacity), it might be useful for the central policy makers and the external team to consider the characteristics of local policy making in cases where SBR is involved.

Note

1 This case study is also published in Bollen R and Hopkins D (Eds) (1987) *School-Based Review: Towards a Praxis*, Leuven, Belgium, ACCO, as part of the OECD/ CERI International School Improvement Project (ISIP) series. Permission to reprint is gratefully acknowledged.

LEA Initiated School-Based Review in England and Wales[1]

Philip Clift

Introduction

The provisions for the control of state education in England and Wales were established by the Education Act of 1944. Responsibility for the administration of education is devolved to autonomous local education authorities (LEAs), now 104 in number. With regard to the curriculum, the only national statutory requirements concern religious education. For the rest, responsibility is further devolved to boards of governors appointed by the LEA to each individual school or college. Thus, in principle, schools have almost total autonomy in curriculum matters. In practice, of course, there is a broad consensus concerning what should be taught, imposed by professional custom, popular expectation and, in secondary schools, also by the syllabuses of the various public examining boards.

The monitoring of the quality of education provided by state schools is done at two levels. At the national level, Her Majesty's Inspectors of Schools (HMI) report directly to the Secretary of State for Education and Science. Prior to 1981, access to their reports was restricted to the school or college concerned, its LEA and the Department of Education and Science. Since 1981, these reports have been openly published.

At the local level each LEA has a team of advisers, sometimes called inspectors, reporting directly to their chief education officer. Their function is rather loosely prescribed. In practice they tend to act as 'go — betweens' for the teachers on the one hand and the administration on the other.

Neither HMI nor the LEA inspectorates have any direct authority over schools but both wield enormous influence. This is particularly true of the latter, who advise on the resourcing of individual schools and the promotion of individual teachers.

Since the mid-1970s there has been evidence of growing public disquiet over the quality of education provided by state schools in England and Wales and of political pressure to make schools and teachers more publicly accountable. This has resulted in two changes in the law. The Education Acts of

1980 and 1981 required schools to provide parents with more information about the curriculum and school organization and to publish their results in public examinations. At the same time, falling school rolls (a consequence of an earlier decline in the birth rate) made it possible to give parents the right to choose which of the various local schools they would send their children to. These changes were accompanied by the decision (noted above) that HMI reports on their inspections of individual schools should be de-restricted.

The increase in the public accountability of schools and teachers indicated by the publication of HMI reports has not been accompanied by any great increase in inspection, however. It was tacitly accepted that this was impracticable given the relatively small number of inspectors compared with the number of schools. An enlargement of inspectorates, HMI or LEA, of the magnitude necessary would have been prohibitively expensive. Nor was an increase in inspection deemed to be the most effective means of bringing about school improvement. Rather, schools have been exhorted to take the responsibility for systematically reviewing their own performance (DES, 1977, 1979, 1981 and 1983) and for making any changes subsequently seen to be necessary.

In reponse to this exhortation, by the middle of 1982, four-fifths of the LEAs in England and Wales had been involved in devising schemes for systematic school-based review (generally called 'school self evaluation' in England and Wales) and about one-third had already published them (Elliott, 1982). There is a predictable variety amongst these schemes. Most are voluntary, a few are not: most are 'free standing', some are the counterpart of programmes of testing or inspections. They have one major common feature however: virtually all include a booklet of classified questions or statements about schools and schooling. The contents of these booklets differ mainly in detail only: there is a broad consensus in the national agenda for school-based review which they present. It is a professional's catechism: there is little evidence of any lay influence in the various booklets (Open University, 1982). This case study of LEA initiated school-based review in England and Wales includes reports on research into the use by schools of three contrasting examples of such LEA schemes.

The LEA Schemes[2]

The reports which follow are of research into school-based review in the Metropolitan District of Solihull, the County of Oxfordshire and an Outer London borough. They exemplify the variety of approaches to school-based review adopted by LEAs in England and Wales:

- voluntary review, without any requirement to present or even produce a report;
- compulsory review, followed by the production of a report to be presented to the Education Authority;

- compulsory review, followed by the production of a report to be presented to the LEA which is then 'audited' by the LEA inspectorate.

Each scheme is described, the aims of its originators presented and its effectiveness in achieving those aims assessed on the basis of empirical evidence collected during a programme of research carried out in the School of Education at the Open University over the past six years.

The Solihull Scheme

Solihull has developed a voluntary scheme for school-based review. A booklet for secondary schools (Solihull, 1979) was published in 1979, and one for primary schools (Solihull, 1980) the following year. A limited number of these booklets was distributed free to each school in the authority. This case study deals with the scheme for secondary schools only.

The contents of the Solihull secondary school booklet (Solihull, 1979) are arranged in four main sections, as follows.

EVALUATING ORGANIZATION AND MANAGEMENT
A framework for evaluating the organizational and management work of the school as a whole, of groups of staff such as departmental and pastoral teams, and the work of individual staff in their organizational and management roles.
1 Objective setting.
2 Planning:
    (a) general considerations;
    (b) staff recruitment, selection, allocation of tasks and development;
    (c) the provision and use of material resources and finance;
    (d) the sequence and timing of activities.
3 Decision making.
4 Distribution of responsibility and authority.
5 Group and personal relations, motivation and morale.
6 Communication, including routine administration.
7 Coordinating and supervising the system.
8 Evaluation and review of a working group.

EVALUATING SPECIFIC ASPECTS OF THE SCHOOL'S WORK
1 The curriculum.
2 The pastoral system.
3 School 'climate' and discipline.
4 Extra-curricular arrangements.
5 Health and safety.

6 The library.
7 Careers and further and higher education guidance.
8 Pupil assessment, record keeping and reporting.
9 The school's external relations with:
(a) community;
(b) parents;
(c) other educational establishments;
(d) education office and welfare agencies.

FURTHER ANALYSIS OF TEACHERS' ROLE

1 Analyzing the subject teacher's role.
2 Analyzing the teacher's pastoral role.
3 Analyzing the teacher's role as a member of the school and the teaching profession.

IN-SERVICE EDUCATION AND STAFF DEVELOPMENT
Response Sheet for In-service Enquiry.
1 Curricular aspects.
2 Pastoral aspects.
3 General and interdepartmental aspects.
4 Services offered by external agents.
Sample evaluation reponse sheets.

The way in which schools should use these booklets is not closely prescribed. Implicitly they seem intended for use in a collegial fashion, however. Teachers are expected collectively to consider the various statements within each section (the number in a section ranges from less than ten to over fifty), then to rate them in terms of importance vis-a-vis their particular school, and the effectiveness of their school vis-a-vis that statement, making use of the response sheets provided. The purpose of the scheme is thus school improvement rather than school accountability. The function of the scheme is diagnostic and remedial. Teacher participation supposedly ensures consensus concerning school needs and commitment to bringing about improvements.

In keeping with the voluntary nature of the scheme, no timetable for use of the booklet is laid down by the LEA and no report on what is revealed by the review is required. No formal procedure has been set up by the LEA to ensure that, or even to ascertain whether, agreed developments are implemented by the schools. Indeed, there is no explicit requirement that schools should make use of the booklet at all.

Research

Our involvement in Solihull began with two case studies of the impact of the LEA's scheme on two of its secondary schools (Turner, 1987a). They were retrospective studies: of school-based review activities that had taken place two years previously (*ie* in 1980); of any school improvements which had occurred and of the extent to which such improvements were seen to be the direct consequence of the school-based review by the teachers involved. We later followed up these case studies with a survey of a representative sample of Solihull secondary school teachers (Turner and Clift, 1985).

The Solihull case studies

There was a marked contrast between the two schools in the enthusiasm with which the Solihull booklet was introduced. In the one school, the head and senior staff very actively promoted the school-based review exercise; whereas in the other, senior staff had expressed reservations about its value, particularly as manifested in the Solihull booklet. In this school, few shortcomings were perceived and hardly any improvements were subsequently proposed. Indeed one teacher commented that, during the exercise, much satisfaction with the *status quo* had been expressed by all concerned (Turner, 1987a). In the other school, discussions had led to proposals for a number of improvements. Such improvements as subsequently were made, however, were of a relatively trivial nature and did not seem to persist, and at the time of the case study interviews (late in 1982), many of the teachers involved had only vague recollections of what had taken place. Paradoxically they remained enthusiastic about the value of school-based review as a means of bringing about improvement. Indeed it was by popular request that a particular section of the Solihull booklet was used again in that school early in 1983.

The Solihull Survery

We designed a questionnaire in two parts. Part 1 was concerned with the Solihull booklet specifically, and part 2 with school self-evaluation generally. Part 1 ended by asking about actions taken as a consequence of the use of the booklet and the overall acceptability of the scheme. Both parts included Likert type attitude scales, developed from statements made by teachers in the case study schools. The responses to these items were subsequently factor analysed to investigate, teachers' latent attitudes towards the Solihull booklet and towards school-based review as a general notion.

The survey points to two major weaknesses in the Solihull voluntary scheme. The first is lack of familiarity. Three years after its publication, less than half of Solihull's secondary school teachers claimed to have seen the booklet, and a much smaller proportion claim to have read it all, or to recall it at all well. Thus for the majority, it has neither communicated a newly emphasized professional responsibility, nor has it provided an agenda for school improvement.

Despite its general popularity amongst teachers in schools where the Solihull booklet had been used, the evidence from the survey is that little or nothing changed in consequence. It is a reasonable assumption that improvement can be made even to the best of schools. The second failing is thus lack of effectiveness: of failure to guide and motivate school improvement.

It may well be that this is a weakness inherent in any scheme for school-based review, with its characteristic assumptions of egalitarianism and fraternity. There is always bound to be a considerable vested interest in the *status quo*, particularly amongst the most entrenched and powerful individuals in any institution: the way things are generally suits them well enough.

The evidence from this survey tends to support this view. The most consistently positive attitudes, towards the booklet and towards school-based review in general, are held by the most junior teachers. It may be that, for them, the attraction of school-based review in general, and of this scheme in particular, lies in the opportunity it appears to offer for them to take part in decisions about school policy. Its non-threatening nature, being focussed at an institutional rather than a personal level, is a further attraction. Institutional review and participation in policy decisions which are then not acted upon are, however, largely sterile occupations and the time consumed by what, on the evidence of this survey, is an ineffective process, is difficult to justify.

To offer an external agenda for school improvement, such as the Solihull booklet, in a spirit of *laissez faire* is thus doubly insufficient. As well as ensuring its widest possible dissemination, external means are also needed to encourage and support its use and to support the reforms its use suggests.

The Oxfordshire Scheme

The Oxfordshire scheme was published in 1979. It has two stated purposes:

   (i)   to promote the greater accountability of schools by requiring them to report on their practice to their governing bodies and to the LEA;
   (ii) to promote the improvement of educational practice by requiring schools to undertake a review of their activities.

It is in three parts. Parts 1 and 2 involve school-based review and part 3, the external validation and moderation of school-based review through comparisons with national standards in public examinations, HMI visitations and inspections and, resources permitting, inter-county exchanges of advisers and headteachers.

Part 1 of the scheme is a 37 page booklet: *Starting Points in Self Evaluation*, (Oxfordshire, 1979a) colloquially known as the 'pink booklet'. A copy of this booklet, of nearly 10,000 words, was given to every teacher in Oxfordshire. Its purpose is set out in a foreword by the Chief Education Officer:

This document is intended to be:
1   an aid to teachers individually or collectively, and schools in examining the value of what they do;

2   a starting point for discussion and further questioning whenever a
     school as a whole, or a department within a school, considers it
     appropriate to take stock of what it is achieving.

It consists of classified list of questions about various aspects of school and
has obvious similarities with the ILEA booklet *Keeping the School under
Review* (ILEA, 1977).

A three-page specification for school-based review, entitled *The Four
Yearly Report*, (Oxfordshire, 1979b) constitutes part 2 of the scheme. It sets
out the general arrangements for school reviewing and reporting in three
brief paragraphs:

1   The four-yearly report shall be confidential to those involved in its
     preparation, preservation and receipt. It will be the headteacher's
     responsibility to produce the report after consultation with the staff
     and help from the advisory services and such other lay or profession-
     al involvement external to the school as may be appropriate.
2   The report shall be presented to a meeting of the governors/
     managers at which the Chief Education Officer or his senior repre-
     sentative shall be present.
3   The report, together with the governors' minute on the report, shall
     be forwarded to the Schools Sub-Committee in confidential session.

It then lists eight topics which each school must consider:

4   The report shall have the following sections:
       (i)   Aims and Objectives
      (ii)   Factual Background
     (iii)   Care and Guidance Arrangements
      (iv)   Curriculum Arrangements
       (v)   Pupil Progress
      (vi)   Staff Development
     (vii)   School and Community
    (viii)   Future Directions

The rest of this brief document expands on this agenda, listing the
matters which should be considered under each heading. Nowhere in this
document is any reference made to the 'pink booklet', nor is there in the
'pink booklet' any mention of its use in connection with the preparation of
the 'Four Yearly Report'.

The third part of the scheme has never been formally implemented.

In order to operate the scheme in such a large LEA, a reporting cycle
was established. In 1979 it was announced that all schools were to present
reports every four years, the first schools in autumn 1980 and the last by the
spring of 1986, by which time the first schools to present their reports would
be into a second cycle. The scheme has since been amended to a five-yearly
reporting cycle because of the considerable administrative workload it produced.

The length of reports is not specified, it is merely stated that this depends on the size and type of school. Moreover, no guidance is given in the document as to how schools are expected to conduct the review required in order to produce the report.

Research

Our involvement with the Oxfordshire scheme began in 1980 with a case study of one of the first primary schools to carry out a review and present a report (Open University, 1982; Clift, 1987). This was followed by a case study of a much larger secondary school and when the first cycle of reporting was almost at an end, by a survey of a representative sample of Oxfordshire teachers, primary and secondary.

The primary school case study

The strategy adopted by this school for their review was simple in the extreme. The teaching staff set aside a number of late afternoon sessions during the second half of the spring term and the whole of the summer term, meeting as soon as possible after the children had gone home. At these meetings they discussed a series of papers prepared by the head or his deputy and circulated several days in advance. The papers dealt in turn with each of the eight topics ((i) to (viii) above). The only planned departure from this essentially responsive stance was for the last topic, *Future Directions* for which each member of staff was invited to prepare and present a paper. (In the event they elected not to commit themselves to print, but to present their ideas orally.)

It was rare for anything other than changes in emphasis in these papers to be requested, thus the version of each which appeared in the final report was virtually the same as it had been when it had first been presented.

The report was criticized by the LEA officers most closely connected with the school for not being sufficiently self critical: not self evaluatory in tone. A more searching examination of every aspect of the school should have been attempted, they said. One went further and said that in his opinion it was not even a particularly good description of the school. No changes in the school's internal policies and practices resulted from the review, but several shortcomings, which were the responsibility of the LEA and which had been identified by the teachers and included in the report, were subsequently remedied.

The secondary school case study

We then carried out a case study of a (much larger) secondary school preparing its report (West, 1987). The whole process took almost two years from the planning of the review to the presentation of the report to the LEA panel. Initially, the head had tried to persuade his colleagues to conduct the review on the basis of an agenda of issues cutting across the existing subject specialist and pastoral organizational hierarchies. The teachers resisted this and presented him instead with a series of departmental reviews, from which he then attempted to construct a report which reflected his original intentions. As with the primary school, the methods used in conducting these reviews were technically naive, involving little more than teachers meeting to discuss their policies and practices and to decide what to write about their department. The final report made over sixty recommendations for reforms, all apparently grounded in the reviews. It was later admitted in the school, however, that most of these reforms had been pending before the review even began.

The Oxfordshire survey

As for Solihull, we designed a two-part questionnaire based on the issues which had arisen in the case study schools (Clift and Turner, 1987). Teachers in primary, as well as secondary, schools were included, however. The questions in the first section concerned the Oxfordshire scheme specifically. Those in the second section asked about teachers' general perceptions of school based review and were virtually identical to those asked earlier in Solihull. We were thus able to compare the reactions of teachers to the contrasting schemes of these two LEAs.

In marked contrast to Solihull, in Oxfordshire, by the end of 1984, four-fifths of teachers had already been involved in a whole-school review. This mass acquaintance with Oxfordshire's scheme must be counted to the credit of its mandatory nature. Knowledge of a scheme and indeed making use of it, does not, however, demonstrate that it is of any particular merit. This may best be judged by how well it satisfies its own stated intentions.

Accountability

In principle, the first of these intentions has certainly been fulfilled. At the time when the survey was conducted, the vast majority of Oxfordshire's schools had already reported the results of a whole school review to their governors and to the LEA and the rest were about to follow suit. Beyond this fulfilment of the scheme in principle, however, lie doubts about how thorough were these reviews, how competent were the teachers as reviewers, how comprehensive was the reporting.

The vast majority of Oxfordshire's teachers claim that they were involved or very involved in their school's review, an equally large majority (four-fifths) felt competent to carry out a review and that their review was thorough or very thorough. But their inexperience in these matters is revealed by their admission that, prior to the introduction of the scheme, little or very little formal review activity had ever taken place in their school. The impression of incompetence is heightened by the data on review methods, the main ones used being 'staff discussion' and 'individual introspection'. Methods derived from educational or social science research are conspicuously absent. At best, the thoroughness of the reviews must be in doubt. Perhaps it was a realization of this which had led teachers overwhelmingly to characterize their own reports as 'descriptive' rather than 'judgmental'. In all this, the teachers can scarcely be blamed: the LEA offers no advice or help anywhere in its published scheme on how to collect valid and reliable data about a school, how such data might be judged or any standards against which such judgments might be made. Some teachers were aware of this lack and had turned to curriculum publications such as *The School Curriculum* (DES, 1981) for guidance. Given their view of the reports as generally descriptive, it is hardly surprising that few teachers felt that having to submit a written report on their school was professionally threatening to them. The case studies had indicated that, in the school studied, the Oxfordshire scheme for school-based review was relatively ineffective as a means of increasing contractual accountability. The survey suggests that this conclusion is generally true of schools in the county.

School improvement

It is even more doubtful if the second intention of the LEA: to promote the development of educational practice, has been fulfilled by the implementation of the scheme. Although two-thirds of Oxfordshire teachers consider that the scheme has been useful in producing proposals for change in schools, the actual changes claimed are rather nebulous and a quarter of all teachers are unsure as to whether their review has led to any changes at all. Despite this, the majority of teachers are in favour of going on to another round of reviews and reports. Clues as to why may be found in their attitudes towards school-based review as a general notion (that is, not specifically linked to the LEA scheme). The factor which accounts for the bulk of the variance in their responses is composed of attitudes towards the process of school-based review. Attitudes towards the school improvement appear as a separate factor: it is as if involvement in reviewing and reporting is a valid experience in its own right. Oxfordshire teachers do not appear to see a link between school-based review and school improvement. This suggests a weakness in communication on the part of the LEA with regard to its second intention.

The general conclusions drawn from the case studies in Oxfordshire schools were that teachers were responding ritualistically to the scheme by conducting relatively superficial and naive reviews of their schools, presenting reports which were mainly descriptive in their nature and not linking the review to any active programme of school improvement. The survey supports these conclusions. To date, the Oxfordshire scheme has at best only partially met its stated intention to increase the (contractual) accountability in schools. It has done little to develop in Oxfordshire teachers an awareness of the knowledge and skills necessary in order to conduct a searching and objective evaluation of their schools and the attitudes necessary to follow evaluation with school improvement.

The Audited Scheme

The scheme operated by the Outer London borough is also mandatory. A school-based review is followed by an inspection by a team of LEA advisers. Thus it possibly avoids some of the weakness of other schemes for school improvement, whether voluntary or compulsory, which involve school-based review alone.

The LEA has produced a document outlining the scheme. First it requires schools to produce a report under eight headings:

1   The school background — the philosophy of the school, its aims and objectives and the local community.
2   The staff generally — their responsibilities, qualifications, classes, communication procedures and policies for induction and inservice training.
3   The curriculum and school organization — including examination results, careers education, health education, provision for children with special needs, provision for equal opportunities and education for a multi-cultural society.
4   Pastoral care.
5   Capitation and financial matters.
6   Accommodation.
7   Health and safety.
8   Reports from each department — including staffing, aims and objectives, assessment of pupils, examination results, accommodation, capitation, resources and policies and procedures within the department.

The review is followed by an 'audit' carried out by the LEAs inspectorate ('advisers'). The procedure is follows:

1   The adviser in charge of the inspection shall meet the head and teaching staff and discuss with them the aim of the inspection.
2   The head and staff shall be informed of the areas proposed for inspection.
3   The terms of reference for the inspection should be decided and defined at meetings to be held before the inspection takes place.
4   Visits to observe lessons should only be made by prior appointment with the headteacher, all concerned knowing of the visit well in advance.
5   No discussion should take place during a lesson without first obtaining the permission of the teacher concerned.

6   The adviser's advice shall be no more than advice. Advisers should have no power to press their suggestions or to determine the curriculum.

7   Before the preparation of the final report, the person in charge of the inspection should meet the head and staff and discuss the outcome of the inspection. Copies of the initial draft of the report should be made available and time allowed for observations and objections to be made which could be incorporated in the final report.

8   Copies of the final report should be provided for the head and each member of staff.

9   Comments identifying individual teachers should not form part of a general report.

10 If an adviser proposes to comment adversely upon the work of an individual teacher at a meeting he should inform the teacher and give him an opportunity to reply. Only the head should have access to any adverse report.

11 The report should be confidential to the staff of the school, the governing body and the Education Committee.

Research

Our involvement with the audited scheme was confined to one case study, of a large secondary school (Turner, 1987b).

The school-based review

When introducing the scheme to the school, the Director made it clear that it had two purposes: accountability and school improvement, but with the emphasis on the former. Throughout the period of the school-based review, the conflicting purposes of accountability and professional development led to divergent perspectives among teachers as to what they were trying to do. On the one hand some teachers saw the process as a hindrance; as something they had to do for the LEA and which would have little consequence for themselves. Others wanted to reconceptualize it as a process which could be of benefit to the school and their department in particular. Thus some teachers, including the head, saw an opportunity in the school-based review for special pleading on staffing and resources. However, the extent to which any thorough evaluation took place within the school is questionable. Classroom observation and surveys of opinion within school were entirely absent from the process: the method most widely used was that of departmental discussion. However, in many cases even this did not take place and the school-based review was restricted to teachers reflecting on past events and reproducing information for the benefit of advisers.

The inspection

The first stage of the inspection consisted of the 'shadowing' of pupils by advisers. Six pupils were selected, one from each school year. The object of this exercise was for advisers to experience the school day as the pupils did. After the shadowing, regular visits began by all advisers to observe subject teachers at work and to look into the policies and procedures of the school.

This visit period lasted for half a term, although for some subject departments it was completed in only four weeks. Some teachers described the regime during the inspection as very artificial and claimed that in general their colleagues were not giving 'normal' lessons: for example, some teachers were making lesson notes for the first time in years. However, the majority of teachers who were interviewed claimed that they had not done anything different from what they would have done were they not being observed, except perhaps prepared lessons and thought things through more carefully.

The report

The first part of the report was mainly descriptive, much of it drawn from the report on the school-based review. Most of the rest consisted of departmental sections, mainly reflecting what advisers had already presented orally in feedback sessions, in some cases briefer and without any reference to actual individuals. Each was accompanied by a list of recommendations. A short section containing the principle recommendations for the school was included at the end.

School improvement

As a consequence of the advisers' recommendations, the LEA made substantial changes in staffing and resources. A new head of history was appointed to release the pastoral coordinator from a 'caretaker' role as head of history; a scale 3 second in department for English was appointed by promoting an existing member of the department. Some departments also gained material resources. For example the craft, design and technology department received money to replace inadequate stock and the Home Economics department was allowed to buy badly needed equipment. The head was able to use the report to argue successfully against a proposed staffing reduction of 7.4 teacher-equivalents, planned by the LEA as a consequence of diminishing rolls and reductions in local authority spending imposed by central government. The outcome was that the school lost only one teacher and its pupil/teacher ratio thus improved. The head said that he was 'highly delighted' with the outcome and claimed that the complacency of the LEA towards the school had been disturbed.

These were all improvements in what the LEA provided, however. The one change in practice, recommended to most departments by most of the advisers concerned an increased in the amount of oral work done with the pupils. Some of the teachers considered this to be a spurious recommendation born of the artificial conditions under which the lesson observations had taken place. Apart from this, few teachers were able to cite definite proposals for changes in internal policies and practices which were a consequence of the process of review and inspection.

The Value of LEA Initiated School Based Review

It is proposed now briefly to consider these three examples of LEA initiated school-based review in terms of a Matrix developed by members of the ISIP Area 1 (SBR) group (Bollen and Hopkins, 1987).

Preparation

In none of these cases were the teachers adequately prepared. Their past experience of school-based review, or of anything remotely resembling it was non-existent. Solihull LEA did little other than publish its voluntary scheme in the form of a booklet and distribute a limited number free to each of its schools. Oxfordshire took elaborate steps to ensure the political feasibility of its obligatory scheme whilst doing little to ensure its technical feasibility. Every teacher in the county was given an opportunity to meet its youthful and charismatic Chief Education Officer and to hear from him personally of the nature and value of what was proposed. The conditions for teacher participation and control of information were documented simply and unambiguously. This was true also of the audited scheme where the Chief Education Officer also introduced it personally to the teachers in the school which we studied, but in terms which placed stress on accountability. In no case was training in the skills necessary for school-based review offered: indeed there is no evidence of any realization on the part of those in authority that such training might be necessary. Similarly, no help with resources for carrying out the reviews were offered: it was tacitly assumed that the schools would 'find the time'.

Late in 1983 and early in 1984, Oxfordshire LEA undertook an 'evaluative exercise' in respect of the nature and workings of its scheme. This exercise resulted in a report to the Schools Sub-committee (Oxfordshire County Council, 1985) which set out the history and practice to date of the scheme and proposals for its modification. With the exception of a proposal that the next round of evaluation should be focussed on a particular aspect rather than the whole school as in the first round, these proposals concern the reporting procedures following the evaluation. Otherwise they simply reiterate what was stated in the original 'Four Yearly Report' document and still do not contain anything to help schools with evaluation processes.

The Reviews

Perhaps as a consequence of this lack of training and resources, the reviews were characterized by a naivety of approach. No use was made in the reviews of the methods of social science research. The most popular methods (and in many schools the only ones) were personal introspection and group discussion. Little data was collected specially for the review: little use was made of data already in existence in schools. Where reports were required, they were generally acknowledged to be descriptive rather than judgmental. No distinction was made between an initial and a specific phase of review. Only one of the LEAs included procedures to validate the school's conclusions. Here, the 'audit' conducted by the LEAs advisers (inspectors) was so different from the review that it was almost an unrelated exercise.

Development

Such school improvements as resulted from these reviews were mainly in terms of extra resources from the LEA. In this, the mandatory schemes were much more successful than the voluntary one: there is an obvious moral obligation on an LEA which requires it schools to conduct reviews, to remedy any shortcomings in its responsibilities revealed in consequence. This moral obligation does not necessarily apply where the reviews are voluntary.

Institutionalization

In Solihull, school-based review is a voluntary activity and it seems now to have virtually ceased. In Oxfordshire, the first cycle of reviews and reporting is now complete and a second is about to begin. Changes in the scheme are proposed which are concerned mainly with narrowing the focus of the reviews. No provision is proposed for the technical preparation of the teachers as reviewers. In the case of the audited scheme, other schools will proceed with reviews but there is no expectation on the part of the teachers who have already completed theirs that they should be involved in review activities until it is their turn again in some years time.

Conclusions

At the beginning of this paper, it was suggested that there is a belief in official and professional circles that, for schools to take responsibility for reviewing their own performance is the most effective and efficient way of bringing about national school improvement. These studies suggest that in England and Wales school-based review, in accordance with LEA initiated schemes, has not been effective in the ways intended. It does not seem to have generally motivated the teachers involved to make tangible changes in their working practices or to redeploy the resources already available to them to any greater effect. There are indications, however, that it has been effective in ways not necessarily intended. The process of school-based review inevitably reveals shortcomings in the resources provided by the LEAs and the identification of these shortcomings and the use of reports as a basis for successful 'special pleading' has been a feature of the mandatory schemes.

This failure to operate in the way intended seems to be due to teachers' lack of experience and expertise in the process of SBR and perhaps to a lesser extent to their lack of commitment to a scheme originating outside their school. For school-based review to be of any real value, therefore, substantial resources need to be devoted to the in-service training of teachers as evaluators. School-based review is also time consuming and demanding, requiring teachers to divert substantial amounts of their time and energy to it from their other duties. This has obvious cost, or at any rate, 'opportunity cost' implications. It is also questionable, therefore, whether school-based review, as practised, is an efficient means of bringing about school improvement.

Notes

1 This case study is also published in Bollen, R and Hopkins, D (Eds) (1987) *School-Based Review: Towards a Praxis*, Leuven, Belgium, ACCO, as part of the OECD/CERI International School Improvement Project (ISIP) series. Permission to reprint is gratefully acknowledged.
2 It should be borne in mind that the research reported in this case study is into procedures in force in these three LEAs in the early 1980s and that these procedures may well have been modified since that time.

References

Bollen, R and Hopkins, D (Eds) (1987) *School-Based Review: Towards a Praxis*, Leuven, Belgium, ACCO.

Clift, PS and Turner, G (1987) 'Teachers' perceptions of a mandatory scheme for school self evaluation', in Nuttall D *et al* (Eds) *Studies in School Self-evaluation*, Lewes, Falmer Press.

Clift, PS (1987) 'Self evaluation in an Oxfordshire primary school' in Nuttall, D *et al* (Eds) *Studies in School Self-evaluation,* Lewes, Falmer Press

DES (1977) *Education in Schools: A Consultative Document*, London, HMSO.
DES (1979) *Aspects of Secondary Education in England: A Survey by HM Inspectors of Schools*, London, HMSO.
DES (1981) *The School Curriculum*, London, HMSO.
DES (1983) *Teaching Quality*, London, HMSO.
ELLIOTT, G (1982) *Self-evaluation and the Teacher: Part 4 — Report on Current Practice*, Hull, University of Hull (mimeo).
ILEA (1977) *Keeping the School Under Review*, London, Inner London Education Committee.
NUTTALL, D L, McCORMICK, R, TURNER, G, HOLLY, L, JAMES, M, WEST A, and CLIFT, PS (1987) *Studies in School Self-evaluation*, Lewes, Falmer Press.
OPEN UNIVERSITY (1982) *Course E364: Curriculum Evaluation and Assessment in Educational Institutions*, Milton Keynes, Open University Press.
OXFORDSHIRE (1979a) *Starting Points in School Self-evaluation*, Oxford, Oxfordshire County Council, Education Committee.
OXFORDSHIRE (1979b) *The Four-yearly Report*, Oxford, Oxfordshire County Council, Education Committee.
OXFORDSHIRE COUNTY COUNCIL (1985) *School Self-evaluation in Oxfordshire*, Oxfordshire Education Department (mimeo).
SOLIHULL (1979) *Evaluating the School: A Guide for Secondary Schools in the Metropolitan Borough of Solihull*, Solihull, Metropolitan Borough of Solihull Education Committee.
SOLIHULL (1980) *Evaluating the Primary School: A Guide for Primary Schools in the Metropolitan Borough of Solihull*, Solihull, Metropolitan Borough of Solihull Education Committee.
TURNER, G (1987a) 'School self-evaluation and its impact: The effects of a voluntary LEA scheme on two secondary schools' in NUTTALL, D *et al* (Eds) *Studies in School Self-evaluation*, Lewes, Falmer Press.
TURNER, G (1987b) 'Self-evaluation linked with inspection: A case study of an urban comprehensive school' in NUTTALL, D *et al* (Eds) *Studies in School Self-evaluation*, Lewes, Falmer Press
TURNER, G and CLIFT, PS (1985) 'Teachers' perceptions of a voluntary LEA scheme for school self-evaluation', *Educational Research*, 27, 2.
WEST, A (1987) 'Self evaluation in an Oxfordshire secondary school' in NUTTALL D *et al* (Eds) *Studies in School Self-evaluation*, Lewes, Falmer Press.

School-Based Review: A Response from the UK Perspective

Philip Clift

I would like to begin this response by reiterating some of the points my good friend Robert Bollen has made concerning the nature of what we in ISIP term school-based review. I propose then briefly to describe the approaches to SBR, as thus defined, which have been evident in England and Wales over the past decade. Finally, I shall consider the implications for SBR in the UK contained in the ISIP conceptualization, as presented by Robert Bollen.

The SBR Concept

Fundamental to the nature of SBR (ISIP version) is that it is systematic. As Robert points out, it is not new as a notion: teachers have always reviewed their work to a greater or lesser extent according to temperament and head-teachers have reviewed the corporate work of their schools. What is new is the systematic and formal approach, involving agreed routines and procedures, agreed agendas of what to review and an integration of these into complex school management procedures.

Thus SBR involves us in the development of techniques: of data collection, of data analysis, of the evaluation of these data and of linkage of this evaluation to programmes for improvement. SBR can thus be viewed as a means to an end: a way of systematically identifying weaknesses and shortcomings and providing corporate motivation to improvement.

But perhaps the most important — and subtle — perspective on SBR which has emerged from our ISIP activities which Robert draws attention to, is SBR as an end in itself. This conceptualization, which Robert sees as potentially the most fruitful one, rests on the belief that systematically going through a process of institutional review raises the corporate self-awareness of a school to an extent which is a major school improvement outcome in itself. For it automatically promotes the enhancement of internal communication, the sharing of aspirations and the motivation to professional and institutional development. In making this argument, Robert also points to the incongruity of associating SBR with any kind of contractual accountability.

As a natural outcome of the systematic and formal nature of SBR as thus conceived, Robert rightly draws attention to its demanding nature; to the fact that it cannot be conceived of as a fringe activity to be done in 'a bit of the slack' time which teachers may be able to find in their termly routines. SBR needs time and energy in its own right.

This raises the question of whether SBR is really an incongruous notion, given schools as they are. The issue may well be: is it an ideal process applicable in reality only to ideal schools, or can it create those ideal schools and, if so, what policy changes in our education system are necessary in order to permit schools to make the change and what would the costs of such changes be?

SBR in England and Wales

The form which SBR has tended to adopt in the UK is Robert's 'most potentially fruitful', that is, the school improvement strategy in itself. We can discern three distinct, but related, approaches. First there are the LEA initiated schemes, of which about fifty have been published to date. These may be sub-divided into three types:

- voluntary review without any requirement to present or even pre-pare a report for the LEA;
- compulsory review, followed by the presentation of a report to the LEA;
- compulsory review, followed by the presentation of a report to the LEA, which is then 'audited' by an inspection.

The evidence from the UK case study suggests that these schemes have fallen short of the ideal in their actual operation.

The second form which SBR has taken in the UK is a wholly school generated one. The contents and procedures of the LEA schemes have in many cases influenced these school generated schemes but otherwise they are free of outside pressures and agendas. Such evidence that we have concerning these schemes is that they tend to lack form and substance and thus again fall far short of the ideals of SBR.

The third form, and perhaps the most hopeful, is represented by the GRIDS project (McMahon *et al*, 1984). GRIDS is an acronym for 'Guidelines for the Review and Internal Development of Schools'. The Schools Council sponsored it in its latter days and its successor, the School Curriculum Development Committee, has continued to do so. GRIDS has also had a considerable influence on SBR in other parts of Europe as a consequence of the ISIP project.

The principle of GRIDS is to retain the benefit of structure inherent in the LEA schemes, whilst at the same time engendering commitment in schools by permitting teachers to decide on what to review and how. We have some evidence that GRIDS in some places and to some extent reaches towards the ideals of SBR.

Implications for the UK

The collective ISIP experience of SBR in a variety of member countries points to the following tentative conclusions:

1 SBR requires that teachers be trained for it. Precisely how and in what ways is not clear — perhaps the methods of social science research and the skills of social science researchers provide the best model. A search for objectivity is the keynote.

2 SBR requires that schools devote a substantial amount of time, energy and resources to it. Nowhere has it succeeded as a 'fringe' activity.

3 In its idealized form, SBR requires idealized schools (or perhaps creates them?) in which collegiality, cooperation, open communication, and fraternity rule; and where professional development and professional self-respect go hand in hand. A measure of egalitarianism is probably vital. Not many schools match this in reality.

4 Even in its more instrumental (means to an end) form SBR requires that resources for improvement be made available. It is not the cost free means of obtaining school improvement which some writers have implied. Nor is it remotely a successful means of enforcing 'standards' on teachers.

5 Any close association between contractual accountability and SBR leads to the impoverishment of the latter and to an ineffective assertion of the former.

In summary, SBR presumes a highly professional teaching force — well trained in the skills of institutional review, aware of their own professionalism possessed of the high morale necessary to seek for constant improvement and confident of support in what they desire from the other stake-holders in education. It also presumes a very different apportionment of teachers time and energy than that existing in most schools at present.

Reference

McMahon, A, Bolam, R, Abbott, R and Holly, P (1984) *Guidelines for Review and Internal Development in Schools*, (Primary and secondary school versions) York, Longman, for the Schools Council.

4 The Role of Headteachers and Internal Change Agents in School Improvement

Introduction

The key role of the school leader is not necessarily confined to the head but can also include heads of department or any individual who assumes a leadership role within a specific context: 'internal change agent' is a term that also describes that role. Although there is now general agreement on the crucial importance of the role of the school leader in school improvement, there is still a certain degree of opaqueness associated with the skills involved and the most effective ways of developing them.

Eskil Stego tackles these problems directly in his paper. He first discusses the importance and the role of the school leader: second, he outlines in some detail the training needs of school leaders at various stages of their development; and third, he discusses the contribution of the school context to and the role of the educational authority in school leader development. What clearly emerges from this discussion is the importance of the personal qualities of the school leader, the qualitatively different nature of the role qua teaching, the need for long-term planning in the development of the role and the crucial contribution made to this process by the educational authority.

The case studies in this chapter are at the mirco level; they record attempts by headteachers in particular settings to improve the quality of education offered in their schools. The cases are taken from Italy and England but are not intended to be representative of school leader activity in those countries.

The headteacher of the Leonardo da Vinci Middle School is experienced but new to the school. The school is in a high socio-economic area, is regarded as a 'good' school and has concentrated on traditional, cognitive approaches to teaching and learning. The head attempts two kinds of improvement: the first is to broaden the teaching approach; and the second is to achieve a closer link between the school and the surrounding community. Her improvement strategy includes: identifying needs; utilizing specialist resources and facilities available from external sources; harnessing the resources of the local community (including another local middle school); avoiding 'conflict or crisis management'; identifying and working with 'key stimulators' and providing visible models of the desired improvements. It is interesting to reflect on the generalizability of her improvement strategy: what personal capabilities are required to pursue such a strategy successfully? And how effective is the evolutionary or process view of improvement that she adopted?

The case study from England is in fact two 'mini cases' of head-teachers who introduce change. The cases focus on two secondary schools (one 11–18 the other 13–18) in which the heads (both new) attempted a considerable number of similar changes with contrasting success. The head of school A used a strategy similar to the one in the Italian case: consultative; facilitative; evolutionary; and made skilful use of external opportunities. Teachers' perceptions imply a considerable degree of success for this strategy, although the examples and some of the head's comments show that he sustained some disappointments and did not make as much progress as he had hoped. The head of school B used a much more directive strategy, initiating all changes himself, overruling the recommendations of working parties which he had set up and failing to take on external initiatives. This approach produced widespread staff alienation, a very critical resolution from the Staff Association and an adverse external review. With reference to these cases it is interesting to reflect on the head of school A's 'opportunistic innovations' which used external initiatives: should this approach be encouraged and if so, how? Also how might the head of school B have been helped to avoid the difficulties he encountered? This case raises again the fundamental question of whether new heads should be prepared for the task of leading school improvement? If so, when and how should this be done?

In making his response from the UK perspective, Ray Bolam elaborates on the points made in the presentation and cases by discussing the work of the National Development Centre (NDC) for Management Development (MD). The NDC define the ultimate aim of MD as 'improving the quality of teaching and learning in schools'. The immediate aim, however, is to improve the management performance of those with school management responsibilities. At the school level this requires a policy and a programme within which the professional development needs of the individual manager are balanced with the institutional development needs of the school. At the LEA level this requires a policy and a programme within which a range of needs are balanced. At both school and LEA level it requires a recognition that the MD needs may well vary significantly between individuals and groups of individuals. At both school and LEA level it must also be recognized that management development is a human resource strategy rooted in the organizational structure and therefore requires appropriate staffing and organizational arrangments for its implementation.

Perspectives on School Leader Development

Eskil Stego

What Is School Leader Development?

It seems as though school leaders in most OECD countries work within two broad but closely connected functional areas. On the one hand, they are responsible for executing the intentions of superior authorities by administering and organizing school activities according to existing aims and regulations. On the other hand, they function as active organizational leaders who utilize and develop the abilities of the people who work in the school. Where the emphasis of the school leader's work effort is placed, with this functional perspective as the point of departure, varies from country to country. In some countries school leaders are expected to be chiefly executors and to implement the decisions of the education authorities. However, it seems as though there is a growing interest in the need for the school leaders to play a more active leadership role — a role which means leading and improving the school in accordance with the conditions which exist in the individual school and the norms and rules which the members of the school have established. The work of a school leader seems, therefore, increasingly directed towards:

- utilizing and developing the professional ability of personnel;
- building up, 'maintaining and improving a well functioning social system where the personnel and the pupils in collaboration define the ambitions of the school in accordance with the general aims of the school, try out different work procedures, follow up on how school work is carried out and what results are achieved;
- taking the initiative for the continuous assessment of school work and leading improvement efforts aimed at increasing the quality of schooling.

School leaders at different levels and with different responsibilities will, more than ever before, be dealing with change. They can be changes which one would like to effect in order to achieve specific goals or changes forced on the school by outside circumstances. Such changes can sometimes occur rapidly, sometimes they develop gradually. Changes can be the result of changed values or a desire from individuals to take increased responsibility for their own actions or increased control over what they do. Changes can also be based on an increased consideration for an individual's needs, particularly where cooperation between people plays a central role. Often, quick, surprising and obvious changes, which have effects on the individual organization and its leadership have their origins in economic changes or demands for greater effectiveness. Whatever their source, changes always make demands on the school and on its leaders who have to be prepared to meet the challenge of improvement and to give it a positive direction.

The above examples for possible changes point towards a leadership role which is primarily characterized by flexibility and cooperation. Such leadership makes demands on the leader in the form of a capacity for self-knowledge, self-renewal and emotional maturity. None of these characteristics can be developed only through theoretical studies. They are primarily developed through contact with other people. It is in practical activity that the leader can test their knowledge, skills and attitudes and assess their real worth.

Programmes for school leader development should therefore be designed to give each school leader increased ability to shape his/her leadership into an instrument for systematic school improvement aimed at:

- an increased social interplay among the school's members and between them and the environment;
- increased pedagogic efficiency; and
- increased democracy in the school's internal work.

Programmes for school leader development should therefore strive to increase the capability of school leaders to understand their own school and its own system, the people working there and its connection with the world around. This understanding should find concrete expression in real problems; school leaders therefore need to have good insights into the factors which, taken together, mould the conditions for schooling. They ought to be able to systematically analyze their own school, its dependency on outer and inner forces and what the potential problems are. This calls for school leaders who are able to use adequate improvement models. Moreover, school leaders must be able to develop action plans which harmonize with their own ideas and those of their staff regarding the school and its improvement.

Glatter (1981) suggests 'that there are at least three other factors which, together with an individual's capabilities, will interact to determine whether the management practised by that individual in a school is effective' (p154). The other factors are:

- the school leader's position in the school hierarchy;
- the organization and micro politics of the school;
- the nature of the environment immediately surrounding the school and beyond.

Glatter also argues that school leader development can emphasize one or other of these factors, and which of them is emphasized depends on the views of those designing the particular scheme.

This statement leads us to conclude that development of school leaders can occur in different ways:

- it can be formulated as professional development measures that are adjusted to the development needs of individual school leaders, their schools or school authority;
- it can occur through different development efforts in the organization of the local school; and
- it can also be influenced by development of the school system both nationwide and inside the actual region or municipality.

These elements of school leader development are illustrated in figure 1; and are discussed in some detail in the following sections.

Professional Development of the Individual School Leader

A school leader's capabilities can be developed in different ways, both through knowledge — and/or experience based approaches. There are various approaches to developing individual capabilities such as self development, formal training programmes, courses or other training experiences. As Glatter (1983) says in referring to Burgoyne (1976):

> ... being taught was only one of a number of perceived sources of their managerial skills and qualities. Others included 'modelling' (copying from a respected other), 'planned discovery' (learning from experiences planned to produce learning), 'vicarious discovery' (learning from observation of others' successes and failures) and discussion (usually with those in similar situations). (p102)

Figure 1: Elements of School Leader Development

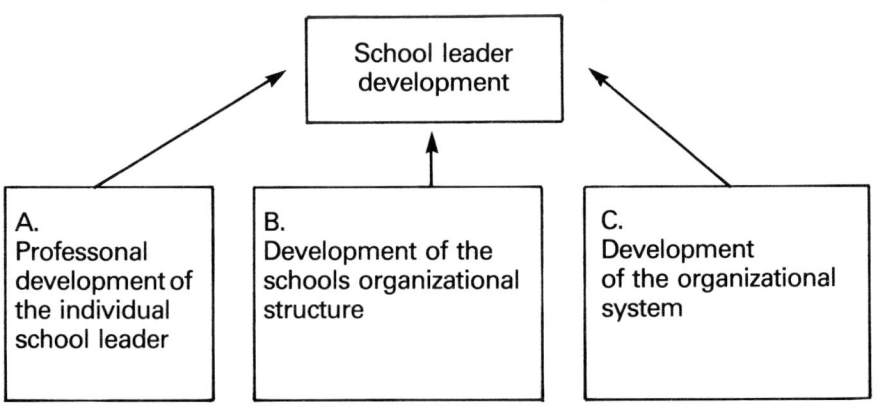

There are three main interest groups which are involved in the professional development of school leaders: the school leaders themselves; the school authorities and the institutions which contribute with different kinds of developmental support. By 'education authority', we mean the authority in the school hierarchy which is the school leader's immediate superior and has administrative responsibility for school education in the area in which school leaders work (for example, school districts in the US, local education authorities in the UK, local boards of education in Sweden).

Professional development occurs both in a planned and unplanned fashion, both through conscious and unconscious socialization processes as well as through formal education. Professional development is obviously given different emphases depending on whether the target group is composed of prospective or newly-appointed school leaders or a school leader with many years of experience.

Prospective School Leaders and Their Need of Professional Development

After having studied how the professional development needs of prospective school leaders are met at the present moment in different OECD countries, we have come to a number of conclusions. It is extremely important that the training of future school leaders involves not only a traditional administrative programme at a university but also participation in various activities which can give them practical experience of exercising leadership on their own. The education authority should therefore establish a development programme for those who intend to make a career as leaders in the school system. The programme should be formed so that the school leader candidates have the opportunity of:

- extending their general competence in such fields that academic courses do not provide. It is important in doing so, not only to bear in mind routine administrative duties but also to elucidate the school leader's role in school improvement;
- establishing close contacts with active school leaders and following them in the exercise of their professional duties and to give the future school leaders the opportunity of analyzing the expectations of interested parties concerning the school leader's role;
- practising leadership actively themselves at various levels in the school as head teachers, head of departments, resource teachers, leaders of development projects, investigators, as temporary assistants to inservice school leaders or by substituting school leaders on leave.

The education authority should also give future school leaders the opportunity of discussing their experiences with existing school leaders. Such exchanges of experience ought to take place in parallel with their work in different management positions.

To those who are thinking of becoming school leaders, we would like to offer the following advice:

1 Make a survey of what leadership/management experience you already have and try to analyze what competence and which personal qualifications these experiences have given you.

2 Try to investigate what hindrances there are to your achieving your ambition of becoming a school leader and how you can eliminate or reduce the effects of these obstacles.

3 Set up a plan for your career as a school leader — by taking stock of the leadership duties you need to fulfil in order increase your management experiences.

4 Take part in a training programme. If you do not have access to such education, plan how you can increase your competence in some other way. This can be done, for example, through self study or by participation in short educational programmes which concentrate on subjects which you judge to be important for your own improvement.

5 Examine your education authority's policy in order to enable you to plan your school leader career. Also, show an interest in and take part in the various activities which are arranged for future school leaders.

The Newly-Appointed School Leader's Need of Professional Development

The new school leader's work situation is particularly difficult when taking up the first appointment. It is, therefore, of particular importance that the education authority is prepared to help and guide the new school leader in growing into the professional role and in acclimatizing to the new workplace.

An induction programme should be tailored to the newly-appointed leader's actual work situation and his/her need of professional development. The nature of this professional development depends, obviously, on whether the leader in question has participated in some form of pre-training. These conditions are important in determining the scope of the type of training included in an induction programme.

During the first year of employment, the new school leader should be helped to grow familiar with the new environment. A representative of the education authority or an older colleague should take on the responsibility of being a 'supporter' who gives advice for example, on:

- the conditions which influence and control the school leader both internally and externally; or

- making a comprehensive plan of the directions that the management work should take during the first year.

The new school leader should, from the beginning of his/her career, be given the opportunity of developing their ability to work on a long-term basis and in a systematic way. This systematic work should, above all, be directed towards areas where the new leader feels a need for increased knowledge. The older colleague should help analyze the results of this systematic work.

It is not only during the first year of employment that a school leader needs help and support. An induction programme should also extend over the following two to three years. During this period, the new school leader should have the opportunity to increase his/her competence in the skills of school improvement. Experiences should be analyzed together with the experienced colleague and become an important foundation for learning.

Important premises for induction planning

If an induction programme is to be experienced as a meaningful activity it need to be based on the following principles:

1   First there is the *duration of an induction programme*. Adult learning often takes place in competition with many other activities so motivation is needed. School leaders seem to be preoccupied with the short-term benefits of what they learn but the short-term perspective is an unsuitable foundation for a development programme. The profession of school leader is not by nature an extension of the teaching profession: it is qualitatively different. Most new school leaders have not received any direct professional preparation through their previous employment and have only had limited leadership assignments. Consequently, they have to learn directly from the practice of their new role. Since competence in every aspect of the profession needs to be developed, different induction activities have to extend over a relatively long period of time.

2   Another premise is that school leaders are frequently assumed to *learn reflectively*. Reflection is meaningful because it leads to a wider understanding of one's own personality and role: so school leaders also learn by translating their own reflections into practice. The implication is that if school leaders are placed in instructive situations where opportunities for learning are created, they can use their previous experience of learning and draw conclusions for their own school situation. Here also, the assistance of qualified colleagues or consultants is necessary as the developmental process proceeds.

3   A third premise is that most school leaders seem capable of permanent learning *if learning focusses on concrete and immediate parts of their*

lives. If learning is made to focus on immediate details, this will enhance motivation for absorbing the lessons due to the potential usefulness of what is learned.

4 A fourth premise in the choice of development strategy is that *school leaders learn best from and with their colleagues.* Even if the school leader understands a new working method, it will not be put to use unless it has been shared by others in the school. To alleviate the negative effects of this well-known pattern, school leaders can be helped from the very outset to involve fellow school leaders in the work of learning. This can be done in many different ways; colleagues can observe and constructively criticize the professional activity of the participating school leader; they can present viewpoints concerning development tasks which the school leader is trying to accomplish and so on.

The Need for Developing Competence on the Part of Experienced School Leaders

The direction of the professional development of experienced school leaders is influenced largely by those persons who analyze and assess their development needs. These needs should grow through continuous assessment, not only of the individual leader's own activities but also of the school organization's efficiency and of the pedagogical and social work in school. This means that more interested parties than just the school leaders themselves should be involved in a survey of the school leaders' professional development needs. It concerns primarily the school personnel, pupils, parents and representatives for the education authority. Which development measures should be used in order to increase the individual school leader's capabilities should therefore be judged from different points of view. These can be:

- *the school's need* of leader development surveyed in connection with planning and carrying through of various school improvement projects;
- *the individual school leader's need* which is investigated by the school leader himself/herself, often in collaboration with representatives of the education authority; or
- *the education authority's need* of renewing and making more effective the work done by school leaders, with the education authority's general policy for school administration as the point of departure.

Watertight divisions between these several needs do not exist. The education authority should, however, consider it a duty to coordinate the needs expressed by different parties and work out a long term plan for school leader development.

School Improvement — The Foundation for Professional Development

In several OECD countries and increasingly elsewhere, there seems to be a connection between school leader development and school improvement. It seems that professional development is one of several important instruments for school improvement. But the dominant point of view is still that professional development primarily satisfies the individual school leader's needs for school improvement. However, professional development for school leaders is increasingly used as a means for the education authority to direct, initiate, support and stimulate long-term, planned improvement of the school. Because of this, it is the school's improvement ambitions which, to some extent, will decide the direction and content of school leader development. Consequently, the priority given by the education authority to leader development will depend increasingly on the individual school's improvement programme rather than on the school leader's personal needs. This means, among other things, that many school leader development activities will be carried out as team activities *ie* several people from the same school taking part in current development programmes. In this way, it is not only the school's formal leaders who acquire a wider proficiency but also representatives of the staff who can function as internal facilitators or 'change agents'. Leader development which has as its point of departure the improvement needs of the individual school, should be planned on a long-term basis. This calls for thorough preparatory work. One needs, among other things, to specify:

- which staff should participate;
- which leader capabilities the development programme is intended to strengthen;
- what the content of the programme should be;
- what expectations there are regarding the participants' contribution to the school after the development programme; and
- what different professional activities should be coordinated with other current improvement work in school.

The school leader's individual development needs

Much leader development will occur by the school leader's participation in specially arranged professional development programmes connected with various development projects in the school. However, school leaders need also to have the possibility of developing individual leader capabilities within areas where the school leaders themselves estimate that their qualifications are insufficient or out-of-date. This more traditional form of leader development is carried out at present in relatively unplanned and unsystematic way. The development needs which are provided for are often dictated by the fashion of the moment. Development efforts are thereby dominated by a marketing of 'news' — new work routines, new work procedures, new leader philosophies, *etc.* It is seldom that there are long-term and well planned development programmes which build on a continuous and conscious assessment of the school leader's current capabilities within different fields of activity in the school. Presumably this is due to the fact that, in many OECD countries, there is no tradition of the school leaders themselves or the school leaders in collaboration with a superior, repeatedly following up and checking the effects of their own leader work and individual professional capability. Such repeated assessments need to be taken into account in the education authority's goals and expectations for leadership work in the schools. This leads to an individually adapted development plan. In this plan should be specified:

- in which management areas performance needs to be reviewed;
- which leader capabilities need to be developed;
- how development programmes should be organized to meet these needs;
- how the effects of the improvement should be followed up.

The Education Authority's Responsibility for the Professional Development of School Leaders

Leader development in various forms is one of the education authority's most important means of directly influencing the organization and direction of school work; in connection, for example, with implementation of improved working methods and new work routines, or as a result of a more general and comprehensive assessment of the quality of schooling. The education authority should also be responsible for enabling school leaders to familiarize themselves with and analyze far-reaching social questions which, in the long run, will reflect on school activities.

The School Leader's Role as an Active Participant in Leader Development

Although many development activities are addressed to a school team, much leadership training is still aimed at the individual school leader. Individuals, however, can create the experiences which lead to further development. The following propositions relate to school leaders as active participants in different professional development activities:

1 A person taking part in a scheme of professional development has primarily the task of learning. Leader development, in order to be successful, must be built on the assumption that participants will learn because they experience a need for more knowledge.

2 An important prerequisite is that school leaders are prepared to play an active part in the improvement work. In order for this active

participant role to be attainable, it is an advantage for the school leaders to have realism in viewing their own role within the school community.

3   An important part is played in leader development programmes by the school leader's own enquiries and experimentation. In this connection s/he must be able — either directly during specific training times or indirectly during the development work which follows at school — to have his/her management style critically scrutinized by participating colleagues.

4   Programmes addressed to a school leader team should be based on the expectation that the school leader will play an active part in the planning, implementation and follow-up of the development activity concerned. Active participation is required not only in the seminar sessions but also in the work at school. In order for leader development to serve its purposes, the ambitions and plans evolved by the school leader must be rooted and processed in the working community of the school. It is the school leaders who are primarily responsible for solving the problems they have chosen to tackle. The school leader must be prepared to assume and share the risks involved by looking for a solution. It is also the school leader and his colleagues who evaluate the result and decide whether or not the solution is acceptable.

Organization Development as an Instrument for Leader Development

Development of the school's management functions can, as we saw earlier, also be achieved by changing the aims and general direction of the school management in the individual school. This form of school leader development can occur in many different ways. Here we shall only indicate some examples. We have found that leader development occurs if:

1   responsibility and work assignments are redistributed between different categories of leaders in the school, between the school leader team in a school and the education authority or between the school leaders and various decision making groups inside and outside the school. This kind of redistribution has often led to the school leaders being able to change their work priorities and assume a more active role in school improvement;

2   a hierarchical leadership structure is turned into a more democratic leadership team structure, or if an organizational system with autonomous decision making groups is created;

3   the capacity of the school administration to lead school improvement is reinforced by appointing resource teachers, facilitators, change agents or project leaders.

We have also discovered examples of leader development which build on changes in the school's decision making system, changes in the form of co-determination for the school personnel, pupils and parents, changes in information and communication systems in the school, *etc.*

Different Development Measures Within the School System

The education authority has numerous possibilities for directly influencing the extent and the direction of initiatives aimed at school leader development. We have already noted that it is important for the education authority to work out and present aims which specify the authority's views regarding the school leader's work and its general direction and the standards required for different categories of school leaders.

Such a statement can be the basis for a series of measures which the education authority should take in order to influence school leader development. It can, for instance, be used for:

- determining the policy of the education authority regarding identification, recruitment and career movement;
- allocation of work and responsibility between the education authority and school leaders;
- assessment of school leaders in the exercise of their professional duties;
- the building up of various collaborative channels between the education authority and the school leaders and between the individual school leaders themselves.

The education authority should have the ultimate responsibility for school leader development. This means, among other things, that a comprehensive strategy for leader development should be worked out and based on the:

- analysis of internal and external improvement needs and diagnosis of the consequences for the school organization and the school personnel;
- formulation of a school leader development policy that indicates strategies to realize desired school improvements;
- preparation, design, planning and execution of different measures and programmes that accomplish these improvements.

The choice of school leader development programmes depend on the analysis of forces which impinge on the behaviour of school leaders. Some of these factors are: composition of the management team, leadership styles, teaching duties, organizational complexity, availability of external support, *etc.*

The work behaviour of school leaders can also be influenced by a number of factors. Individual attributes are crucial but situational factors can also be of major importance. If the goal is to improve the behaviour of school leaders — then it is not sufficient simply to change the capabilities or attitudes of school leaders. We need also to take into account the situation and the climate within the school. These can enhance but also block change in behaviour. Therefore, school leader development should optimally focus on organizational development. Looked at in the opposite way, any structural change in the school as an organization requires specific skills from school leaders to support the specific change.

Finally, in many cases, the education authorities themselves need support from external professional organizations in order to carry out different development programmes for school leaders. This support is necessary in the form of consultant contributions directly aimed at the improvement of the individual schools, or of their leaders, or which are intended to support the education authority in working out strategies such as:

- recruitment and selection of school leaders;
- preparation and induction programmes;
- models for self assessment as a basis for identifying individual school leaders' development needs;
- creating networks of school leaders within and outside the education authority's area of responsibility; and
- 'peer consultation' programmes.

A Note on the Work of Area 2

Area Group 2's most ambitious undertaking is clearly the three-volume series on school leaders and their development. The first volume (Hopes, 1986) *The School Leader and School Improvement: Case Studies from Ten OECD Countries*, comprises a series of papers that discuss and analyze the current state of school management and school improvement in particular ISIP member countries or regions. Each country analysis includes a case study focusing on one or more individual schools from that country which give examples of school leader involvement in school improvement.

The second volume (Stego, *et al*, 1987) *The Role of School Leaders in School Improvement*, is in effect, a response to volume 1. It takes the data contained in the country analyzed, and particularly in the case studies, and analyzes it across national lines, using international perspectives to illuminate both what we already know and what we hope to learn about the school leaders' role in school improvement. The cases are generally accounts by school leaders who give their personal interpretation of events and processes. Thus, while the cases are valuable they may also portray a school leader bias. Although the book draws heavily on the case studies, they are not in any sense to be construed as representative of the state of schools or school improvement in their respective countries; rather, they are concrete examples of individual schools which illustrate the diversity and range of possibilities, problems and solutions open to school leaders in every country.

The final volume of the series is envisioned as a source book, consisting of training materials, programs and specific methods useful in promoting, supporting and extending the professional development of school leaders in the school improvement process.

Part of the impetus for this project was the wish of Area 2 members to meet what they perceived as a lack in the existing literature. Certainly, valuable materials on school improvement already exists — such as the major ISIP volume, *Making School Improvement Work* (van Velzen *et al*, 1985) and the first ISIP technical report by Hopkins (1985). Because of their generic or specific aims they could not, however, pay sufficient attention to the specific functions, needs, and potential for constructive action of school leaders, tending rather toward a broader overview of the entire improvement process. Much of the existing literature originates from North America and the United Kingdom. The contribution of our books is to look across a range of countries and cultures, using cross-national data for purposes of synthesis and analysis. This series then, attempts to explicate more fully and richly the role of school leaders in school improvement. The specific aims of the second book are to answer such questions as what the roles and tasks of school leaders in school improvement are, what capabilities leaders need for these roles and tasks, how these capabilities can be developed and finally, how school leaders are influenced by contextual factors and by their preparation for their school improvement roles.

References

BURGOYNE, JG (1976) 'Learning processes in the acquisition of managerial skills and qualities', *Management Education and Development*, 7, 3.

GLATTER, R (1981) 'Developing Staff for School Management' in Block 6, Open University Course E323 *Management and the School*, Milton Keynes, Open University Press.

GLATTER, R (Ed) (1983) 'Implications of Research for Policy on School Management Training' in HEGARTY, S. *Training for Management in Schools*, Windsor, NFER-Nelson for the Council of Europe.

HOPES, C (Ed) (1986) *The School Leader and School Improvement: Case Studies from Ten OECD Countries*, Leuven, Belgium, ACCO.

HOPKINS, D (1985) *School Based Review for School Improvement*, Leuven, Belgium, ACCO.

STEGO, E et al (1987) *The Role of School Leaders in School Improvement*, Leuven, Belgium, ACCO.

VAN VELZEN, W et al (1985) *Making School Improvement Work*, Leuven, Belgium, ACCO.

A Shot at Improvement: A Case Study from Italy[1]

Eliosa Ricatti

Arese is a satellite town in the neighbourhood of Milan. Its urban development scheme changed when the Alfa Romeo automobile plant was built
there some years ago. Other multinational industries were then established in
the same area and the sociological features of the resident population changed
dramatically. Blue collar workers employed in the big industries and factories
tended to move to neighbouring villages, whereas the middle management
staff and directors chose Arese as their place of residence. The Leonardo da
Vinci Middle School was built at the extreme end of this catchment area
which consists of cottages and blocks of flats surrounded by attractive gar-
dens. The pupils do not come from the original local community but from
the new settlements: some of them moved to the new, higher status area
from the oldest section of Arese.

The middle school was built six years ago as part of a multifunctional
centre including a creche, nursery and primary school. The creche has never
been used as such because of lack of demand and the building has recently
become part of the middle school. The middle school building is a two-
storey construction full of light: it was designed for twelve classes but at
present there are twenty-two in operation which means that some of the
laboratories are used as regular classrooms. The teaching activities take place
in the morning; optional activities (for example, sex education) and adult
education courses take place in the afternoon. The school is open from 8 in
the morning to 8 in the evening. There is no resident warden.

This is a typical school, easy to identify among the other buildings. The
socioeconomic level of the surrounding community is middle class and there
are no socially or culturally deprived pupils. Many pupils, however, come
from immigrant families, *ie*, one or both parents come from a foreign country; they do not mix with other foreigners or with the local community and
tend to profit from individually arranged cultural experiences.

All kinds of sports and cultural performances are offered by the Town
Council (for example films, theatre, concerts) in an attempt to build up a
feeling of community. The housing structure, however, consisting of indi-

vidual cottages or self sufficient blocks of flats with their private swimming-pool, gym, clubhouse does not favour social mixing. In addition, because no upper secondary school has yet been established in Arese adults tend to develop interests and acquaintances elsewhere; mainly in Milan, where the further and higher education institutions are concentrated.

The school population consists of 527 pupils, fifty teachers and fifteen non-teaching staff. A section of the school is based in the Salesian Brothers Institute that runs special courses for socially disturbed children which serves another forty pupils.

The school has a reputation of being a 'good' school: most teachers reside in Arese and regard themselves as serious professionals. They certainly care about the school, particularly because it is also their children's school. The fact that the cultural standard of the local population is high has created unusual expectations for the school. There are pressures for keeping traditional and high quality standards within the school and the teachers have responded positively to this demand. A sort of cultural control is consequently exercised by the parents and the teachers, for their part, concentrate their efforts on developing cognitive learning (a safe and visible traditional approach) at the expense of other skill building activities.

It is very difficult to introduce innovations in such a situation because this would involve not only inviting teachers to change objectives, procedures and approaches that had led to successful stable results so far, in order to favour other approaches that may be a failure; but also, raising new expectations in the parents, *ie*, to make them aware of different needs. The first step however, is to make everybody aware of the need for innovation.

The headteacher of the Leonardo da Vinci Middle School has been in post for one year. She is an experienced headteacher who has also worked as a teacher trainer in the Milan area: she knows Arese well because she was previously the headteacher of another Arese school. She is a headteacher on a permanent contract. She is helped by a deputy headteacher, who is released from teaching for eleven hours a week and by two *collaboratori*, *ie*, teachers with full-time teaching loads, who have been elected to act as counsellors in the decision making process. The deputy headteacher is in charge of checking the daily attendance of teachers and arranging supply cover for absent teachers. The headteacher maintains final supervision, however. The deputy headteacher also has the task of supervising the pupils when they enter the school building and of seeing to the regular start of the school day. The *collaboratori* meet with the headteacher once a week for one or two hours; they discuss how to face emerging problems, how to structure the activities of class councils, when to convene staff assemblies, how to introduce an experimental project *etc*.

From the beginning of her tenure, the headteacher had in mind to try to change the attitude and environment of the school towards innovation. She first analyzed the situation in order to understand the people and their positions, and to identify latent or existing problems. She found that the keynote of the context was 'isolation', both within and outside the school. For example, the pupils were not involved in extra curricular activities organized by the school; neither did their parents participate in the cultural events taking place in Arese. The school also was not partaking in the rich innovative stimuli that were emerging and taking shape in the Lombardy region. This seemed to be due to the fact that local teachers were not stimulated to participate in new projects or in INSET activities because that would involve having to travel from Arese to Milan to attend sessions which would be a nuisance. This was also unnecessary given the fact that parents were satisfied with present practice.

The headteacher's first effort was at this point to identify internal resources that would support the idea of change for improvement. Then she tried to reinforce this position by encouraging participation in INSET. For example:

- the school participated in a pilot project for health education, that involved many Lombardy schools under the coordination of the Regional Council;
- some teachers agreed to participate in a residential refresher course for middle school teachers and to report to their colleagues;
- the headteacher circulated documents and reports concerning innovative efforts that were taking place in other schools. Specific attention was focussed on those educational approaches that were aimed at moving from purely cognitive to more educational objectives.

The headteacher also invited a psychologist to the school to meet the teachers and to discuss problems connected with the need for guidance that pupils at this age have. The different class councils were then invited to plan interventions aiming at the development of self awareness in their pupils, and the psychologist was made available as a support to the teachers' work.

The headteacher was careful not to create conditions of frustration among her staff. She began by helping her teachers to become aware of the meaning and value of what they were doing and she acknowledged the merit of their efforts and knowledge. She also, however, encouraged them to enlarge their own visions and define their objectives in educational terms and make their practice more congruent with the established goals of the *scuola media*. What she introduced was the concept of improvement; this does not necessarily criticize established practice, nor does it originate from conflict or crisis management but results from a search for betterment.

The other main improvement effort concerned a better integration of the pupils into a school community. The basic idea was to promote social contacts and multinational insights and perceptions. The social objective was to facilitate social and international integration through common semi-structured activities; the education objective was to make the pupils understand that their reality is not the reality but a way of being among others.

When the Provincial Education Office contacted the headteacher suggesting that a course in Dutch could be run in the afternoons on the school premises for children in primary or middle school coming from Dutch families residing in the area, she welcomed the idea and supported the initiative throughout the school year. She already had some Dutch pupils at her school and she saw the educational value of giving them opportunities to reinforce their cultural background. This was also an opportunity for enlarging the range of experiences of the other pupils in the school. All classes were informed of the initiative, of its meaning and its value and, in addition, the headteacher created opportunities for establishing links between the Dutch children and the school pupils. The latter visited and interviewed them about their country, looked at their posters and pictures and made friends. At the end of the school year they organized a performance together: the Dutch children sang Dutch folksongs and danced, the school pupils provided the accompanying music. When these pupils leave school, they will have made new friends whom they would never have otherwise met even though they lived in the same area.

Another opportunity for improving the integration of the local community was given by a survey of the nationalities living in Arese. The results showed that 110 pupils at primary school level and fifty-five at middle school level came from foreign families and although they lived in Arese they attended international schools in Milan or in Varese. The survey also showed that forty out of the 527 pupils of the Scuola Media Leonardo da Vinci came from families where one parent was a foreigner.

On the basis of this data, the headteacher suggested that her pupils organize an international day and invite all foreign children of their age to an afternoon snack in the school. The school pupils organized entertainment, showed their guests around the school, established new links, shared experiences and began to create a community climate.

There was also no community feeling among the Italian residents of Arese. There is, however, another state middle school in Arese, in another quarter. The headteacher of the Leonardo da Vince Middle School thought that the two schools could make joint efforts towards creating opportunities for social integration among the young. The headteachers of the two schools agreed to organize a joint research study to be conducted by two classes, one in each school. The selected topic was 'Ways in which the young spend their time in Arese'. This initial link, supported by a common task, developed into other coordinated activities; for example, organization of sport events with participation of both schools. Consequently, the previous indifference between the two schools was changed into mutual involvement and support.

Through her enthusiasm, capacity and dedication, the headteacher succeeded in gaining the support and trust of most of her teachers, of the parents and of the local authorities. She also introduced new criteria for class formation, extra curricular activities organized during regular school time, guidance provisions for all pupils, *etc.* She also encouraged her teachers to

discover their own creativity. Consequently, the climate changed tremend-
ously in the school with flexibility taking the place of rigidity. A continuing
problem, however, is how to involve all teachers, including those who are
resistant to change, in developing a process of continuous innovation for
improvement based on needs identification and research.

If one looks at the different stages in the improvement process, one can
see that in this instance the headteacher acted as the change agent. She was,
however, very careful to build consensus around her proposals; she initiated
change by exploring needs, existing resources and the possibilities for short
term success. She did not work with the entire staff; she identified key
persons who were already creative and developed their enthusiasm. She
believes in motivation through good examples. The headteacher's driving
goal was a vision of the Leonardo da Vinci Middle School as a place for
learning, for educating future adult citizens, for developing social and democratic attitudes and behaviours and for promoting the cultural growth of the
community.

It is instructive to analyze this case into the different stages in the process
of improvement.

Initiation

The first step in the improvement process is to identify needs and to translate
them into clearly defined variables. This operation was done by the headteacher with the help of some teachers and the Arese Town Council who
provided data on the characteristics of the resident population and gave access
to additional information. The results of the survey were then presented to
the school staff assembly so that all teachers became aware of the social
context in which they were operating.

Mobilization

The headteacher discussed ways of getting a certain number of classes involved in a project that aimed at community integration. The chief goal was
to move from a social issue to developing educational goals. The pupils were
identified as the key actors in the project and it was their initiative that made
the idea grow: the teachers were facilitators in the process of planning and
implementation. Also the *organi collegiali* were involved: they were informed
of the initiative and gave their approval and support.

Implementation

The activities mentioned above were regarded as an integral part of the curriculum, they were not considered as extra curricular engagements. In the school there was curiosity about the project because in the participating classes much visible, creative and interactive work was going on, in contrast to the usual structured, repetitive and sometimes boring routine.

Interest Groups

The headteacher established an informal management team for school improvement which was based on voluntary participation in the project. The parents were both puzzled and interested at this new teaching approach. The local authority, though, was quite happy with the work that had been initiated at the Leonardo da Vinci Middle School and appreciated the new links between the school and the community. When the headteacher later made proposals for improving school facilities, the Arese Town Council responded positively and promised funds for the improvement of the school building. The local community was also informed of the initiatives organized at the school through the local newspaper: the headteacher wanted to share information with a wider public so as to reinforce the image of the school and to encourage more community spirit.

Continuation

It is vital that these initiatives become the motivating force for further study and research by the teachers and an occasion for learning and development on the part of the pupils. The educational value of such projects lies not only in the events themselves but in the process that is necessary to make the events possible. What the school has accomplished so far is a short-term objective that requires further effort in order to keep the improvement process alive.

Brief Definition of Terms

Middle Schools

For pupils aged 11 to 14 years. At the end of the third year pupils sit an examination for the award of the middle school diploma; pupils have a different teacher for each subject; each form has its own classroom; teachers move from class to class, except where a specialist room (for example, laboratory) is needed.

Eloisa Ricatti

Collaboratori

Teachers elected by the teaching staff to be consulted by the head, especially when quick decisions have to be made. They teach full time schedules and have no formal management responsibilities.

Organi Collegiali

Structure of participatory bodies at school level representing relevant interests, including class councils, teachers' assembly and school board. The latter is made up of elected parents, teachers, non teaching staff and the head.

Note

1 This is an edited version of a case study of the same title published in Hope, C (Ed) (1986) *The School Leader and School Improvement: Case Studies from Ten OECD Countries*, Leuven, Belgium, ACCO. Permission to reprint is gratefully acknowledged.

Two New Headteachers Introduce Change: A Case Study from England[1]

Dick Weindling, Peter Earley and Ron Glatter

Introduction

These two case studies are derived from a research project entitled *The First Years of Headship* conducted by the National Foundation for Educational Research (NFER) in England and Wales. The methodology involved initial interviews with forty-seven new heads of secondary schools soon after they took up appointment in September 1982. From this group sixteen were chosen in different local education authorities (LEAs), and these have been followed over their first eighteen months of headship. Three visits were made to the sixteen schools and the head was interviewed on each occasion. On the second visit, after the head had been in post for about a year, the researchers interviewed all the deputy heads, the chairperson of the governing body and a senior LEA officer responsible for secondary schools. In the third visit, in addition to the head, the researchers interviewed a cross section of staff in each school: heads of department in English, mathematics, sciences and humanities; heads of first, third, fifth and sixth years (approximate ages of students: 11, 13, 15 and 16–17) and eight other teachers. To illustrate the head's role in change, we have chosen two of the sixteen schools in which the heads have attempted a considerable number of changes with contrasting success.

The Schools and the Changes

School A is a comprehensive secondary school in a small town. The students are aged 11–18. There are 950 students and sixty teachers. The school is being affected by declining rolls.

School B is a comprehensive secondary school for students aged 13–18 in a multicultural inner city area. There are eighty teachers and 1352 students and the roll is rising. The school was built in 1975 to amalgamate a boys' and a girls' school. Most senior staff come from the two previous schools.

As both new heads started in September 1982, the timetable for the year had already been worked out, which meant that no major curricular changes could be introduced until the following academic year (September 1983). During the first year, both heads initiated departmental reviews, established regular meetings of middle management and set up a number of working parties open to any member of staff. Similar curricular, pastoral and organizational changes were introduced at both schools, namely: integrated science, integrated humanities, a timetabled form tutor period and a change of the school day in terms of the length of each teaching period.

School A also had two government funded pilot projects, one concerned with technical and vocational preparation and the other designed for low attaining students. In *school B* a major change was the abolition of corporal punishment and the move from ability grouping to mixed ability teaching for students aged 14 and 15.

While many changes were similar for both schools, the main difference was the rate of innovation. In *school B* all the major changes were implemented in September 1983 at the beginning of the head's second year, whereas in *school A* a number of the main changes had planned start dates of September 1984 and even 1985.

While the staff in *school A* appeared to have accepted change, considerable difficulties were found in *school B*. The research suggests that it was not so much the rapidity or the number of changes that caused the problems but rather the way in which the head of *School B* introduced them.

We will now look more closely at these contrasting processes of change and the head's part in them by examining each school in turn.

School A

Background

The previous head, now retired, has been in the post since the school opened in 1960. He was highly thought of by the staff. He had a very relaxed informal style. He avoided conflict and compromised whenever possible. Some teachers saw him as 'too casual'. He was described by the LEA officer interviewed as 'more of a shepherd than one who leads from the front'. One deputy head stated that the school was in a rut and that there had been no innovation for some time. The majority of staff interviewed thought that change was needed and that things had been 'too complacent'. They saw the school as a caring institution and a good school, so it was not the case that the new head had inherited a 'sick school' that needed pulling up by its bootstraps. Some commented that for the last few years there had been no innovations or new ideas but, nevertheless, the previous head was seen as 'a hard act to follow'.

The senior management team (two deputy heads and two senior

teachers, who have all been at the school for at least fourteen years) was generally seen by the new head and by the staff as being not very effective in curriculum leadership. One of the deputy heads had applied unsuccessfully for the headship but did not show any antagonism towards the new head.

The New Headteacher

He had previously been a deputy head for five years in a city comprehensive school. He defined his style as operating in an open way, spending much time getting to know staff, approachable, leading from the front and not being office bound. He wanted the staff to see him as the leading profession-al. He was on christian name terms with them. The head felt that relations with staff were of paramount importance. Unlike this predecessor, he in-volved the senior management team in everything.

At the first staff meeting he told staff what he wanted for the school. One of his initial acts was to see all the heads of department. He tried to see one teacher every day for half an hour. Occasionally, he observed someone teaching. He made little overt reference to his previous school.

Senior and junior staff saw the new head as tactful, open and accessible, very friendly, having a sense of humour, incredibly hard working (leading by example), very determined, intolerant of slackness and good at public relations. They saw him as listening to views and making his own decisions.

He had given the school a sense of direction and expected a lot from the staff. He was considered generally to have a philosophy similar to that of his predecessor (some teachers thought this was why his application was success-ful), although he was seen as having a much wider grasp of educational issues.

The Introduction of Change — The Head's Approach

The head's approach to introducing change, derived from an interview with him, can be summarized as follows.

It is important to be accessible and welcome views from the manage-ment team and below. It is very important to know your staff as, when you do, you know what can be done. You must prepare the ground and thus create a climate for change. Decisions about innovation should be reached by consultation. Compromise where possible but occasionally a minority deci-sion may be necessary. It is best to introduce only superficial change initially. The long-term project is to prepare the ground for more fundamental change. A headteacher should 'sow the seeds', initially with senior staff and then middle management. Senior staff must be united. You must allow adequate discussion with interested parties so that there are few, if any, 'surprises' when the head's document or paper is presented. Do not use the 'steamroller approach'. It is also important that staff learn to initiate changes themselves.

The Head in Action: Some Examples

1   Improvements/decorations to buildings were seen as a top priority by the new head, possibly so that staff and pupils could see the direct effects of the new regime. The head was very good at getting resources from the LEA and led by example in decorating the school, with teachers and parents involved.

2   The biggest problem that the head identified, at the first interview, was getting staff involved and the lack of new ideas from the deputy heads. Some heads of department needed a serious shake up and the head's strategy here was to observe some lessons, express concern and ask for a scheme of work. The head feels that new appointments which have been made to these departments will help to bring about change. (In England and Wales, heads have a substantial influence in staff appointments.)

3   One clear example of the head's facilitative approach was when he capitalized on the interest expressed by the head of the science department in integrated science. The head of science wanted to introduce integrated science into the upper school and the head was also keen for this to take place. Four out of the eight teachers in the science department were in favour, although two others were against such a move. The head spoke to these two teachers. The LEA was also in favour of the new course and an intensive county-wide INSET course was based at the school (twenty schools were involved). The head of science stated that the head had been extremely supportive of his ideas regarding science in the school. Here the head was helped by having a committed head of science. This was not the case in relation to some other departments.

4   The head was in favour of introducing school uniform but the majority of staff were opposed. The head decided not to force the change through.

5   One of the deputy heads had been given responsibility for the time-table and resources and was asked to chair a working party. None of these tasks had been done well. The head had tried to allow the deputy head to get on with the jobs but was then annoyed with himself for not monitoring more closely. It had proved necessary for the head to take over the chairmanship of the working party. The head used the senior management team a great deal and tried to involve many staff through working parties. The head would have liked a good curriculum deputy head to provide support and to give

feedback. He felt that he was doing jobs that the deputies should have been doing . The team worked efficiently on day-to-day matters but not on the curriculum. The team was fully supportive of the new head and appreciated being more involved in things. They had not tried to obstruct any of his initiatives.

6   Included amongst the many changes taking place in *school A* are what might be termed 'opportunistic innovations', where the head was made very good use of external initiatives to facilitate or implement change. For instance, the LEA had requested a curriculum report, which the head has used as a reason to initiate discussion of the curriculum and therefore to help towards creating the right climate for change. Other examples include national projects, one concerned with technical and vocational preparation and the other with low attaining students. The head was extremely keen to get the school involved in these two external initiatives and saw them as important stimuli and a convenient mechanism for getting the changes he desired. Change was therefore possible yet, at the same time, responsibility could be attributed to external agencies. The low attainers' course was particularly significant in that the two departments mainly involved were sterile and hard to move. The initiative had therefore provided a much needed stimulus. In this particular example, the head had to work very hard to get the course off the ground. The technical and vocational preparation scheme had also involved the head in an enormous amount of extra work and attendance at LEA meetings. Nevertheless, in retrospect, it was thought to have been worthwhile. The head had also been able to link the two initiatives by proposing a technical and vocational course for low attainers and arranging a meeting of those responsible in the LEA for those external initiatives. The next step had been to get those involved in the school to devise an appropriate course.

Support from Outside Agencies

LEA support for the internal initiatives was mixed. There had been very little contact with the advisers and even this had been initiated by the head. The LEA had provided some funds for building improvements and decoration, INSET and integrated science. The LEA officer was very helpful and did his best to support changes and meet the head's requests. The staff saw the head as having been very successful in obtaining extra resources and facilities. The governors had been helpful and supportive although, like most governing bodies, they do not have the necessary curriculum expertise to permit detailed discussion of the changes being introduced.

Some Reflections by the Head

'I'm rapidly coming to terms that in this school, major change will take time. I feel you must carry people with you.'

'There are no strategies for introducing change that will work in all situations. You must know the previous head and the way that he operated, and you must be very careful not to create disaffection amongst your staff.'

'I do not advocate a steamroller approach — a management technique deliberately used by some heads — as this can be counterproductive and in times of little teacher mobility it means you can be harbouring a lot of resentment on the part of your staff. In the long term, this is not in the pupils' interests. I prefer to wait and ensure that the staff are on my side, try and get them to see the need for change and to get them to think that the ideas are theirs.'

'Introducing lots of change rapidly can look good on paper or on your *curriculum vitae*, but at the end of the day it's people who suffer and the staff commitment will not be there. It can't therefore be good for the development of the school.'

'I don't think there is a period when it is easy to introduce change. You need to create the right kind of atmosphere and get staff involved in things like INSET, then changes will gather momentum and people will begin to approach you with new ideas. Given this approach, then, there isn't a honeymoon period but rather you create a critical climate about things that we do in school.'

Teacher Reactions

From the teacher interviews it appeared that all staff had been a little anxious and concerned that the new head would bring in sweeping changes very quickly and they were all happy that he did not do this. No changes had taken place in the first term. All thought change was needed after the previous head's very long period of office. The head was about to help the school 'evolve'. Only one teacher thought the decision making process was too long-winded. The majority seemed pleased to have been involved in the discussion of change and the decision making process. A few junior staff felt they did not have an opportunity to be involved apart from staff meetings, although they recognized that they could join a working party if they wished. The general reaction of the staff to the head and the changes introduced was very favourable. They all respected his hard work and his leading by example. He was seen as supportive of staff and he publicly praised them for their efforts.

A representative selection of comments from teachers follows. The last four are from more senior staff (heads of departments and year):

'The staff can now see that there is a vehicle whereby they can carry out new ideas. I felt as though I had been able to innovate and do things and, when I talk to the head, he gives ideas of the sorts of things he wants.'

'He has done things very gradually. He has made some fairly big changes without people realizing. He hasn't upset anyone. He did not say at the outset "We are going to do this and that". He has done it through discussions and consultation.'

'We feel we are a team going somewhere together with a good leader.'

'Before we were never really asked to discuss matters. The new head will involve us in discussion which will produce a result. The senior teachers here at first felt immature, they were as green as grass. It was a new experience for us. For any thinking person in the school, this was the experience. It was like going from second gear to fourth. Our early discussions were at a very poor level. I think INSET was needed for us.'

'We are looking at one step at a time. This is important so people do not feel threatened.'

'Curriculum development and change has been done in such a way that all those who wanted to be involved could be; nothing has been imposed. The changes that no doubt the new head wanted have come about.'

'He's not dictatorial and no one resents his attitude, he's very diplomatic and very kind. No one feels genuinely threatened, rather that they ought to shape up.'

School B

Background

The previous head had been head of the former boys' grammar school and had taught in the area all his life. He was described as 'traditional', 'authoritarian', 'very autocratic', 'ex-army and very efficient', 'a competent and business-like manager', who knew exactly which way he would go. He was not seen as an innovator — 'very conservative, played it safe' — but had done a good job in bringing the two schools together. He would listen to staff but was very obstinate: 'a fat cat boss'. Over his last three to four years he became ill and morose and running a large comprehensive became too much for him. It seems that one of the deputy heads basically ran the school over this time. She had been deputy head for seven years since the new school opened. She had applied unsuccessfully for the current headship but did not show any bitterness towards the new head. The other deputy had been in this position for fifteen years and had started his teaching career in the boys' school with the previous head.

The New Head teacher

The new headteacher had previously been a deputy for four years at a very innovative school and spent five years as a head of department at another progressive school. He described his style of headship as 'charismatic', 'consultative', but also 'manipulative at times'. Teachers felt that the new head was approachable and would listen but was not at all open to their views. Many thought him devious and did not trust him; some even called him a liar. Although he said he wanted democracy and consultation, the staff felt this was not the case in practice: 'he sees himself as a great democrat and then behaves in a very autocratic way'. The staff, and apparently the pupils, saw him as 'soft on discipline'. The relations between the new head and the female deputy were quite good. She felt he certainly listened and considered her opinions. However, relations between the other deputy and the head were very poor, to the extent that the deputy had taken out a grievance procedure against the head. (This concerned the removal of his role as head of resources and the giving of the job to another teacher, without consulting him.)

Introduction of Change — The Head's Approach

The new head produced a 'school audit' of 111 pages for the first governors' meeting. This was really a review and report by each department. The head felt that ideally he should wait a year before introducing change but decided that he had to start straight away to achieve anything in five years, so he was going like a 'bat out of hell'. 'I found that so many things had to be started at this school that I couldn't be democratic. I had to provide the institution with a philosophy and the institution needed a wallop. I had to hit them when they were down.' At the beginning of his second year, he felt he could relax the hard leadership line and move step by step.

In the third interview, the head said that he had brought in all the changes he sought but the 'real change' he wanted to achieve was a change in teachers' attitudes and teacher-pupil relations. He felt that a difficulty for a new head was 'seeing the consequence of your actions. It is hard for the staff to adjust to these changes. I think your objectives are not as important as your methods.' (Ironically, it seems that the staff largely objected to the head's methods rather than his objectives.) 'If I had to do things again, I think I would be more precise about working parties. I would also pay more attention to the staff than I did and I would be more careful about what I said. But I think rapid change is still necessary and change means you are attacking people's sacred cows.'

It would appear from our data that the new head was the initiator of all the changes which were introduced. He does not seem to have acted as a facilitator for other people's ideas within the school nor to have taken on any external (national or local) initiatives. With regard to delegation and consultation, he set up a working party on the school day chaired by one of the deputies and a second working party on active tutorial work (ATW) chaired by the other deputy. The head said he wanted to move to a 3 × 1½ hour period day. The working party did not recommend this and were unable to find any schools which operated such a system. They had even contacted the Department of Education and Science (DES) to obtain the names of schools using this system but the DES could not provide any. The working party on ATW recommended that one 50-minute period should be timetabled for this work. These recommendations were discussed at staff meetings and senior management meetings and in general the staff seemed in agreement. However, the head overruled both working parties and introduced the three period day with 1½ hour's ATW on Friday afternoon.

Support from Outside Agencies

The new head felt he could have received more support from LEA officers and advisers, but recognized how busy they were. (This was echoed in the interview with the LEA officer.) The governors had proved supportive although the Chairman said in his interview that now he was not sure the head was the right man for the job and that he had much to learn about 'man management'. The new head felt he had received most help from the other heads in the authority who had been 'absolutely outstanding'. (The schools are not in competition, as the rolls are rising.)

Teacher Reactions

Things went badly wrong during the new head's first year. Towards the end of his first term, the two main working parties on the school day and ATW had reported back and he had overruled their recommendations. The Staff Association voted overwhelmingly in favour of a resolution expressing their concern about poor discipline and the 'inconsistent and ambiguous leadership' of the head. (This came very close to a total vote of no confidence.) The governors were informed and a small sub-committee interviewed the head and a few teachers representing the Staff Association. The sub-committee recommended that the LEA advisers should carry out a major review. This took place at the beginning of the head's second year and all staff were interviewed by a small team of advisers who produced a finely balanced report.

At the beginning, the majority of staff seemed optimistic but during the first two years the head appeared to have alienated almost all the staff. Their views ranged from extreme anger to general unhappiness. (Note the high turnover of staff in the first year: twenty-four out of eighty left.) 'We' re not a bolshie staff.' 'It's a lovely staff here but we felt threatened by all the rapid changes.' All the teachers interviewed recognized that change was needed at the school and they expected the new head to introduce changes but over half stated there has been too many changes, too quickly. 'Change is like a tidal wave, we felt we were drowning. It was hard to keep our heads above water.' They felt the new head had a blueprint for the school. He had ignored their views and imposed his own, saying that it would work because it did at his last school. In general, however, it was not the changes themselves that generated the adverse response from teachers, it was the ruthless way the head had imposed them. The overall teacher reaction to the advisers' report was positive, with most seeing it as brief but balanced.

Some Reflections by the Head and Deputies

On our third visit, after the advisers' report, the head said:

'I think most of the changes are going better than I hoped and I am glad I did them all early. I think you have to hit people hard, you mustn't allow them to dig in their heels. They had to cooperate to keep their sanity. We can now modify things to the demands of the teachers. I would certainly do it again the same way. Even though it means going through all the trouble we had, I would still do it.' 'If I'd done what the staff recommended, it wouldn't have gone far enough.'

When asked if he had deliberately used conflict as a strategy to achieve change, he replied: 'I haven't got this at a conscious level and I don't know whether I deliberately engineered confrontation.' 'I think staff are glad that the advisers' visit and the report are all over. It gave them more exposure than they wanted but it has flushed things out and that is good.'

The female deputy felt that changes were needed and agreed with most of the things the new head had tried to introduce, but she completely disagreed with the way he had acted. 'I would have found out what the teachers felt, tried things out and moved much more stealthily.' She said that: 'One of his great strengths is that he is full of ideas but this is part of his weakness: his ideas are not thought out clearly. He is trying to employ management techniques but he can't put them into operation successfully. He is good on theory but is poor on the practical applications. He doesn't really know how to move people in the direction that he wants.'

The other deputy was not in favour of most of the changes introduced by the new head and certainly was opposed to the methods used: 'He just came in and swept things away.' This summed up the feeling of many staff.

Note

1 This case study is also published in HOPES, C (Ed) (1986) *The School Leader and School Improvement: Case Studies from Ten OECD Countries*, Leuven, Belgium, ACCO. Permission to reprint is gratefully acknowledged.

Management Development: A Response from the UK Perspective[1]

Ray Bolam

In this response I have tried to do three things: first, to review the current position in England and Wales with respect to management development; second, to identify some of the implications in the ISIP Project for England and Wales; third, to look ahead to future developments.

The Current Position in England and Wales

At the National Development Centre (NDC), we define a school manager as somebody who works through other people, particularly professionals, to achieve the goals of the organization. On the basis of that definition there are approximately 130,000 school managers or leaders in England and Wales. This estimate includes heads, deputies, heads of department and heads of year.

As far as professional development is concerned, what do we do for them? The first thing we do is to appoint them and, as we know from the POST project (Morgan *et al*, 1984), that in itself is problematic. Next, we offer them award-bearing in-service courses in a variety of institutions, particularly universities and polytechnics. Third, we offer them short courses of various kinds in LEA teachers' centres, in institutions of higher education, in other LEA institutions like the North West Education Management Centre and the South West Primary Management Centre, in industrial and commercial training centres and also, and we should not forget this, through various kinds of project support for leaders in their school improvement role.

The most significant of these recent developments, however, are those courses which have come about as a result of the specific grants introduced by the government in 1983 on which approximately £2½m a year has been spent over the past three years. There are two types of course: the One-Term Training Opportunity (OTTO) programmes and the twenty-day or basic programmes. In the three-year period since 1983, approximately 5000–6000 people with school management responsibilities will have gone through approximately ninety-five courses at approximately forty institutions. One significant conclusion confirmed by this experience is that external courses are not an especially effective means of bringing about change. We already knew this from previous work on school-focussed in-service education. Short courses are, of course valuable and important but they have serious limitations. Dr Tony Bailey has recently carried out a study at the University of Sussex for the Department of Education and Science which has looked at preparation, support and follow-up for heads attending twenty-day and OTTO courses (Bailey, 1985). This research found that although preparation and follow-up are regarded as essential for course impact, very little actually occurs. The NDC experience is similar: it is that the most significant criicisms of the twenty-day and OTTO courses has been directed at LEAs because they did not provide adequate preparation and follow-up for heads, deputies and others. Partly as a result of these findings, the NDC initiated a project on management development with eight local authorities and about fifty schools, to explore ways of supporting LEAs and schools as they seek to plan, implement and evaluate coherent and systematic management development policies and programmes.

Some Implications of ISIP

The first thing I was very pleased to note from Eskil Stego's paper is that our recent work is in line with informed professional opinion and experience elsewhere. This is not to subscribe to the view that we have nothing to learn. Quite the reverse. As professionals, we have a responsibility to share with colleagues from other countries and to learn from them. It is thus encouraging to learn that other countries are exploring the use of the 'stages of development' concept (*ie*, that professionals have different training needs before they are appointed, in their early years in post and when they are experienced) and have also concluded that local education authorities must accept more direct and explicit responsibility for this professional development.

Three other points which struck me in Eskil's paper are ones which we are becoming aware of but not yet paying sufficient attention to: first, the importance of self-development and the need for individuals to take ownership of their own learning; second, the value of reflective learning — I think that most of us learn from reflecting upon what we actually do and I think we need to explore methods of helping school leaders to do so more effectively; and, third, his stress upon the way in which individuals can be helped to become more effective through organization development was, for me, especially important.

Ray Bolam

The Future

The policy and financial framework for the future of this work in the UK is reasonably clear and, although we all feel somewhat uncertain and ambivalent, the general view is that the post-1987 funding arrangements do offer major opportunities. A lot will, of course, depend on whether authorities get more, less, or the same funding and also what this impact will be upon award-bearing courses and institutions of higher education. Nevertheless, I think we all look towards the future reasonably optimistically. The reason for this is that the new arrangements stress the need for coherent LEA and school staff development policies within which management development programmes can be formulated, implemented and evaluated. In expressing this optimism, a note of caution is also appropriate. Most LEAs and schools are not used to working in this systematic and comprehensive way on staff and management development. It will, therefore, take time to get it right and we all need to support each other in the complex business of individual and organizational learning.

In speculating about the future, I would like to draw your attention to what I think are the gaps in our knowledge; between what we know at present and what we need to know. I think we now know a fair amount in research terms — about the roles and tasks of school leaders. The implicit framework within which this research appears to have been conducted is represented in figure 1.

Its main purpose seems to have been to deepen and extend our understanding of school management roles and tasks and, as a result, we can now make certain statements with some confidence, particularly about the roles and tasks of secondary headteachers: hence the two boxes in unbroken lines. However, the rest of the field is riddled with unanswered (and often unasked) questions: hence the broken lines and question marks. Thus, the articulation between the work done on roles and that on tasks is unclear. I do not think

Figure 1: The Present State of Research Knowledge on School Management in England and Wales

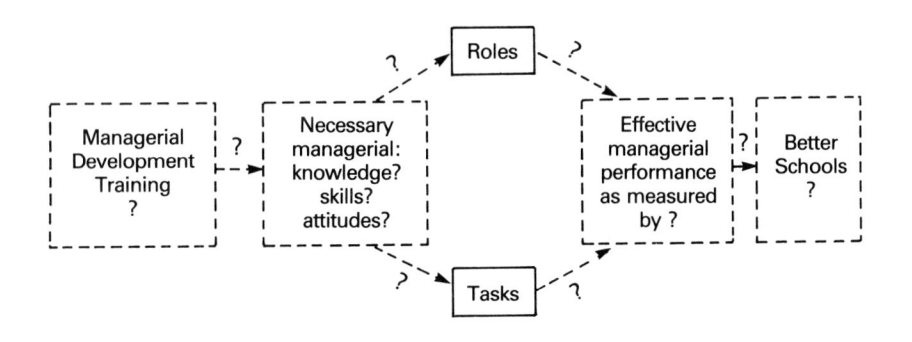

we yet have robust enough research knowledge about what we really mean by 'better schools' (although, as professionals, we may have good practical knowledge), nor are we sure what we mean by 'effective leadership perform-ance' or what 'effective' managers actually use by way of knowledge, atti-tudes and skills.

Finally, it may be important to consider just how realistic it is to look to research and social science knowledge as a likely source of information and how far we should look to practitioner knowledge — informed, reflective, practitioner knowledge — as the principal source of experience and help.

Note

1 Portions of this paper are based on a previously published article by BOLAM, R (1986) 'The National Development Centre for School Management' in HOYLE, E and McMAHON, A (Eds) *The Management of Schools*, London, Kogan Page. Permis-sion to reprint is gratefully acknowledged.

References

BAILEY, A (1985) *Support for School Management: Project Report*, Sussex, School of Education, University of Sussex.

MORGAN, C, HALL, V and MACKAY, H (1984) *The Selection of Secondary School Headteachers*, Milton Keynes, Open University Press.

5   The Role of External Support in School Improvement Processes

Introduction

External support is the help provided to schools for improvement purposes by those outside the school. In the UK the major sources of external support include the advisory/inspection service, local teacher centres, university and college departments of education, the School Curriculum Development Committee (SCDC) and the schools psychological service. Until recently, external support systems have not been formulated within a school improvement framework. Although their potential contribution to school improvement is now being realized, much still remains to be done in developing a rational system for external support that is both visionary and responsive to school needs.

David Crandall's presentation discusses the ways in which external support is being conceptualized within ISIP. He defines the concept, explicates the various roles associated with it and gives examples. He also offers a variety of models for delivering external support: the regionalized staff model (a UK example would be LEA teacher centres); the centralized staff model (the LEA advisory service is a UK example); the regionalized brokerage model (for example the Open University's local centres); and the centralized brokerage model (the National Development Centre is a UK example). These models are, of course, not exclusive and some agencies such as the SCDC may use more than one delivery system. Crandall then discusses the various activities an external support provides: for example, needs assessment, curriculum development, dissemination, training. His presentation offers a useful way of organizing our thinking about what may be an unfamiliar concept.

David Crandall is also responsible for the case study on external support in the United States. In this he further explicates the concept by providing an analysis of the various support systems which exist in that country. These include: school district specialists; teachers' centres; colleges and universities, offering courses and consultancies; intermediate units pro-

viding resources and courses; federal government funded regional laboratories which serve as information centres for school improvement. There is, however, no central coordination among these agencies of external support. Initiatives for school improvement come from a variety of sources — by law, from the federal and state governments, from the local school board, and some from the schools themselves. Strategies for school improvement vary widely but there is less flexibility than is normally assumed. It is generally agreed that the primary responsibility for education lies with the local community. But the tension between local and external control is very apparent and increasingly federal funding is having 'strings' attached to it. There also appears to be a high degree of overlap between different support agencies working in the same field. Traditionally schools and support systems in the United States are characterized by their diversity; these factors and the others just mentioned are problematic for the development of a coherent system of external support.

Don Cooper's case study of the introduction of the General Certificate of Secondary Education (GCSE) examination examines the issue of external support from a different perspective. Whereas Crandall examined a national system, Cooper takes a single innovation and looks at its external support implications. Cooper argues that the GCSE, which stresses the role of the individual student, contains several distinctive features designed to bring about school improvement. These are: all syllabuses and examinations will be based on national criteria; great emphasis will be put on 'differentiation'; all subjects will normally be required to include assessment of course work. The implications of the introduction of this examination include teachers: having to develop their assessment skills; becoming familiar with moderation procedures; and viewing students as individual learners which will mean a reappraisal of methods and teaching styles. To facilitate this, a cascade model of in-service training is being employed using materials developed by the Open University in conjunction with the Secondary Examination Council. This account of GCSE raises some obvious and fundamental questions: Is GCSE a school improvement strategy? Is the 'cascade' model of in-service training an effective external support strategy? If not, what other forms of external support are required for the effective implementation of GCSE?

Keith McWilliams implicitly responds to some of these questions in his 'response from the UK perspective'. He stresses the importance of a broad based network of support and points to some promising codevelopment activities. The multiplicity of and lack of coordination between support agencies are, however, a major stumbling block to effective school improvement in the UK. McWilliams argues strongly for coherence, coordination and balance within the external support system.

External Support for School Improvement: Constructs from the International School Improvement Project

David Crandall

Introduction

Every country has the means for supporting the efforts of schools to improve. This support often comes from a variety of organizations, including universities, government (national, state, local) and research and development institutes. In the last twenty years it has become apparent that such support is valuable but costly and that it is both more effective and more efficient if the support is systematic and organized, rather than random and uncoordinated. While many countries have made deliberate decisions to enhance and coordinate external support to schools, there has been no clear, solid knowledge base about which structures and activities succeed in which political, cultural and economic contexts. As the knowledge about school improvement has increased, so too has the knowledge about how it can best be supported (Louis *et al*, 1985). It is now an auspicious time to examine the systems that have been developed to more fully understand where improvements might occur and what designers of future support systems should consider.

This has been the purpose of the External Support Area Group of the International School Improvement Project (ISIP). From 1982 to the present, area group members have discussed external support within their countries, comparing and contrasting the structures, strategies and policies that support schools to improve. Early in the discussions we recognized the need for a common language, a way to talk about the different systems so they could be more readily compared and analyzed. With such descriptions, communication could be greatly enhanced between individuals representing various countries, organizations and perspectives.

Other ISIP books describe what is known about school improvement (*vide* van Velzen *et al*, 1985) and external support and the different configurations of external support in developed countries (Louis *et al*, 1987). The purpose of this paper is to introduce how we are coming to think and talk about external systems (*vide* Loucks-Horsley and Crandall, 1986).

General Charactersitics of the System

We define 'external support system' quite broadly (Louis *et al*, 1985):

> External means outside of the school building. This excludes teacher-to-teacher help and assistance from a building administrator or principal; it includes support provided by a variety of units outside the school (for example, school districts, county or intermediate units, and state/provincial and national agencies and projects).

> Support means the process of aiding or helping school improvement, and may take the form of training, consultation, provision of information or materials. It excludes purely regulatory functions that assess a school's performance or dictate certain processes or activities; such regulatory functions also provide no help in using evaluation data or carrying out the directives.

> Finally, we use the word 'system' to mean an interacting set of two or more people and processes with a common mission that serves more than one school. This is in contrast to individuals, who may provide assistance to a school to meet a need but are not part of a larger system. (p198)

Thus, an external support system can range in scope from a single INSET program to train teachers to use microcomputers, to an entire country's coordination of its educational service centres, research institutes, and universities whose activities seek to upgrade the organizational effectiveness of the country's schools.

Two examples illustrate the range of activity that ISIP's Area Group on External Support has included within its purview:

> The SIPRI Project in Switzerland has three goals: to study essential aspects of the current situation of the primary school; to formulate suggestions for concrete improvements; and, where possible, to try them out. Individual schools work with a 'school companion' (Schulbegleiter) to analyze their situations related to four themes: student evaluation, teaching methods, coordination of kindergarten and primary teachers, and parent participation. The school faculty develops and implements a plan for change in one of these areas, with resources and technical advice from expert groups.

> The Harvard Principal's Centre provides school leaders from the Boston/Cambridge, Massachusetts, area and beyond with opportunities for professional development and networking. With a membership of over 500, it offers after school workshops on timely topics; regular meetings of small groups that focus on specific concerns; a summer institute and a newsletter.

Clients

Who is served directly by the external support system? Some systems approach teachers directly (for example, INSET programs), while others primarily serve building administrators (school leaders) who, in turn, work with teachers within their schools (for example, the MAVO Project in the Netherlands). Some systems train trainers only (for example, the National Training Laboratory in the US), and others target decision makers in state or national agencies (for example, training in Sweden for National School Board members). France's regional academies provide INSET for teachers, their primary targets. Occasionally there are also offerings for school administrators.

The design issues here are quite interesting. Many believe that if schools are to be more effective in teaching children, then what teachers do should be the focus of improvement. Teaching changes can be aided through direct training of teachers by external assisters. But there are several alternatives. First, a restructuring and refocusing of the school environment could well support changes in teaching; school leaders are in the best place to lead such restructuring and refocusing. Thus an external support system could target school leaders and affect teaching — and for a much larger number of teachers.

Another approach to upgrading teaching is to improve the skills of others (than school leaders) who come into contact with teachers. Thus, external support systems could have as their clients district level coordinators, supervisors and/or inspectors; university faculty; and teachers' or principals' centre staffs. Again, by the 'multiplier effect', this strategy may allow a great many more teachers to be reached by those who have been served by the external support system. However, one must consider the possibility that the assistance that actually reaches teachers might be diluted or changed so significantly by the intermediary that the original intent is not carried out.

Finally, staff of the central government's ministries are important. Rarely do these people receive information or training related to school improvement, yet they make or recommend policies that can tightly constrain or inhibit the efforts of local schools. They also have the power to stimulate and support school improvement. There are currently a few external support systems that have these individuals as clients. For example, the Technical Assistance Base of the US's National Diffusion Network helps federal staff to learn the needs of their contractors working with schools nationwide, so they can develop policies and procedures that promote more and higher quality improvement efforts.

Design of Delivery Systems

Is the support system centralized (for example, are services delivered from one central location) or regionalized (for example, are services coordinated from a central location, but delivered from different places throughout the service area)? Does the support system have its own staff who deliver services, or does it broker delivery of services (for example, arrange for others to deliver services or refer clients to others)?

Figure 1 illustrates some examples of different combinations of these design options (Williams, 1982). The first, the regionalized staff model, has the support system host agency coordinating a number of units in the field whose staff provide services to schools. An example is the Ontario (Canada) Ministry of Education which was regional offices whose staff provide assistance to schools implementing new curriculum guidelines.

The second model, the centralized staff model, has the host agency providing direct support to schools. The Catholic Pedagogic Centre in the Netherlands housed a MAVO Project staff that worked with schools throughout the country who were in the process of becoming MAVO schools.

In the third model, the regionalized brokerage model, a central agency again coordinates regional service units. In each of these units staff arrange for experts in areas of need to deliver services directly. An example is the French regional academies which develop an INSET catalogue from an assessment of needs in the region, then locate consultants who conduct courses or consult with schools in the areas they choose for concentration.

In the fourth model, the centalized brokerage model, the central agency arranges for individuals outside of its own staff to deliver services. An example is in the National Diffusion Network (US), where some project developers prepare 'certified trainers' in different parts of the country, who can be called upon to provide training to schools whose needs match their own particular experiences or expertise.

Regionalized services have distinct advantages over centralized; most importantly, the services can be more clearly targeted to the unique needs of the region. This is particularly important when regions vary in their community type (for example, urban, rural), wealth (for example, school expenditures) and the policies that govern them (for example, in the US, states will have very different mandates that regional support agencies can attend to better than can agencies with a national responsibility). Centralized systems, however, have more opportunities for quality control and for avoiding potentially wasteful overlaps in service.

Brokering services offer a support system a great deal of flexibility to meet specific, individual needs of its clients. The disadvantage is often in the lack of commitment of individual consultants to a comprehensive view and strategy for school improvement and to the long-term assistance needed for success. Brokerage systems often foster short-term, small scale, uncoordin-

Figure 5:1 Examples of External Support System Organizational Designs

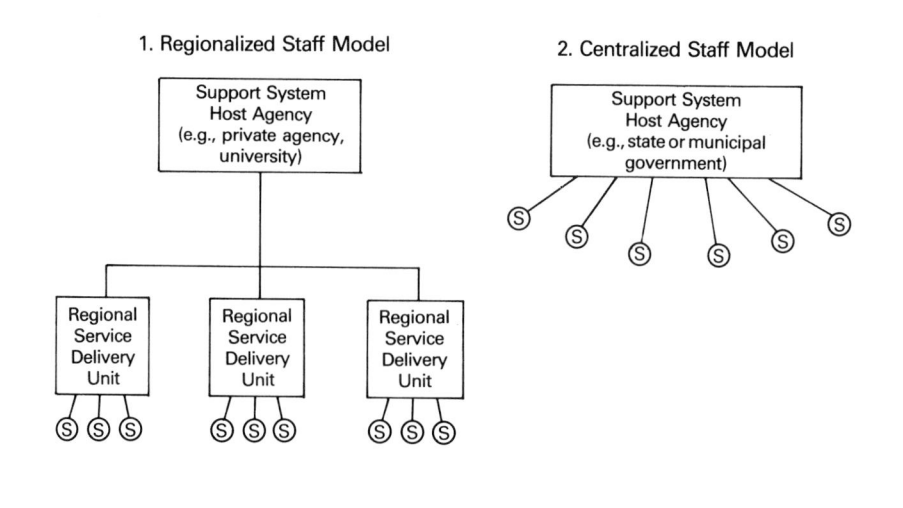

1. Regionalized Staff Model

2. Centralized Staff Model

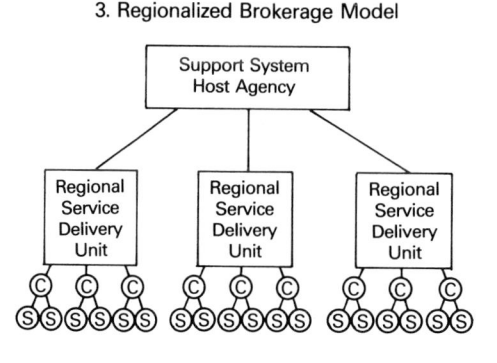

3. Regionalized Brokerage Model

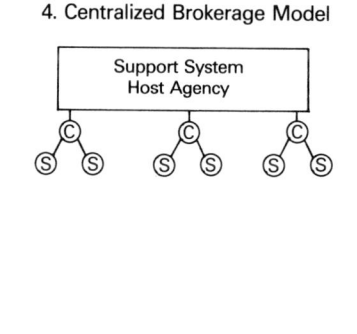

4. Centralized Brokerage Model

S = Schools
C = Consultants/Experts

ated services, whereas staff who work full-time with a set of schools or school people or have responsibility for a given need area (for example, science or technology), have, by role definition, a broader commitment to improvement.

Note that some external support agencies use more than one delivery model. For example, the School Curriculum Development Committee, serving England and Wales, sometimes provides direct assistance to schools, as in the second model; for other tasks, they operate a brokerage model, using LEA and higher educational associates and consultants.

External support systems come into being from a number of different sources. Legislatures, municipalities, ministries, university directorates — all can initiate, and thereafter regulate, external support. A good example of this is provided by the school services function of the Ontario Institute for Studies in Education (OISE) which is mandated by the Ministry of Education for all faculty members. Another example is the establishment of the three pedagogic centres for the Netherlands authorized by the National Legislature.

Activities of the External Support System

To pursue its mission, an external support system conducts certain kinds of activities. These vary widely depending on many factors, among them resources, cultural norms, mandate, and client needs. Eleven kinds of activities, encompassing the broadest possible range, are listed below, with several examples under each.

Needs Assessment

Needs assessment is an activity used by many external support systems to determine precisely what kind of help its clients need. Some systems begin a client relationship with an assessment of needs; other systems assess needs throughout a relationship with a client. Some assessments are formal, others informal.

An example of formal, initial and ongoing needs assessment is drawn from the US where 'effective schools' programs are being adopted by schools throughout the country. Several external support systems, among them regional laboratories and state education agencies, begin their work with individual schools by having a school staff assess their school along a number of dimensions. This assessment, which is repeated periodically throughout the one-to-two year relationship, allow external support system staff, together with school staff, to determine what to work on and how. The assessment component of many school self evaluation processes used in the UK often resembles this procedure.

Other external support systems, such as those that sponsor INSET activities, determine their offerings through an informal assessment of what teachers need to know or learn in order to improve, made prior to the arrangement for and announcement of INSET offerings.

Development

Many external support systems develop materials for distribution to schools. Such materials include research briefs, curricula, guidebooks, software, *etc.* Others develop new practices, for example, new approaches to teaching, organizing classrooms and schools, and serving disadvantaged groups (for example, language minority and handicapped students). Still other systems develop evaluation or assessment instruments that can be used to diagnose and/or evaluate children, teaching, and organizational effectiveness.

Development activities can also involve assisting clients to do their own development — again, of materials, practices, and assessment instruments. Support systems may also help schools develop plans for improvement, which may involve restructuring, adding programs and inservice activities.

Examples of development support abound. Teachers' centres in the UK and in the US typically support teachers to develop material to use in their teaching. The Tests and Measurement Centre in The Netherlands designs new instruments for use in Dutch schools. County school board staff in Sweden assist schools to develop and implement individual school plans.

Research/Analysis

Some external support systems conduct research and analysis activities with the aim of improving school practice through the development of new knowledge. This research may be basic or applied; it may involve analyzing information, trends and context factors in order to develop, recommend, or critique educational policies.

Canada's Ontario Institute for Studies in Education is an example of a support system that engages in all of these activities. The Federal Republic of Germany and the US both support a series of research centres that focus on different aspects of the education enterprise. Universities in several countries, such as Japan and Sweden, perform this function.

Dissemination

Dissemination is the activity that links schools to sources of information. Some external support systems exist solely for this purpose, such as the National Diffusion Network in the US. Others, such as research centres in several countries, may disseminate their findings as a secondary activity. What is actually disseminated varies widely — curriculum materials, research findings, new practices. Some external support systems, such as the Ontario Ministry of Education and most educational authorities that also support school improvement, disseminate information about new policies and requirements. Finally, some external support systems help schools disseminate their own materials and practices. In the US, a number of quite different strategies are used. For example, regional educational laboratories of the US Education Department's Office of Educational Research and Improvement (OERI) set up mechanisms by which schools that have developed their own good programs can share their success with others. The National Diffusion Network assists educators who have developed unique practices to create effective materials and training programs so others might adopt the practices.

Planning

External support systems may also help schools to plan for improvement. Swedish County School Boards have staff specially trained to help schools develop their required school plans. The NETWORK's National Assistance Project for Special Education Technology sponsored by the US Education Department, helps school-based teams plan for the application of technology to their programs for handicapped students.

Networking

Networking can be an extremely effective activity for an external support system, largely because, if clients actively network with each other, the support system has less direct assistance to give. Networking maximizes the expertise and experience of the system's clients and takes advantage of peer-to-peer learning.

Several examples of such networking exist in ISIP countries. The Swiss SIPRI Project links schools involved in each of its focus area. The UK's School Curriculum Development Committee sponsors networks of 'associates' in LEA teacher training institutions, teacher unions, subject associations, *etc.*

Implementation

Providing implementation assistance is an increasingly common role for external support systems. In Canada, the Ontario Ministry of Education's regional offices help local schools implement curriculum guidelines. The Netherland's three pedagogic centres have a variety of strategies for helping schools implement national education policies. Where local schools select their own curriculum, such as in the US, external support systems often make schools aware of the programs that are available and help them select, adapt, and implement the one(s) that meets their needs.

Training

Some external support system staffs conduct training for school people. INSET activities sponsored by universities are common. Other support systems, such as the school leader training program in Sweden and the internal coordinator training conducted by the Catholic Pedagogic Centre in The Netherlands, are not part of university INSET activities. External support systems may not actually conduct training but arrange for others to do so. This is the case in France's regional academies, for example.

Evaluation

Some external support systems have evaluation as part of their mission. Staff of the Catholic Pedagogic Centre in the Netherlands, for example, carefully evaluate the implementation of large-scale reform efforts. In the US, a series of regional technical assistance centres are sponsored by the federal government to help schools evaluate their programs for disadvantaged students, funded largely with federal monies.

Another evaluation activity is the search for exemplary local school practices, conducted by a number of external support systems in the US. In these efforts, when practices (they may be science programs, applications of technology, whole schools) are nominated as effective, formal evaluations take place (either examining existing data or collecting information through testing, site visits, *etc*) and practices that pass scrutiny are designated exemplary. Typically, such recognition qualifies the practice for dissemination through a proactive external support system like the National Diffusion Network, or through listing in a directory of promising or effective practices. A current project that seeks to develop and refine this process for entire schools is the US Department of Education's Technical Assistance for Successful Schools Project (TASS), now underway at the NETWORK.

Capacity Building

The purpose of some external support system activity is to help local schools and school people develop the ability to identify and solve their own problems, and to plan for and implement their own improvements. Thus, the focus is not on implementing a specific improvement but on developing the skills and knowledge necessary to be self directed in improvement related activities. In some cases, this is done through organization development activities which may include training in problem diagnosis, problem solving, decision making, goal setting conflict resolution, and action planning.

Mandating

Some external support systems have a role to mandate certain procedures, outcomes, and/or materials for use by local schools. Most of a country's education authorities are included in this category. There are some important issues involved in whether and how a given external support system can both mandate and assist or support local schools in implementing the mandates. Often school people find it difficult to ask for help from someone who also is checking for compliance, since help requires problems and difficulties to be identified. Likewise, external support system staff, whose roles have always been to monitor schools for compliance, are not prepared to deliver assistance or support in change efforts. Yet in many countries, staff or authorities such as local or national inspectorates (for example, in Belgium, the UK and France) and state and national agencies (for example, in the US states and Sweden) are changing or have changed from monitoring to assistance responsibilities, or to a combination of both. This often requires retraining and reorientation for both inspectorate, staff and school people alike.

Finally, going back over the listed eleven activities just presented and estimating what percentage of resources (staff time and budget) are spent on each, allows one to determine the priority each is given in the current system. In practice, some subset of the foregoing activities comprise the primary strategy mix that has been developed or has evolved for a given external support system. Our work in ISIP has enhanced our ability to expand our business and consider altering or expanding the strategy mix made available to improving schools.

References

LOUCKS-HORSLEY, S and CRANDALL, D (1986) *The External Support System Profile: Analyzing Support for School Improvement*, Leuven, Belgium, ACCO.

LOUIS, KS, VAN VELZEN, WG, LOUCKS, S and CRANDALL, D (1985) 'External support systems for school improvement', in VAN VELZEN *et al Making School Improvement Work,* Leuven, Belgium, ACCO

LOUIS, KS, VAN VELZEN, WG and CRANDALL, D (Eds), (1987) *Supporting School Improvement*, Leuven, Belgium, ACCO

VAN VELZEN, W, MILES, M, EKHOLM, M, HAMEYER, U and ROBIN, D (Eds) (1985) *Making School Improvement Work*, Leuven, Belgium, ACCO.

WILLIAMS, M (1982) *Designing and Planning External Systems to Support School Improvement*, Andover, MA, The NETWORK Inc.

The Structure of External Support for School Improvement in the United States

David Crandall

When schools in the US desire or are required to make improvements, they can go to a number of different sources for assistance. However, because of the 'local' character of American schools, the availability of help and resources varies widely. It depends in part on the location characteristics, and 'assistance acquiring' capabilities of the given school. Support is not apportioned equally to each school; rather, it is funded by a large number of agencies at all levels (local, regional, state, federal) and is available in different forms through largely intermediary organizations. The discussion that follows attempts to bring some order to this obvious chaos by explaining and illustrating characteristics of the US system(s).

The Nature of External Support in the US

In this section several of the characteristics of external support systems in the US are discussed.

Support for Improvement Comes From Many Different Levels

From the vantage point of an individual school, support for improvement is available from a number of sources. School district central offices, for example, are often staffed with specialists in curriculum and instruction. These staff can provide help in a number of areas, depending on both their availability and the philosophy of the district decision makers (school boards and superintendents). Sometimes district staff are on call to help schools with whatever areas or problems they are interested in; at other times district staff concentrate on helping schools to use the curriculum and instructional approaches determined at the district level. Some districts are losing, or have lost, most of their capacity to provide either kinds of support, due to budget decreases.

Still at the local level, some schools can call for help from teachers' centres and similar centres serving principals. For teachers, these centres often sponsor workshops for their clients and provide space and materials for meeting, designing, writing and discussing and creating new instructional approaches and/or materials. For principals, similar centres provide opportunities for discussion and training in new supervisory, management, and organizational approaches. While these centres, by definition, are focussed on the needs of individual school staff members, rather than the needs of the school as a unit, ideas and materials brought back to the school often are the catalyst or form the core for school wide improvement.

A similar source of support for improvement is the large number of colleges and universities. While the support is often in the form of individual courses and individual faculty members available as consultants, more and more higher education institutions are seeing it as their responsibility to help schools improve. Thus, many sponsor summer institutes or reach out to 'adopt' individual schools and provide negotiated assistance.

Often school districts lack the resources and/or personnel to meet their needs for improvement. A solution many districts have used is to join several districts together into an 'intermediate unit' (IU). While some IUs are used solely to provide resources for ongoing programs (for example, special education, financial support services), others are used to support improvement efforts. When the latter is the case, IU staff are available to work with districts or individual schools. The IU may also provide meeting space, maintain a professional library, and/or sponsor in-service training opportunities for school staff.

States also provide external support for school improvement, sometimes through the establishment of the IUs described above (75 per cent of the states have IUs), other times through direct staff help or resource provision. Much of this support is provided by content area, *ie*, it is categorical. In many states, fairly new 'school improvement programs' have been developed to encourage, or in some cases, require, school to assess systematically their improvement needs and develop and implement plans to meet them.

Finally, although the federal role in education has decreased in the last few years, the government still provides some support for school improvement efforts. Some of this is in direct aid to schools; most goes through states in a number of ways. The nature and forms federal support take are discussed later.

Support for Improvement From the Federal and States Levels is Often Categorical, ie, It is Aimed at Solving Specific Educational Problems, Usually for a Specific Population

For example, the federal government's response to the large numbers of students from poverty-level families, whose educational needs are greater than others, is to provide extra funds to districts based on the number of students who qualify. These 'chapter 1' funds are to improve the education of this special population. Likewise, other resources are made available by federal program offices for schools seeking to develop new approaches to handle problems of their 'special' populations, among them the bilingual, migrant, handicapped, and vocational education students.

In most cases, the resources available from these sources, both direct aid provided on a formula basis (chapter 1) and development funds awarded through a competitive process (bilingual, migrant, *etc.* 'demonstration' grants), are backed up by special 'technical assistance' projects or centres. These centres provide help to schools in a number of different ways, assisting them to use their funds and extra resources more effectively. For example, the six chapter 1 technical assistance centres geographically dispersed around the country, are focussed primarily on assisting schools to evaluate the effectiveness of how they use chapter 1 monies. The federal bilingual program office funds regional 'multifunctional support centres' to help local projects with development, training, management and other areas of need.

Another source of categorical support is for schools interested in (or required to attend to) issues of race and/or sex equity. The federal government supports regional desegregation assistance centres whose staff help districts grappling with the problems of purposely changing the racial mixtures in their schools. Regional centres also provide help to schools interested in eliminating inequities for different sex and national origin groups.

These examples illustrate the categorical nature of much of the external support for schools. While the source of funding for all examples is the federal government, most of it that is not used to support the regional and national centres is given directly to the states. Again, since most state education agencies are arranged in similar categories, the support reaches schools in that way. States add their own resources in most areas, often providing assistance directly to schools using specialists from their agency staffs.

Some External Support Structures Exist for General School Improvement Activity

Most notable are the nine regional laboratories. Funded by the federal government, the mission of these laboratories is to ensure that schools are made aware of the available knowledge and resources that can be brought to bear on an improvement effort. Each lab functions somewhat differently. Some provide direct service to schools in their region; others work only with staffs of state education agencies. Some conduct only dissemination and technical assistance activities; others have major research components which they believe will fill gaps in the knowledge base needed by their region or the country as a whole. Most labs concentrate on collecting the latest research information and school improvement resources so they might be available for use in schools.

David Crandall

External Support Comes in Many Forms

These forms include: funding (both unrestricted and project specific); training, consultation, process assistance; procedures, instruments, materials; and exemplary programs. Funds for improvement are available at every level. Some are distributed to schools on a formula basis while others are granted through a competitive process in which schools propose to develop a program targeted specifically at a local need. While the chapter 1 funds are one attempt by the federal government to meet the needs of a special population, chapter 2 funds are given to school districts for more general purposes. They are distributed by the states, which have the option to designate them for specific improvement efforts; if the states do not so designate, then districts have that option. A recent survey of district use of such funds found them used for instructional materials — in large part computer hardware and software.

While extra funds give schools important slack resources needed to improve, other personally delivered support is also available. At many levels, there are opportunities for learning new information and skills through training. In some cases, individual consultation is available for work on specific problems or interest areas. Some external support is in the form of process assistance, where an external assister guides a school through a process of problem solving and solution implementation. Districts, IUs, state agencies, and federally-funded assistance projects are producing and/or compiling increasingly more materials, procedural guidelines, and assessment instruments to assist schools in each stage of improvement.

Finally, there is increasingly more attention devoted to identifying effective practices and programs, verifying and validating their effectiveness, and creating mechanisms for schools to learn about and be supported in implementing ones that were developed in other settings. States have 'promising practice' files and diffusion programs in many different areas (for example, special education, individualized instruction). The federal government supports a sophisticated system to validate effective programs through the Joint Dissemination Review Panel and disseminate those in areas of national concern through the National Diffusion Network (NDN). The NDN works through a system of facilitators in each state (state facilitators) whose role it is to make schools aware of the programs available and link them to the program developers (developer/demonstrators) for training and ongoing support. NDN programs were among those evaluated in the Study of Dissemination Efforts Supporting School Improvement (DESSI) conducted for the US Department of Education by The NETWORK Inc, from 1978–82.

Relationships Between External Support Structures

In the US there is no coordination among all the sources of external support. At times, individual support systems coordinate their work. For example, when several states decided to encourage and assist their schools to conduct 'school improvement projects', state agency staff link with state facilitators of the NDN, who help schools locate and implement exemplary practices to meet their improvement needs. In another example, some states have taken the categorical funding from the federal government and, rather than passing it on directly to districts, funded IUs to help districts make improvements in the areas covered by the funding. In yet another example, school districts may link with colleges and universities and IUs to establish collaborative teachers' and principals' centres to upgrade the skills and approaches of school staffs.

The kinds of relationships that exist between external support structures are just as varied as the support structures themselves. Often it takes an individual with a vision for school improvement to coordinate and integrate the support and maximize its effects on schools. There are cases where state agency directors or chiefs, IU coordinators, and district superintendents have played this role.

Initiative for School Improvement and Access to External Support

In the US, the initiative for school improvement can come from any level with a legal responsibility for schooling. It can be the result of a direct mandate (a law, a court decision, an action by a school board) or an indirect 'mandate' (such as the pressure resulting from the recent surge of commission reports and studies of schools). An individual school can initiate an improvement effort, as can a district or a state. The federal government can likewise initiate an improvement effort, as it did with legislation for education of the handicapped.

From the perspective of the school, neither the source of initiative for school improvement, nor the diverse, uncoordinated sources of help, cause a particular problem of access to assistance. Schools never see all the possibilities; more often they see few, if any.

Often but not always, when the initiative for improvement is external to the school, its source can either provide assistance, or link the school with sources of assistance. If a court mandates a system to desegregate, it can refer the schools to a desegregation assistance centre. If a state agency mandates school improvement plans or projects, agency staff are usually available for consultation or, at minimum, prepare procedural guidelines or lists of referral agencies. When districts launch improvement efforts central office staff or external consultants (often from universities) are typically available to assist.

When a school initiates its own improvement effort, another story unfolds. The school must take the initiative to find support and its success depends on many factors. It is possible for a school to be geographically out of range of help; likewise, it is possible that support agencies or projects in the school's area conduct no outreach and so are unknown to the individual school. The extent to which a school or, better said, individuals within the school, are active seekers of information and opportunities, will often dictate the extent of resources that are ultimately brought to bear from external support structures. For this reason, the role of a local 'facilitator' — a person in a school, or more likely, central office, who is responsible for scanning the environment for all forms of support — is increasingly important. (It is ironic that economic conditions have caused a severe decrease in the number of people in these positions.)

While this picture has come out rather dimly, it is important to note that there is a rich array of external support for those schools and districts who take action to access it. As states and local districts initiate more improvement efforts, they are becoming more intelligent about where support exists and how to access and integrate the various sources.

Basic Strategies for School Improvement

Because of the overriding belief in the US that the responsibility for education resides in the local community, there is no end to the variety of school improvement efforts that exist. To meet the needs of these efforts for external support, it is logical that structures for external support vary widely and that the support strategies they use vary as well. By providing the local schools with a variety of support strategies, the concept of 'local choice' is enhanced.

While this rationale is sound, and the support strategies available are in fact diverse, there is less flexibility and adaptability than may be assumed. For example, schools in different states are supported in their improvement efforts in very different ways. In Maryland, a district is supported in their selection and implementation of one of four exemplary instructional strategies; in Connecticut, schools receive help in proceeding through a long, complicated assessment and problem solving process; in other states, schools are given access to information about education and are on their own to use it. The 'luck' of being nearby, having a subscription to, or being funded for a particular federal demonstration project, can dictate the kind of support system and, therefore, the improvement strategy a school will experience from an IU or regional centre.

External support structures vary in their approach to providing new *practices* or ideas to school staffs. Some federal categorical and state programs support schools in developing their own practices; others, such as the NDN and some state diffusion programs, support schools in adopting and implementing practices developed elsewhere. In the latter case, some support systems such as the NDN emphasize careful match of the needs of the local school to the practices available. Other support systems mandate specific practices; this most often happens at the school district level, again because of local control.

External support systems also vary in the *process* they use to help schools improve. Some state systems mandate improvement processes, others let the school develop its own. Some external support systems take a broad, comprehensive view of improvement, emphasizing the assessment of all facets of school life and only provide help with the 'big picture' in mind. In fact, many stop at 'capacity building' and never offer specific help. Other systems, such as the NDN, use a strategy based on the idea that a narrowly focussed change can best stimulate change especially at the teacher/student interface where it must occur to make a difference. Most NDN practices are classroom-focussed, aim at a particular content area such as reading or science and are not radically different from accepted approaches.

External support systems also vary in their approach to the *people* they employ to provide the support. Most fund their own staff to work with schools; some, however, are becoming more aware of the importance of internal expertise, and identify, and at times even fund, an 'insider' to collaborate with and carry on the support function. Many systems employ specialists to provide help: evaluators, program developers, content area experts. Other systems have cultivated the role of 'generalist', a person who understands the change process and can guide clients through it, linking when needed to specific expertise.

Strategies used to provide external support often cluster, resulting in some common approaches to school improvement. These clusters vary on two dimensions: whether the improvement is mandated or voluntary, and whether the change involves implementation of a certain practice or practices, or use of a rational problem-solving approach.

In the US mandated change always preempts voluntary or localized change. When a mandate comes down, locally-initiated efforts are set aside. Mandated changes have two general natures: some require use of a specific practice (such as a particular science curriculum) or procedure (such as individualized educational plans), or give schools the choice between a limited number of specific practices or procedures. Other mandated changes require a specific process to be undertaken by the school — usually a rational problem solving procedure by which the school will identify and plan to ameliorate its most pressing need(s).

Voluntary or localized change is usually an 'organic' phenomenon when a school (or person within it) stimulates attention to an interest or a need. In the US, this is typically supported by development funds to design a practice or program to best meet the need. This involves engaging experts, usually from a nearby university or college; and/or training staff, by enlisting the help of an IU or NDN state facilitator for help in identifying new ideas or effective practices that might be implemented; and/or by focussing time and attention on an internal problem solving process that will engage staff and develop commitment to improve. While the development or adoption of new practices might be funded through federal programs such as the NDN or categorical grants, most voluntary local improvement efforts receive their assistance from nearby sources (IU, district, universities). They are rarely without 'pressure' to improve, from district or community, although in the strictest sense, no mandate has occurred.

Tensions in Implementing School Improvement

The tension between local and external control is nowhere more apparent than in the United States. While no one disagrees that primary responsibility for education lies with the local community, there has been much ado about the role of the federal government. From the late 60s when federal resources were used to equalize opportunities for underserved populations and to provide opportunities to innovate, there became more and more 'strings attached' to the resources. Likewise, the intervention of the courts has brought with it a considerable amount of federal control.

Support systems linked to federal funding efforts are not designed to enforce compliance. This is the role of other systems. Rather, they are to relieve the burden of the requirements put on schools by federal expectations. They are, for the most part, reactive to the needs of schools; they do not force schools to use their services. Because research and experience have both indicated that the most effective support services are ones who take the initiative to reach out to schools, the dilemmas of leadership and locus of control are ever present.

The responsive character of external support systems dictates much of how they work with schools. Since few exist to support a specific mandate (*ie*, implementation of a particular innovation), schools have many options in the relationship. Often they can choose whether or not to contact the system; they can choose among delivery modes (for example, information, training, process consultation); they can choose in which phase of the change process to initiate the relationship and when to terminate it; and they can accept any or all assistance and then implement what they want, ignoring what they do not.

The 'local choice' causes dilemmas for external support systems, which have tried in their design and their policies to avoid providing support that will have no effect. Some support systems, such as the NDN, require an agreement to be signed that the adopting school will use the key components of the practice in which they are trained. This eliminates both a wasted training session and the possibility that what is used of the practice will have no effect on students. Other support systems, such as some state agencies, require that the whole district be involved, or at least be tangibly supportive of the effort, when it works with an individual school. This circumvents the possibility that a district initiative will undermine or detract from a school's effort to improve. Likewise, some support system staff will not work with teachers without the principal's commitment. All these measures are taken to increase the probability of success. And all follow from the fact that external support is voluntary — schools that will not accept the conditions need not volunteer.

Collective bargaining is a political factor that has altered some of the ways schools implement improvements, as well as how they seek and use external support. Teacher involvement at every stage of the effort takes a high priority where collective bargaining exists. Further, requiring teachers to attend the preparation, training, and follow-up sessions needed to change successfully is complicated by work hour and release time agreements. In places where teacher unions are strong, the external support structures must be flexible and staff must spend much time involving and working with the right parties.

One reason the teaching population is increasingly demanding to be involved in improvement efforts is that it is ageing and relatively immobile. External support systems working with young mobile teachers, where new blood and turnover is common and burnout is rare, have a different task than those working with the current population. Now, it is necessary to do more up front 'marketing', engaging teachers as advocates, move slowly and carefully, take advantage of teacher expertise as trainers and ongoing support, and use numerous other different approaches.

Another political factor that requires attention is the 'hodge-podge' of roles and responsibilities caused by the complex structures and players providing support. Inevitably, somebody's territory will be, or will appear to be, invaded. For example, federal technical assistance centres are often funded to work directly with interested schools or demonstration projects being developed by individual schools. Sometimes, when the state agency or regional IU also has a responsibility in the particular area of interest, there is resentment when help comes from out of the region or the state directly to the schools. External support agencies need to be careful to notify, coordinate and at times, mollify, agencies with overlapping responsibilities.

Closing

Schools in the US are best characterized by their diversity, as are the support systems which provide them assistance in their efforts to improve. While there is no doubt that this diversity will remain, the nature and source of support may change within the near future, given the variety of cultural and political issues that are raging and competing for attention. Although educators are currently in a precarious position, at the same time there is a window of opportunity to shape unusual alliances and formulate intriguing images for the kinds of support and resources needed in our rapidly changing world.

The General Certificate of Secondary Education (GCSE): A Strategy for Improvement in the UK

Don Cooper

Examinations — General Background

> Examinations are tools, designed for various purposes and to perform various operations. No tool can be perfect but some can be more precise than others and even a good instrument can be mishandled. (Morris, 1961)

Giving a historian's view of examinations, Morris describes the uses to which examinations can be put. Briefly he argues they can be used:

- as a means of maintaining standards;
- as incentives to effort; and
- as tools of social engineering.

Before relating these and other factors to the GCSE, it may be useful to examine each more closely and to bear in mind questions about evaluation generally. Of particular importance are the questions concerned with the reasons for examining, and those relating to the advantages and disadvantages that the process of examining has for the various people concerned with the enterprise.

Examinations as a Means of Maintaining Standards

Sometimes an examination is designed to preserve the efficiency of some system or institution and the needs of the candidates as individuals are of secondary importance. When this occurs, the examination becomes an instrument of policy, seeking as it does to maintain preconceived standards, or to improve standards as is the case with GCSE. There are at least three types of examinations designed for the purpose — those which regulate entry by competitions; those which give qualifications for jobs (licences); and those used for the purpose of inspections.

Competitions

There are very many examples of examinations which are in reality competitions designed to eliminate the majority of candidates and to allocate the remainder to a specified number of vacancies. One of the best known competitive examinations was the 11+ in which standards varied from LEA to LEA according to the numbers of places available. The common entrance examination fulfils a similar function with the candidates scoring the highest marks generally gaining admission to the more prestigious schools. Another example concerns the GCE 'A' level which is being used increasingly to satisfy the entrance requirements of university departments. For example, candidates may be offered places provided they obtain 2 'Bs' and a 'C' or 2 'As' and a 'B', the standards varying from university to university.

Licences

Doctors, lawyers and teachers are obvious examples of people who sit examinations which will give them licences to enter the professions of their choice. They are examined to determine their professional and technical fitness. If they are successful, they are given the right to practise but they are not given a job as of right. Sometimes, licensing is used as a means of progression from one examination to the next. Thus the candidate has to be successful in a series of examinations to achieve the final qualification.

Inspection

Teachers use this method to determine and maintain standards in their classes. They have tests, sometimes at very frequent intervals, and use term and yearly examinations to inspect attainment as well as to motivate pupils. This use of examinations has been in existence for many years. One of the earliest examples at a national level occurred in 1846 when the inspectors realized that the only efficient way to assess a school was to examine the pupils or at least a sample of the pupils. More recently the work of the APU provides a good example of the technique of attempting to determine standards by means of the assessment of a sample of pupils.

Examinations as a Device for Stimulating Effort

For many years the argument has been put that working towards examinations stimulates effort. Nowhere has this been seen more clearly than in work for 'O' and 'A' levels and for the CSE. Indeed, one of the criteria used to judge a school, by some parents, is the way in which it exhorts, cajoles, encourages or persuades its pupils to undertake large amounts of homework to achieve good examination results. The school will be judged on its passes and thus every effort will be made to stimulate pupils to achieve the best possible results. After all, those results will be published and the school judged accordingly. Thus examinations are used not only as a device for stimulating pupils but also for stimulating teachers — they too will be judged on their success rate. Without presuming to argue how deeply a desire for success in external examinations does motivate students, the history of examinations suggests that setting children against one another in trials and competitions has always been a respectable means of encouraging them to greater efforts.

Examinations as Tools of Social Engineering

As examinations take place in a social setting, it is useful to consider how far they have been used to modify society or retain the status quo in that society. One of the most important functions that examinations have had in this country is the way they have been used to allow mobility within the class structure. Since the Middle Ages there has always been the possibility for children of poor parents to receive schooling and, by so doing, to move up the social scale. Even so, this social mobility has affected only a few children — not enough to disturb the social structure itself. It is only with the rapid growth in the numbers of pupils sitting for GCE 'O' level in the secondary modern schools, together with the advent of comprehensive schools, that the routes to the most senior posts in the country have become open to all.

Morris (1961) points out that whilst examinations can become tools for ensuring social mobility, they can never be more than tools. As such they will be used or not used according to the will and philosophy of those in a position to guide society. The interesting feature about the new GCSE is the place it will occupy in the social structure of our society. Some may argue that it will have a neutral role — the evidence from history indicates that this is unlikely.

The General Certificate of Secondary Education (GCSE)

For over a decade successive Secretaries of State for Education and Science have been urged by teachers and others to introduce a common system of examining at 16+. In June 1984 the government announced its decision to establish the GCSE to replace 'O' levels and the CSE. The original proposals had been put forward to guarantee amongst other things a balanced curriculum and to act as a further reward for the highest level of attainment. Indeed, the Secretary of State published, for consultation, proposals for the introduction of distinction and merit certificates but in the light of comments from many quarters, these proposals were dropped.

There are distinctive features about the new examination which it is felt will affect most teachers in secondary schools. These features are:

Syllabuses and examinations will be based on national criteria. These consist of a series of general guidelines for the examination as a whole (general criteria) and subject specific guidelines for twenty selected subjects.

Great emphasis will be put on 'differentiation'. Generally speaking all good examinations discriminate between candidates but in the new examination the emphasis will be on differentiation as well as discrimination. Thus differentiated papers or differentiated questions within papers will be required. These will provide a positive experience for all candidates at all levels so that they should be encouraged to demonstrate what they know, understand and can do.

In the GCSE all subjects will normally be required to include assessed course work. The hope is that this course work will offer the opportunity for new forms of assessment with candidates getting credit for more of the regular day to day classroom activities — recording observations, using research skills, manipulating equipment and materials *etc.*

There can be no doubt that the introduction of this examination will involve many teachers in developing further their assessment skills and in becoming familiar with moderation procedures. The emphasis on the assessment of course work will mean that teachers will have to view their students as individuals within the classroom and this in itself will entail for many teachers a reappraisal of their methods and teaching styles. Newsletter Number 1 of the Secondary Examinations Council (SEC, 1985) indicates the patterns of inservice work planned to help teachers with the task of implementing the new examination.

A partnership has been set up between the SEC, the Open University and the British Broadcasting Corporation to produce materials for the SEC in support of the in-service training activities. Five TV programmes have been prepared covering course work, assessment, differentiation, oral English, oral French and experimental work in science. Early in 1986 every secondary school teacher received a manual to the GCSE in his or her own subject; 440,000 free guides having been made available. The guides and the TV programmes have been designed both for self study and to support group activities. They offer suggestions for a range of different activities, both to stimulate reflection and to propose action to prepare new courses and assessment plans.

The guides are designed particularly to provide a resource for group work since another major component of the GCSE inservice training programme was a series of seminars and briefings held in the spring of 1986. These seminars were conducted by group leaders recruited for the task by the examining bodies and organized in cooperation with the local education authorities who received funding from the government to help with the costs of providing cover for teachers attending the seminars. The seminars were designed to last for the equivalent of two-and-a-half days and were aimed principally at heads of department and other subject leaders. About 60,000 teachers attended these courses nationwide.

After the initial training of heads of department a 'cascade' model of dissemination came into play. Most of the 60,000 teachers who attended the courses in the first phase were asked to play some part in local activities and also to train others within their departments.

The GCSE in-service training programme is probably the largest exercise of its kind ever conducted in England and Wales. Its unique blend of national and local activities and of distance teaching and group work, signals a new approach to in-service provision as well as new generation of examinations.

Finally, it should be noted that the stated objectives of the government in setting up GCSE includes; the raising of standards across the whole ability range, the support of improvements in the curriculum and the way in which it is taught. Thus the GCSE is designed to improve schooling. Many previous curriculum development projects have had similar aims but they have had to persuade teachers of the value of their work. The GCSE is different — it is a fact which will affect the lives of most secondary teachers and their pupils. In a sense many of the problems associated with the GCSE have been identified already — all that remains is for the teachers to address those problems for themselves.

Facts — Secondary Examinations Council (SEC)

1   The Secondary Examinations Council was set up by the Secretaries of State in May 1983.
2   The SEC oversees and advises on examinations and assessment issues in the secondary education sector.
3   The Council itself consists of fifteen members appointed by the Secretary of State after consultation with the many interests involved.
4   The Council was unanimous in advising the Secretary of State to introduce a single system of examining at age 16.
5   Council meetings are attended by assessors from the DES, HMI, the Welsh Office and the SCDC.
6   There are thirty-five standing committees of the Council with other working parties and 'ad hoc' committees dealing with specialist issues (grade criteria in GCSE is one example).
7   All Council committees and working parties include representatives of the education service. Among these are teachers, examiners, lecturers, HMIs and LEA advisers.

Facts — The GCSE

1   The GCSE is a single system of examining in separate subjects which will replace the 'O' level and the CSE.

2   The GCSE will be examined by five examining groups monitored by the SEC.

3   Syllabuses and examinations will be based on national criteria.

4   National criteria have been developed by committees of teachers, examiners and others. The SEC and the Joint Council of GCE and CSE boards reached agreement on the draft criteria. They were approved by the Secretaries of State in January, 1985.

5   Grades will be awarded on a 7-point scale, A-G. The standards expected of candidates will be no less exacting than in the existing examinations.

6   The GCE Boards will bear special responsibility within the examining groups for maintaining the standards of grades A-C.

7   The government's objective is to raise the standards of attainment by stretching and stimulating pupils throughout the ability range.

8   The GCSE will be for all candidates who are able to reach the standards required for particular grades.

9   All GCSE syllabuses must comply with the national criteria. The SEC is responsible for seeing that all syllabuses, all assessment, moderation, grading and certification comply with the national criteria.

10   All syllabuses will be subject to approval by the SEC either directly for Mode One syllabuses where they are subject specific criteria, or by sampling for other syllabuses.

11   In the GCSE examinations assessed course work will normally be a requirement.

12   A major thrust of the new examination will be to ensure that candidates will be regarded for their positive achievements. This is the reason for the requirement that there should be differentiated assessment in all subjects. Possible methods of differentiating are:

(i)   by candidates of differing abilities taking different papers;

(ii)   by all candidates being given the same questions but where answers are graded in terms of the positive qualities and achievements demonstrated by candidates. The need for discrimination is still there but what is now needed as well is that candidates at all levels should be encouraged to demonstrate what they know, understand, and can do.

13   Grade criteria will be developed to indicate what skills, knowledge and competence are required to attain a certain grade.

14   As soon as they are developed and agreed, the grade criteria will

replace the grade descriptions that are currently given in the national criteria documents.

References

MORRIS, N (1961) *Examinations and English Education*, Manchester, Manchester University Press.
SECONDARY EXAMINATIONS COUNCIL (1985) *In-service for the GCSE*, News No 1, London, Secondary Examinations Council.
The facts about the SEC and the GCSE are taken from information leaflets published by the SEC.

External Support: A Response from the UK Perspective

Keith McWilliams

Within the context of this ISIP dissemination exercise, it is important to remind ourselves that any definition of 'external support' for schools must not be restricted to the 'educational mafia'. As educationalists it does us no credit whatsoever to assume that we have a professional monopoly on the provision of appropriate support for schools. As David Crandall has reminded us, schools are surrounded by a wealth of talent. It is likely that our colleagues in schools already have a clear perception of the potential value of members of the local community and have enlisted the active participation of parents, employers and many other interested parties. Of course, this is a fine, laudable general principle, but it is very difficult to put into practice, particularly as it is all too easy to become sidetracked by demarcation issues. Nevertheless, if schools understand their need for 'external support' then it follows that a broad based network of such support is much more likely to achieve school improvement. In my opinion, unless school support is seen as a partnership it is most unlikely to facilitate school improvement but such a relationship requires great sensitivity as well as undoubted expertise.

My second point enables me to offer a modestly critical point regarding ISIP. At the Project's inception some emphasis was given to the notion of encouraging codevelopment. It will be evident to everyone that the main vehicle for disseminating ISIP's outcomes is yet again the printed word. Of course, well written reports and analyses have an important role but I am left to question our comparative inability to create the opportunities for codevelopment activities so confidently forecast during the early planning stages of ISIP. In an international project it has proved very difficult indeed to facilitate operational involvement, although it is pleasing to be able to endorse David's comments that there are some important examples within area 3. Indeed, there have been valuable exchanges between the Network Inc. and the School Curriculum Development Committee. Also, out of the ISIP experience came the idea of linking the curriculum development agencies in England, Wales, Scotland, Northern Ireland and the Irish Republic. Starting at the chief officer level, three consultations have already been held. These meetings reveal the wide areas of common concern between the various bodies *ie*, the School Curriculum Development Committee, the Scottish Consultative Committee on the Curriculum, the Northern Ireland Council for Educational Development and the Irish Board for Curriculum and Examinations. The value of sharing news and views should be self-evident but the establishment of a good communication network is but the first stage towards implementing joint activities. It is likely that this further objective will be achieved in the not too distant future, although I must reassure you all that this does not mean that a standardized version of a UK curriculum is imminent! Instead, this is a good example of the beginnings of cooperation and codevelopment where it should occur, closest to home. As David Crandall suggested, it is encouraging to note that elsewhere within the ISIP 'family' it is possible to identify international networks fostered and activated by individual and corporate members of the project.

David's reference to the proliferation of external support agencies in the United States reminds us that a similar comment could be made of the situation in the UK. I have a theory that suggests that as times get harder and resources and rolls decline, so, in inverse proportion, the number of agencies and individuals seeking to offer support to such a system seems to expand. From the point of view of the harassed classroom teacher, head or LEA adviser it may very well appear that there are too many chiefs and not enough indians, that the multiplicity of support agencies can be regarded as competitive and, worse still, contradictory. The question of coordination must be raised. The issue for schools is not so much 'Where can I get help?', but 'How can I find my way through the myriad of options even when I have made the discovery that I might need and benefit from external support in the first place?'. Indeed the membership of the conference reflected the variety and scale of such provision within the UK educational system. Today, skilful practitioners soon learn the art of making submissions, adopting schemes and implementing them, often with money that originally could be deemed to be the proposers. Another question has to be asked regarding the time and energy demanded by this practice. It may be justified if you emerge as a 'likely winner' but it is far less satisfactory if you are an 'unfortunate loser'. There is evidence to suggest that this mode of operation is not only going to continue, but will expand, as, for example, in the post-1987 INSET arrangements for England and Wales. Today LEA officers and advisers have little option but to acquire the necessary skills involved in making successful submissions usually against very tight deadlines. I submit that this emergent high profile aspect of the education service will dominate our work from now onwards.

The current UK situation reveals not only a proliferation of agencies offering external support but also raises the key issues regarding coherence and balance between the wide variety of support services offered. In some situations competition is healthy and therefore it is possible that the combined activities of the Department of Education and Science, the Manpower

Services Commission and the Department of Trade and Industry are good for the service as a whole. On the other hand, the sheer volume of support agencies could create confusion, wasteful duplication and a dissipation of scarce resources. Another prediction hardly likely to cause surprise is that this complicated pattern will continue. Indeed, the recent announcement of the creation of the Microelectronics Support Unit set up to disseminate the outcomes of the Microelectronics Education Programme with specific reference to the whole curriculum, indicates that a diversified, fragmented mode of provision will continue. As a member of the Board of Management for this new body, I am well aware of the scope and urgency of its task in order to establish a support structure in only a few months.

In my judgment it is essential that all of us involved in the external support dimension should take very seriously indeed the need for coherence, coordination and balance. Of course we all shy away from the bogey word, 'control', and many of the agencies involved pride themselves on their autonomous or semi-autonomous status. It is significant that this area of concern is precisely mirrored in the dilemmas enunciated by David Crandall and added to the eleven features of external support agencies he identified. Whatever we may feel about the UK situation, it behoves us all to realize that the context within which we operate is most certainly not unique.

6   The Development and Implementation of School Improvement Policies by Education Authorities

Introduction

The development of policy is crucial to effective school improvement. Policy at national, local and school level provides direction for innovation and the basis for systematic and sustained planning. To be useful for school improvement, policy needs at all levels to be coherent, practical, acceptable and implementation oriented.

Unfortunately, as Hans Tangerud points out in his presentation, this is rarely the case. He argues that the growth of pluralism (or value pluralism in his terminology) in decentralized Western societies has hindered the generation of effective policy. The essential and laudable characteristic of pluralism is that it cherishes freedom of speech and a diversity of opinion but it is precisely that which inhibits the production of clearly defined policy. This occurs at three levels: (i) at the centre where formal policy is developed; (ii) at various layers of the bureaucracy; and (iii) at the school level where there may be value conflict between and among school leaders, teachers, parents, pupils and governors etc. Tangerud suggests that given this inevitable situation, conflict-oriented strategies for the production of policy need to be developed. He makes a start by describing the 'in-between', 'delegation', 'charismatic' and 'direct use of power' strategies.

The case studies illuminate the theme of policy led school improvement in two different situations. In this case study of the 'Role of the Superintendent in Promoting Educational Reform', Richard Wallace argues that the superintendent must assume the role of educational leader. His position is that the superintendent must exert vigorous educational leadership to improve instructional effectiveness and promote standards of excellence in schools. Leadership can be defined in many ways. Expressed very simply, it can be described as a process of working with and through other people to get a job done. From Wallace's perspective, educational leadership requires extensive goal setting, planning, implementation and evaluation relevant to instruction. The case study describes how a local policy, developed along these lines, was successful at achieving educational reform.

By way of contrast Michael Henley and Peter Smith in their case study of the Technical and Vocational Education Initiative (TVEI) in Northamptonshire show how TVEI originated from central government policy concerning national training objectives. TVEI is intended to provide pupils with better preparation in schools and colleges for working life and better arrangements for the transition from full time education to work. It is directed by the Manpower Services Commission through a partnership between it and each LEA concerned. As a policy initiative in curriculum development, the target is the 14–18 year age group of all abilities. Although central authorities provided generous funding and a broad policy framework, the LEA, together with their schools and colleges, prepare the implementation policy for their own project. The development of TVEI is also influenced by regular consultation with interests outside education and with students and parents. TVEI is raising policy issues in a number of key areas: for example, resource levels; regulations covering secondary and further education; models of generalization; curriculum development. The case study demonstrates how some of Hans Tangerud's dilemmas are overcome in practice but leaves open the question as to whether the 'TVEI policy model' is the most appropriate approach to policy development for school improvement.

In his response from the UK perspective, Michael Henley argues for a partnership in policy making and for a policy that is specific and process oriented. He also argues for aims and implementation principles (for example, staff development) to be explicit and coherently formulated in school improvement policies.

The Development of Policy in Pluralistic and Decentralized Societies

Hans Tangerud

Introduction

This presentation does not cover the whole spectrum of topics dealt with in area group 5: nor does it detail the diversity of opinion among area group members. The presentation should be seen as one member's effort to extract from a vast array of material some basic themes and to present those themes in a fashion that may be conducive to further development.

In addition to the specificity of the task undertaken by the area 5 group, their work has been different from that of the other area groups in two ways. First, whilst the other groups have been concerned mainly with what is local, grass roots, from 'bottom up', area group 5 has been dealing with what is 'top down', *ie*, centrally initiated and monitored, at national, state or regional level. This change of focus stems from a concern with the need for policy in its broadest sense which surpasses policy at local or school level. Second, it would be all too simple to say that the work of area group 5 has been performed within the limits of a conflict model as contrasted to that of the other groups which can be seen as based on a harmony model. While it must be admitted that all groups have dealt with harmony as well as conflict, the focus on conflict has been paramount in area group 5 and much more so than in the other areas. Following from this, and in my opinion, the main theme of area group five work has been the role and strategy of central leadership in pluralistic and decentralized western societies.

Pluralism — Its Causes, Dimensions and Consequences

At the 1983 conference in Stockholm pluralism was defined at the general level as a fundamental external factor that interfered in many ways with school improvement efforts. At the Oslo conference in 1985 we dealt more concretely with the concept of pluralism, which was narrowed down, explicitly and implicitly, to 'value pluralism', which seemed the most meaningful and productive definition for our work.

By and large, western societies can be regarded as gradually becoming more value pluralistic over the last century. Today the norms of the ruling class are not accepted by all citizens to the same extent as was the case 100 years ago. Value pluralism seems to develop along the dimensions of social class, generation, ethnicity and charisma, *ie*, religion, politics, interests and hobbies. Value pluralism leads to the development of subcultures, ie aggregates of people holding similar values, giving reciprocal reinforcement of those values and sticking together in ways which reduce contacts with and influence from other sub-cultures. So, sub-cultures become a factor in the further development of value pluralism.

Value pluralism is by itself a highly cherished value in western democratic societies because it stands for tolerance and freedom. When there is value pluralism, there are not only differences of values but a high degree of acceptance of other people's right to think and behave differently. There is also a strong feeling that anybody can and should decide for him/herself, even though this may interfere with professional values and performances. Alternatively, value pluralism means latent or manifest conflict, a fight for power, the formation of alliances and *mesalliances* at all levels. As value pluralism represents a difficulty in any school striving for some kind of consistency, measures have been taken in some countries to expel religion from schools, to support private schools, to give parents the right to choose a school to their liking or to delegate schooling to business or private organizations at local levels all in order to establish a more homogenous setting.

Value pluralism affects centrally initiated school improvement efforts along three dimensions: central decision making, the top to bottom dimension, and the local or school situation.

The Central Decision Making Level

Pluralism at central decision making level may be inferred from two observations. One is the increasing number of consultations or hearings with political and administrative bodies, labour organizations and all kinds of pressure groups that need to be accomplished before any decision can be made. Without such procedures, one cannot be sure of sufficient backing for the intended change to be carried through. As the parties consulted regularly hold divergent or opposing views, there must be compromises. Compromises cannot always be reached and the result is often that official documents contain opposing views, abstract formulations that can be interpreted in quite different ways and/or omissions of whatever is strongly controversial. It goes without saying that such documents form no solid basis for consistent school improvement efforts. In order for well planned and effective change efforts to take place, there must be at least smooth interaction between the spheres of politics, administration and the educational profession, the latter including subject matter as well as process specialists.

The second observation is that such cooperation at an acceptable level is rarely seen. The most usual consequence seems to be that there is first a political decision of a general and ideological kind succeeded by administrative measures narrowing down and even changing to some extent the original political message and the professional is left with little space within which s/he cannot always move meaningfully. Another consequence may be that one has on one side change efforts that are purely administrative without any support from the R & D profession and, on the other side, professional change efforts with no reference to administration. Sometimes politicians, due to lack of professional information, make decisions that have little chance of being effectively carried through.

The 'Top Bottom' Dimension

'Top bottom' pluralism exists at several layers of bureaucracy. Listening to the debates at different levels, one comes to understand that teaching staff, single school leadership, local leadership and regional leadership constitute different sub-cultures with different jargons, problem definition and loyalties, all of them in some contrast to the central leadership. The consequences seem to be a lack of loyalty towards central bodies and an inability to understand and pass on messages from the central leadership. The result seems to be something like whispering games where the message is continually being changed as it is passed on from one to the other.

Pluralism at Local Level

Third, there is pluralism at the local level. First of all there is pluralism within staff. Any change effort will inevitably interfere with staff members' positions as well as established coalitions in ways that may cause some unrest. Second, there is pupils' and parents' pluralism, of which teachers are extremely conscious, leaving them with a kind of paranoia which may in its turn lead to a self censureship as regards controversial topics. Third, there are the influences of the local school board and local pressure groups.

To sum up; the existence of pluralism may result in inconsistent authority, an inability to make decisions, communication difficulties, disloyalty, an inability to make changes based on non accepted values, a fight for power, alliances of labour *etc.* This is not to say that there is nothing but conflict, but conflict is an important aspect of the cultural situation that needs to be taken into consideration.

Measures and Strategies

When considering school improvement from a centralized perspective based on a conflict model, one finds that the measures and strategies usually discussed in the professional literature are not quite adequate. This is understandable as professional literature is usually written by non-political, non-administrative professionals based in a university or in a support organization. This leaves us with a lack of relevant literature.

From a conflict model perspective there is a need to develop conflict oriented strategies of which the following are some examples.

The 'In-between' Strategy

The idea is to make changes only in those areas where there is little or no conflict. One may well doubt whether such areas are big or important enough to be of significant interest. Yet, this strategy seems to be the one most often chosen consciously or unconsciously. If this is the case, it is no wonder that there are often no results or the results are rather different from the intended change. The central leadership is often tempted to choose this strategy as it is supposed to be inoffensive to those involved.

The Delegation Strategy

When there are insoluble conflicts at central level, responsibility may be delegated to the regional or local level in the hope that conflict lines will be less rigid and pluralism not quite as rampant. There may also be delegation to private organizations, which means that the responsibility is turned over to the sub-cultures. A third possibility is delegation to the market, when there is something that can be produced and sold with sufficient profit. Like the first strategy this one is also somewhat weak as it implies reduced direction and control and, therefore, reduced effectiveness at central level.

The Charismatic Strategy

If the minister talks to the people on TV stating what excellent changes he wants to make and his problems with a defensive teacher union and tells the parents what kind of school they should expect and press for, he is using a charismatic strategy. Such a talk may be supported by articles or radio or TV programmes illustrating what good schools and good methods are. Another possibility is to establish alternative institutions with a firm and consistent philosophy and with a highly qualified and loyal staff, that may cause a pressure from many parents to have something similar.

The Direct Use of Power Strategy

Even in highly pluralistic and decentralized societies central authorities are still in a position to exert influence by way of judicial and similar measures. It is interesting to note that school laws and other regulations in the educational field seem to have a lower status as compared to other public sectors in so far as there is little control and very rarely blame or punishment. There are certainly limitations to the use of judicial measures in education but the often frequent use of enormous sums of tax money indicate that the possible uses of such measures have not been thoroughly explored. In addition it is often possible for the central leadership to set aside some extra money that can be used to encourage special developments.

These points should be taken as no more than examples of ways of thinking, that need to be developed further. In addition to the need for more refined and adequate strategic thinking there seems to be a need to do something about the work situation of the decision maker at central level, particularly that of the politician. An increase in pluralism leads to an increase in work load as much more time is needed to explain, convince, seek support and follow up, to a great number of audiences at decision making level and all through the hierarchy. At present, some of the apparently bad compromises which lead to meaningless, impracticable, ineffective and expensive solutions should be regarded as accidents or mishaps caused by lack of real communication.

Note

At the conference, Tangerud's presentation was scheduled as an after dinner session. Feeling that the audience may consequently be less alert to a theoretical presentation, he chose to develop his conflict model of school improvement by presenting a series of myths.

Myths at the central decision making level
1 The myth that politicians decide.
2 The myth that decisions are meaningful.

Myths about the research and development profession
3 The myth that it exists.
4 The myth that it wants to learn from experience.

Myths about the educational bureaucracy:
5 The myth that the bureaucracy is able to understand the political message.
6 The myth that the bureaucracy is able to translate the political message into educational action.
7 The myth of bureaucratic loyalty.
8 The myth of bureaucratic efficiency.
9 The myth of bureaucratic impartiality.

Myths at school level:
10 The myth of the non-existing teacher unions.

11 The myth of the school as an educational institution.
12 The myth that teachers care for children.
13 The myth that pupils are committed to school improvement.
14 The myth that conflicts can and should be solved.

The overall myth
15 The myth that we need a minister of education.

The Role of the Superintendent in Promoting Educational Reform in the United States

Richard Wallace

Introduction

The burden of educational improvement falls heavily upon the shoulders of the superintendents of schools across America. If school districts are to respond effectively to the mandate to improve the effectiveness of American schools, then superintendents of schools must provide vigorous leadership. However, most superintendents have not been trained as educational leaders.

Champagne and his colleagues (1984) who completed a study of programs for administrators in Pennsylvania found some rhetoric on educational leadership but few course requirements for superintendents that focussed on that issue. If these findings were to be replicated nationally, then the lack of offering of courses in educational or instructional leadership may suggest that many superintendents may not be prepared to exert the leadership required by the educational reform movement. Silver (1982) points out that the competencies most frequently emphasized in administrative training programs relate to conceptual and analytic skills that prepare administrators to manage schools.

Superintendents need to apply their analytic skills to educational leadership issues and not just to management issues in school administration. The tools of analysis can be applied effectively to the processing of educational achievement data and other information related to schooling effectiveness. Constant monitoring of data from multiple sources provides the basis for educational leadership. Data such as pupil and teacher attendance, student suspensions, distributions of grades, item analyses of standardized achievement tests are all important sources of information that superintendents should analyze to formulate educational improvement plans.

Analysis and continual monitoring of indicators of educational quality by superintendents form the cornerstone of effective educational leadership. Superintendents should stimulate other educators with specific competencies in instructional matters to develop initiatives to address identified educational needs. Then superintendents should lead their associates with a systematic and continuous monitoring of critical data related to program implementation and outcomes. In this way, superintendents will direct their staff to modify or refine program initiatives to produce optimal results. Careful and continuous analysis of educational information provides the basis for vigorous and effective educational leadership by superintendents.

Needs Analysis in Pittsburgh — The Cornerstone of Educational Leadership

A fundamental premise underlying any educational improvement program is the requirement to have a full understanding of the current state of the school district. This serves four purposes. First, an understanding of the *status quo* provides the basis for a diagnosis of the strengths and weaknesses of the district. Second, it provides important base line data from which one can gauge the effectiveness of improvement efforts. Third, it provides an opportunity for the superintendent to apply his/her analytic skills to the existing data base that will provide the foundation for leadership for planning educational improvements. Fourth, it facilitates the development of political consensus through which a commitment to action can arise.

Early in the fall of 1980 I initiated a needs assessment survey for the district that would provide both the superintendent and the Board of Education with data that could be used to set priorities for the district. In this effort the district secured the assistance of Dr William Cooley and the staff of the Evaluation Unit of the Learning and Research and Development Centre (LRDC), University of Pittsburgh. In their work in the Pittsburgh area, the Evaluation Unit had conducted a number of studies for the Pittsburgh city schools (Cooley and Bickel, 1987) and had developed a database from the records kept at the Board of Public Education in Pittsburgh.

We agreed that the survey would have two foci. One was to sample the opinions of a wide variety of 'stakeholders' in the school district and the community to obtain their impressions of the problems facing the district. They would be asked to identify the district's problems that could be corrected through direct intervention. The second focus examined all the information in the Board's data base to describe in some detail the nature of the problems identified through the survey.

The survey was conducted in December 1980. The survey took three forms: mailed questionnaires, telephone interviews and personal interviews. Most of the educational professionals were surveyed through mailed questionnaires. Parental interviews were conducted by telephone and personal interviews were carried out with community leaders. For some groups, such as the Board of Education and school principals, all members were included in the survey. For larger groups such as teachers and counsellors, a 5 or 10 per cent stratified random sample survey was conducted. Once the data were gathered and processed, the task of making meaning out of the data was shared between the LRDC and the Board of Education staff. The LRDC staff organized a presentation of both the survey data and the longitudinal data.

The Board of Education members met in an all-day session in late January 1981. Drs William Cooley and William Bickel presented the data. The Board engaged in extensive dialogue and questioned the presenters to obtain a greater understanding of the results. The Board spent about three hours reviewing the data. Then they spent an additional three hours arriving at consensus among themselves with regard to priorities for the district. The Board agreed on two major priority areas: (i) school improvement; and (ii) effective management. Under the general heading of school improvement, the Board identified the following six priority areas: increasing student achievement, improving the quality of personnel evaluation, managing enrollment decline, attracting and holding students, improving discipline in the schools and developing a strategy for improving specific low-achieving schools. The superintendent was then charged with the task to develop specific plans to bring about an improvement in each of the priority areas identified.

Improving the Performance of Principals and Teachers

The staff development program known as PRISM (Pittsburgh's Research — based Instructional Supervisory Model) is the primary vehicle to promote the role of principal as instructional leader. It also serves as the vehicle for the revitalization of teachers and the basis for personnel evaluation systems. This section will provide a brief description of the program and a summary of results to date.

At present, there are four variants of PRISM in operation and a fifth in the planning stage. PRISM I is concerned with providing a consistent framework for the description, observation, improvement and evaluation of instruction at all levels in the district. PRISM II is directed towards improving the instructional leadership behaviour of principals, supervisors and central office administrators. PRISM III is the district's effort to improve the quality of secondary education. PRISM IV is designed to stimulate the improvement of our elementary schools, while PRISM V will be directed toward middle school improvement. All five PRISM programs are designed to improve the effectiveness of instruction, promote the instructional leadership role of the principal, improve personnel evaluation and thus lead to a higher quality of student learning in the district. This paper deals with PRISM I, II and III.

Components of PRISM I

There are five essential components of PRISM I:

  (i)   knowledge training;
 (ii)   skill development;
(iii)   practice;
 (iv)   follow up coaching;
  (v)   peer networks.

The knowledge base of the model is derived primarily from the work of Madeline Hunter (1978). Where appropriate, other research findings have been introduced to augment the Hunter model. Skill training focusses on the development of the ability to take anecdotal records of classroom instructional observations that are as close to verbatim records as possible. They are to be used in planning and carrying out the conference with the teacher. The conferring portion of the model is a variant of the clinical supervision model developed by Cogan (1973) and Goldhammer (1969).

How PRISM I Works

Beginning in September 1981, all administrators in the district were required to attend thirty hours of training on the PRISM model. All central office administrators, including the superintendent and assistant principals, and supervisors had received initial training and were using PRISM with selected staff to become more skilled in using the model. In the summer of 1982, the principals taught a special two-week summer session for students. This summer school provided them with an opportunity to teach students themselves and internalize the instructional model to be required of teachers. As principals taught, they were observed by their peers and received feedback from them regarding the effectiveness of instruction. This provided a mechanism through which both instructional and supervisory skills could be refined simultaneously.

During the 1982/83 school year, all principals were expected to conduct a minimum of three observations of teaching each week along with follow-up conferences. They were required to keep records of the observations. The record included the subject and grade level observed and the focus and style of the conference (in terms of the specific improvement strategy). The data describing these observations were carefully monitored by the staff development team. Additionally, each of the staff development team members was assigned a specific number of principals for whom he or she was responsible. These staff development associates functioned as coaches for the principals, and were required to observe and confer with them to ensure that the principals had assimilated and operationalized the instructional model effectively. This same coaching process has been used in each subsequent school year.

PRISM reflects the first segment of the response to the Board's priority regarding effective personnel evaluation. It has established the criteria for effective instruction. PRISM I has provided principals with specific classroom observational skills including anecdotal note taking, analysis of notes to obtain specific data for the teacher conference, conference planning, and conducting conferences to promote instructional improvement. The PRISM model also forms the basis for the district's teacher evaluation system.

Results to Data

In 1985/86 PRISM I was in its fifth year of operation. A survey conducted by Salmon-Cox (1983) provided formative evaluation data to the staff development team. The general results indicated an unanticipated high level of enthusiasm for the program. The data also indicated that the principals are taking the program seriously. Many constructive suggestions were offered by the principals to improve the efficiency of the program. One of the most salient findings of the survey compared responses of principals in 1980 and 1983 with respect to criteria for teacher evaluation. As part of the needs assessment survey, the principals responded to the following question: 'A serious problem I face is a lack of good criteria by which to evaluate teacher instructional effectiveness.' In 1980, 87.5 per cent of elementary principals, 50 per cent of middle school principals, and 71.4 per cent of secondary principals agreed that this was a problem. In 1983 only 13.3 per cent of the elementary principals, 6.7 per cent of the middle school principals, and 25 per cent of the secondary principals responded that this was still a problem. These data are one important indicator of the impact of PRISM on instructional leadership.

Improving the Instructional Leadership of Administrators and Supervisors

PRISM II is the district's program to improve the instructional leadership skills of principals, supervisors and central office personnel. PRISM II has been developed because many of the district's principals were not prepared to cope with the current emphasis on instructional leadership. Not only had their training failed to prepare them to assume this role, past school boards and cabinet level administrators had not expected them to be instructional leaders. Principals often were selected for their positions because they were good at public relations or good at maintaining discipline in schools. More often than not, supervisors of instruction at the elementary, middle and secondary level are somewhat better prepared to offer 'content centred' instructional leadership. However, they lack the status and the power to exercise potent leadership. Thus, with the new emphasis on educational improvement, the Pittsburgh School District found its schools under the direction of principals who were not well prepared to assume this new instructional leadership role.

Components of PRISM II

PRISM II has much in common with PRISM I. The training workshops and the coaching of PRISM I serve as the foundation for PRISM II. The knowledge of the components of effective instruction and skill in observing and improving instruction are the cornerstone for instructional leadership. Beyond PRISM I, however, principals and other administrators must have a knowledge base with regard to curricular models and instructional techniques. Principals need to know enough about organization development and the educational change process to furnish an environment for teachers that is likely to produce a focus on instruction.

Since 1981 the Pittsburgh schools have offered PRISM II workshops for principals to enhance their instructional leadership skills. In the first two years, the programs heavily emphasized classroom observation skills. More recently, the emphasis has shifted to improving conferring skills designed to enhance instructional performance of the good and excellent teachers in the district. The 1985 summer workshops, scheduled for five full days, included a variety of topics dealing with such issues as staff assessment, supervision, curriculum, personal and professional growth. The program includes some core experiences required of all participants as well as elective courses. The major core experiences included a seminar on personal, managerial and organizational productivity. Elective courses included such topics as time and stress management, improving writing skills, disciplining with dignity, and the use of data for instructional planning.

Results to Date

The data gathered with respect to the implementation of PRISM II indicate that about two-thirds of the principals in the district have embraced and implemented the concepts intrinsic to instructional leadership. The remaining third of the principals are still struggling to implement the district's expectations. Administrators have been evaluated over the past four years on the extent to which they have cooperated with staff responsible for the PRISM and the Monitoring Achievement in Pittsburgth (MAP) programs. Evaluation items have been developed to rate principals on their effective implementation of the achievement monitoring and PRISM programs and their use of information that reveals what is going on in the school instructionally. Results to date indicate that principals need different formats for interpreting instructional monitoring information and additional training in use of these data. Dr William Cooley of the Learning Research and Development Centre, University of Pittsburgh, is currently working with district staff to develop and implement a mini computer-based program that will help the principal process the achievement monitoring data at the building level and use the data for instructional planning. It is hoped that more effective analysis of these data can become the basis of enhancing further the instructional leadership responsibility of principals.

The Schenley High School Teacher Centre

In response to a growing concern about contemporary public schooling as well as student achievement, numerous programs have been designed within the past two years to affect directly the product of public education — the student. Few programs, however, have been specifically designed for teachers' needs for continuing education beyond the certification process. Fewer still integrate the continued development of teachers into a public school setting. Nonetheless, it stands to reason that for school improvement to effect lasting change, teachers in the classroom must serve as a focal point of such efforts rather than addressing university training or certification standards alone.

To this end, the Pittsburgh Public Schools have implemented a staff development program for secondary teachers (PRISM III). Beginning in 1982, a number of planning groups (including teachers, administrators, union representatives and community figures) developed an initial set of recommendations for program content, staffing, anticipated outcomes, and evaluation. The formulation of the program was guided largely by a needs assessment of the more than 800 secondary teachers in the district. It explored concerns in five areas:

   (i)   instructional skills;
  (ii)   content area update;
 (iii)   classroom and student management;
 (iv)   human relations; and
  (v)   technical routine management.

The program's planner organized the results of the needs assessment into three broad program objectives:

1 *Instructional Skills Development:* Providing the teacher with a review of recent developments in research on teaching and learning.
2 *Adolescent Development:* Reviewing current research on the psychological development of adolescents, and exploring the relationships between development and academic behaviour.

3 *Content Area Update:* Receiving an update in each teacher's subject, including a review of the district's expectations for that content area.

PRISM III was introduced as the means for describing and improving instructional techniques. The program also subsumes a clinical supervision component in which peers observe one another's teaching and confer about the strengths and weaknesses which were observed. A series of seminars and workshops was developed to improve teachers' understanding of adolescent development. Several strategies, ranging from workshops on questioning skills to extensive curriculum development efforts with the district's supervisory staff, provide the core of a content area update component of the program.

A planning committee, focussing on staffing for the centre, identified four distinct groups that would be needed to staff the teacher centre:

(i) an administrative staff to oversee the program and serve as a liaison between the program and the district's administration and all secondary schools;

(ii) visiting teachers (VTs) who are called from their home schools to participate in the teacher centre's programs for an eight week cycle;

(iii) resident teachers (CRTs) who serve as clinical instructors and workshop leaders for the VTs; and

(iv) replacement teachers who assume teaching responsibilities in the home schools of Visiting Teachers while they are at the centre.

Schenley High School, an existing comprehensive school, was selected as the site of the centre. It opened in the fall of the 1983/84 school year, and it is planned that it will remain operative for four years. The total cost of the initiative is approximately $1½m annually.

Context for Professional Development

The Schenley High School Teacher Centre is one of the major efforts in staff development of the Pittsburgh school district. It is an outgrowth of the Board of Education's priority for school improvement. The structure of the program is consistent with the PRISM I and II programs designed to promote instructional effectivness in teachers and instructional leadership skills in administrators. Through the Schenley High School Teacher Centre and other related programs, the Pittsburgh schools provide a coordinated intervention strategy designed to promote more effective teaching and learning in the city schools and enhanced instructional leadership of its principals.

The Schenley Program for Principals

The district's leadership had assumed that the PRISM I and II training provided from 1981 to 1983 was sufficient for secondary principals to provide effective follow through for their teachers who were returning from the Schenley High School Centre. This was not the case. While monitoring the follow through, the district leadership found that the principals did not have sufficient knowledge of the program at the Teacher Centre to support the faculty when they returned to their own school. Thus, in the 1984/85 school year the district appointed a follow through coordinator whose responsibility was to assist principals and teachers in providing appropriate activities in order to keep the Schenley experience alive.

The district also planned a program for secondary principals that was held at Schenley. Principals, in groups of four, were released from their duties for twenty days during the school year to attend two ten-day programs specifically designed for them. Principals had an opportunity to observe their own teachers engage in Centre activities and participate in programs that were designed to promote the goals of teacher revitalization in their own schools. Principals engaged in discussions about instructional leadership and the specific use of department chairpersons in the promotion of quality education for the youth of the city.

The 1985/86 program for secondary principals focussed on the effective use of instructional cabinets in the twelve high schools of the city. The cabinets were comprised of the department chairpersons and senior teachers selected by the principal. The cabinet's task was to review all pertinent data with respect to the academic performance of students in their school and plan instructional improvement programs.

In summary, the superintendent has taken a proactive role in the promotion of quality education in the Pittsburgh schools. The educational priorities of the district were set up by the Board as a result of the needs analysis conducted in the 1980/81 school year. He then played an active leadership role in the formulation of the PRISM program designed to address the Board's priorities. The Pittsburgh superintendent of schools views a major portion of his role to be that of instructional leader (Wallace, 1985). In this paper, the role of the superintendent has been reviewed specifically as it related to the promotion of the instructional leadership responsibility of principals.

References

CHAMPAGNE, DW (1984) Personal communication.
COGAN, ML (1973) *Clinical Supervision*, Boston, MA, Houghton, Mifflin Co.
COOLEY, WW and BICKEL, WE (1987) *Decision Oriented Educational Research*, Boston, MA, Kluwer-Nijhoff.

Richard Wallace

GOLDHAMMER, R (1969) *Clinical Supervision*, New York, Holt Rinehart and Winston.
HUNTER, ML (1978) *A Clinical Theory of Instruction*, El Segundo, CA, Tip Publications.
SALMON-COX, L (1983) 'Monitoring achievement in Pittsburgh: The teachers' viewpoint', paper presented at the annual meeting of the American Educational Research Association, Montreal, April.
SILVER, PF (1982) 'Administrator preparation' in METZEL, HE (Ed) *Encyclopedia of Educational Research*, 5th edn, New York, The Free Press.
WALLACE, RC (1985) *The Superintendent of Education: Data Based Instructional Leadership*, Pittsburgh, Learning Research and Development Centre, University of Pittsburgh.

The Technical and Vocational Education Initiative (TVEI) in Northamptonshire, UK

Michael Henley and Peter Smith

Introduction

The Manpower Services Commission (MSC) was set up in 1974 to run the public employment and training services. It is separate from the government but accountable to the Secretary of State for Employment. As well as running employment services and schemes for the unemployed, the MSC plays an increasing role in promoting change in training and education. At a time when spending on education has generally been restricted, the MSC had been generously funded and this has encouraged local authorities to respond to the Commission's initiatives.

In 1981 the government issued as a major policy statement a White Paper *A New Training Initiative*. It set out the following national training objectives:

   (i)   modernization of training in occupational skills with particular emphasis on training to agreed standards of skills appropriate to the jobs available;

  (ii) better preparation in schools and colleges for working life and better arrangements for the transition from full time education to work;

(iii) wider opportunities for adults to acquire and improve their skills.

TVEI represents one approach to the second objective listed above.

The MSC assumed responsibility for TVEI because the constitutional arrangements for education in England and Wales could not otherwise easily accommodate it. The MSC is not subject to the kind of close and detailed democratic control customary in local government and it is in a better position to plan ahead securely over a five-year time span.

TVEI Policy

The MSC's stated aims for TVEI are two-fold.

1 In conjunction with the chosen LEA to explore and test ways of organizing and managing the education of 14–18-year-old young people across the ability range so that:

    (i) more of them are attracted to seek the qualifications/skills which will be of direct value to them at work, and more of them achieve these qualifications and skills;

    (ii) they are better equipped to enter the world of employment which will await them;

    (iii) they acquire a more direct appreciation of the practical application of the qualifications for which they are working;

    (iv) they become accustomed to using their skills and knowledge to solve the real world problems they will meet at work;

    (v) more emphasis is placed on developing initiative, motivation and enterprise as well as problem solving skills and other aspects of personal development;

    (vi) the construction of the bridge from education to work is begun earlier by giving these young people the opportunity to have direct contact and training/planned work experience with a number of local employers in the relevant specialisms;

    (vii) there is close collaboration between the local education authorities and industry/commerce/public services *etc*, so that the curriculum has industry's confidence.

2 To undertake what is set out above in such a way that:

    (i) the detailed aims can be achieved quickly and cost effectively;

    (ii) the educational lessons learned can be readily applied in other groups among the 14–18-year-olds;

    (iii) the educational structures/schemes established to further the aims of the initiative should be consistent with progressive developments in skill and vocational training outside the school environment, existing in vocational education for under 16-year-old young people, and higher education;

    (iv) emphasis is placed on careful monitoring and evaluation;

    (v) individual projects are managed at local level;

    (vi) the overall conduct, assessment and development of the initiative can be assessed and monitored by the MSC and the TVEI Unit it has established for this purpose.

3 The MSC's stated criteria for TVEI are summarized as:

    (i) to provide equal opportunities for young people for both sexes;

    (ii) to provide a four-year curriculum with progression year to year;

 (iii) to have clear objectives and encourage skill development;
 (iv) to provide a balance between general and technical education and be related to potential employment opportunities;
  (v) to provide appropriate and planned work experience;
 (vi) to ensure that courses are linked to subsequent training opportunities;
 (vii) to make available a wide range of qualifications;
 (viii) to involve the whole ability range;
 (ix) to involve industry and commerce.

TVEI in Northamptonshire: The County Context

Northamptonshire: Population

The county of Northamptonshire is essentially a rural county within which there are five urban centres — Northampton (population 170,000); Corby (population 48,000); Kettering (population 45,000); Wellingborough (population 40,000) and Daventry (population 18,000) — plus a number of smaller townships. Northampton and Corby had been until recently designated as 'new towns' for many years. Wellingborough and Daventry have been influenced in their growth by population inflow from two major conurbations: London and Birmingham. The population of Northamptonshire is 550,000.

The Northamptonshire TVEI Project: Origins and Characteristics

Northamptonshire's submission as a 'second round' TVEI authority was the product of much thinking at the grass roots in schools and colleges which are organized in the county into groups or 'consortia'. Following a review of proposals from several consortia those from two, based on Wellingborough and Northampton, were chosen. Members of the local inspectorate, careers and youth and community services together with education officers converted the proposals into a county submission and added elements to make a fuller and more appropriate bid.

 Northamptonshire's TVEI project contains the unique feature of 'associate schools', funded by the LEA and acting as a control group so that possibilities for replicability can be better evaluated. The two consortia each comprise one college of further education, three funded schools and three associate schools. In addition there is a third group of associate schools in Corby, forming a third consortium.

 Northamptonshire's TVEI Project is managed by a County Coordinator equivalent in status to an LEA General Inspector, two Area Coordinators and a TVEI Careers Officer. This central team, in conjunction with headteachers and principals of participating institutions, forms a Project Management Committee which manages the Project and reports to the County Steering Group comprising LEA officers and representatives from schools and colleges, the careers service, the youth and community service, MSC, trade unions, employers' organizations and parents. The steering group meets several times a year and acts in an advisory capacity.

Some Aspects of Educational Arrangements in Northamptonshire

Northamptonshire's educational arrangements embrace two secondary school systems, namely:

(i)   a middle (age range 9–13 years) and upper school (13–18 years) comprehensive system mainly in Northampton;

(ii) an 11–18 comprehensive school system in the rest of the county.

Hence, within TVEI the two systems are operating side by side and the attempt is being made to create coherent curriculum development across the project. Traditionally the schools in Northamptonshire (as in the rest of the country) exercise considerable autonomy over their internal organization and their curriculum policies.

There is also a system of colleges providing a wide range of courses of vocational education. These courses may be begun at 16+ (after the period of compulsory full-time education is completed) but many students enter colleges when they are older; for example, at 18 after completing a further period beyond 16 at school. Thus there is some overlap in provision by age in secondary schools and colleges. At colleges attendance may be full-time or part-time.

There are urban and rural secondary schools in the project. Since the 1970s, each major urban zone in the county has become the focus of developing collaboration between schools and colleges through the establishment of a 16+ area committee which aims to share in curriculum development and to rationalize course provision where student numbers are low. Falling rolls, for example in the Wellingborough zone, where for every four students in 1980 there will be three in 1990, are tending to create tensions and insecurity within the schools and colleges. Since TVEI in Northamptonshire was conceived on the consortium principle and requires much closer collaboration from 14+, the implications for changes in organizational structures may become more considerable each year.

The Northamptonshire TVEI Project: Funding, Scale and Present Organizational Impact

Northamptonshire's TVEI project covers five academic years, 1984/89, and involves additional funding for the lifetime of the project of £2,015,000 for the six schools and two colleges. Significant features of this funding are that the resourcing is primarily, though not exclusively, for a named cohort of students and that it is curriculum led.

Each funded school has to recruit forty students per academic year for four years so that in total there will be 960 named students during the life of the project (six schools × 40 students × 4 intakes.) Although the proportion of students is relatively small in terms of the total secondary school population of 45,000, the fact that the cohort must include the whole ability range is a key indicator of the importance of TVEI as an educational innovation.

Arising from the requirements for the financing of a named cohort, there are considerable conflicts of interests and loyalties for the parties involved in the project. The very term 'named cohort' implies to many some sort of 'selection' process, so that the stress is on recruitment of a cohort and the methods by which such recruitment is achieved. Where a school has a 'common' curriculum for all pupils, recruitment is less of a problem in terms of its divisive effects, except where there is competition for scarce resources, for example work experience placements. At a school where an 'option' system exists, then recruitment may become an issue when take-up of appropriate options becomes imbalanced.

Where finance is specially provided for TVEI residential experience, the issue of a privileged group of students is raised. Indeed any resourcing for the cohort produces conflict and schools are endeavouring not to create a school within a school by using TVEI resources to complement existing resources. The process of planning dialogues with the MSC and the frequent planning meetings of headteachers, principals and coordinators are steadily producing clarification of aims and agreed strategies to deliver TVEI.

After one year of the Northamptonshire project, the general view of headteachers concerned is that TVEI has had a major impact on thinking about the secondary curriculum and how it is organized and delivered. As the project develops into the post-16 stage, the impact on all courses is likely to be more extensive, especially as funding can only be granted for courses which are either new or enhanced. This must also be seen against the backcloth of a national review of all vocational qualifications as outlined in a central government White Paper or major policy statement '*Education and Training*' of April 1985. To date, schools have tended to identify post-16 TVEI work in terms of work for additional vocational qualification. A much more fundamental review of education for the age span 14–18 years in terms of purpose, content and organization will be required, however, in order to create greater coherence at the 16–18 stage. TVEI's significance is that it is a test bed for new approaches and strategies to deal with this stage.

Michael Henley and Peter Smith

The Curriculum for TVEI Students in the Two Consortia: An Outline

In the six funded schools the curricula for TVEI students in the first two years of the programmes have individual variations. What is given below represents a synthesis of the approaches in the two consortia:

NORTHAMPTON CONSORTIUM
CURRICULUM FOR TVEI STUDENTS AT 14–16
FROM SEPTEMBER 1985

GENERAL EDUCATION 70%

Social and personal education −7%
Mathematics −10%
English −10%
Languages −10%
Science −15%
Humanities/social science −10%
Music/drama/PE −8%

through which the *TVEI Core Skills* are developed.

TVEI SKILLS 30%

variously delivered through a modular curriculum/options involving:

Information technology)	
Business studies)	leading to
Media studies)	various
Business language)	nationally
Community studies)	accredited
Technology)	examinations

+ Experience of work
+ Careers education
+ Residential education

WELLINGBOROUGH CONSORTIUM
CURRICULUM FOR TVEI STUDENTS AT 14–16
FROM SEPTEMBER 1985

GENERAL EDUCATION 70%

Core programme
English
Mathematics
Humanities
Science
Language

Personal and social education
Development of TVEI core skills

TVEI STUDIES 30%

A number of different schemes in the three schools deliver the listed TVEI studies through:

individual subject options;
or 'packages' of options;
or nationally accredited examination courses;
or through a modular curriculum, including integrating modules.

Industrial society
Technology and design
Business studies
Electronics
Computer studies/information technology
Community care studies
Food studies
Personal services
+ Experience of work
+ Residential education
+ Careers education

Experience of Work: Guidance for TVEI Schools in Northamptonshire

'Work experience' is considered to express the concept in TVEI less well than 'experience of work', which, for TVEI schools, is to be regarded as a curriculum development area of the greatest significance for the project. The outline below which concentrates on curriculum, is supported, for project teachers, by provision of other county documents which define procedural and legal aspects, including insurance regulations.

1 Experience of work is adjudged to be a more appropriate title since it covers a range of experiences in a variety of modes and not simply a common fixed period of time, for example, three weeks hitherto seen as a norm. Experience of work should be used to enable employers to better understand education and to reconsider their own expectations of young people when recruiting and training.

2 Experience of work has the following broad aims:
  (i) to offer the opportunity to pupils to prepare and adjust to the demands of the adult world;
  (ii) to assist in the development of appropriate skills and competencies, for example, life, social and work related skills;

(iii) to assist in creating more relevance in the curriculum to the world of work and creating better pupil motivation, consultation and involvement;

(iv) to assist in the choice of a future occupation;

(v) to increase pupils' awareness and understanding of the nature of industry and commerce;

(vi) to offer, through a variety of opportunities and experiences, different models of adulthood to assist them in defining and developing their own adult identity;

(vii) to offer a greater balance of contexts and modes of learning, moving the emphasis from didactic to experiential learning;

(viii) to widen the resource provision for learning and to add breadth and balance to the nature of teaching styles;

(ix) to enhance the work of the school in the community and the community in the school, by using adults other than teachers in the education process.

3 Effective 'experience of work' schemes must involve a range of social partners — industry, commerce, community agencies, careers service, parents and teachers — if the broad aims are to be achieved. These partners can come to understand education better and reconsider their expectations of young people when recruiting and training arrangements are concerned.

4 Each of the social partners needs to take part in an educational programme aimed at improving the experience of work provision. This activity is designed to develop:

(i) appropriate experiences at work for a total ability range;

(ii) increased teacher and parental awareness of the nature of industry and commerce and the likely changes expected to take place in the next few years;

(iii) increased awareness of the needs of pupils by supervisors and others in industry and commerce;

(iv) greater cooperation between the social partners in developing curricular responses.

5 The experience of work should be part of an integrated scheme providing young people with:

(i) appropriate inductions into the world of work and adult life;

(ii) opportunities to explore a variety of occupational schemes to allow effective reflection and learning;

(iii) experience of negotiating their own objectives in terms of experience of work and adult life and of briefing and de-briefing;

(iv) scope to avoid too early a specialization, particularly in terms of the acquisition of work related skills.

6 Several types of 'experience of work' activity are included in the TVEI programme including:

(i) work observation periods;

(ii)   work/occupational surveys;

(iii)   group activity schemes — for example, local preservation work;

(iv)   entrepreneurial activities — running a business and actually producing a product, for example, a film;

(v)   'sheltered simulated work' schemes in 'training workshops';

(vi)   longer and shorter periods of experience of work dependent on the objectives to be achieved;

(vii)   'shadowing' certain kinds of work roles;

(viii)   simulation experiences.

7   Each student maintains a log look which forms part of a record of personal achievement. Elements of progression from year to year are planned as an integral part of a student's curricular programme. The later stages of the four year course have to be linked effectively to subsequent education/training opportunities. The provision of equal opportunities to people of both sexes and the avoidance of sex stereotyping are particularly stressed.

8   Experience of work in terms of the TVEI project is not only directed to the needs of pupils but also to the needs of staff. Staff have the opportunity of periods in a variety of 'work' contexts through secondments.

9   A range of topics or courses complementary to work experience have been developed within the curriculum to support the needs of students in their experience of work *viz*: health and safety modules, industrial studies, role of trades unions and small businesses and cooperatives.

Experience of Work: Assessment of the Experience

The Northamptonshire TVEI project has links with other curriculum development activities in the county. One such development concerns 'records of achievement' and includes a scheme for assessing the experience students have of work as part of the curriculum they follow. Assessment is seen as a process of gathering information (formative) not the product of this process (summative) though sometimes there is reference to 'the assessment', meaning the grade or make which is produced by the process of assessment. Teachers and employers together with the students join in periodic review sessions which help all concerned to agree on the desired outcomes of experience of work for students, and on the monitoring, debriefing and evaluation arrangements.

Summary of the Intentions of TVEI

By the end of the five-year period during which the Northamptonshire TVEI initiative is to run, there should have been tested and established:

1   Effective collaboration between schools and college for the production of a modular curriculum, embracing certain national examinations, academic, vocational and technical in character.
2   Effective curriculum organization through the modular system to promote equal opportunities and the avoidance of sex stereotyping.
3   Changed learning/teaching strategies involving student negotiation, formative profiling, independent learning and inter disciplinary task centred assignments.
4   Planned work experience over a four-year period, involving work simulation, engagement in mini enterprises, joint planning by schools/colleges and industry seen as an integral part of the TVEI curriculum.
5   An enhanced careers guidance and education programme using computerized learning and simulations.
6   The use of the community as an educational resource on a planned basis.
7   A coherent profiling system embracing both the formative processes and summative record of achievement.
8   The establishment of a TVEI Centre for High Technology, both for teaching and curriculum led staff development in the fields of:

   (i)   business studies and electronic office systems;
   (ii)   computer aided design;
   (iii) computer numerical control systems;
   (iv)   other industrial applications of computers.

9   The establishment of computerized records systems and electronic mail between the central office and institutions.
10 Effective mechanisms for the management of resources through consortium and project developments.
11 Effective evaluation mechanisms using national and local studies and facilities.

TVEI Related In-service Training Scheme (TRIST)

The White Paper of April 1985 entitled *Education and Training for Young People* reviews the progress of the 'new training initiative' begun in 1981 and in particular TVEI which commenced in 1982. It reports that there is an 'emerging nationwide network of TVEI projects within the education system' that is an 'important instrument for change within the educational system'. By 1986, this network covered the great majority of education authorities but only a small percentage of schools within those authorities. The government, recognizing that the pilot projects are only laying a foundation, conclude that there is an urgent need to increase the number of teachers equipped to disseminate the successful elements of TVEI and thus reinforce the broad objective that all pupils experience a relevant and practical curriculum.

Additional resources in the sum of £30 million were made available between September 1985 and March 1987 to support TVEI related in-service training (TRIST). The generalization of the innovation in the curriculum is to be staff development rather than resource-led. TRIST is but a prelude to a new scheme for funding in-service training in England and Wales to be introduced in April 1987. This will involve a new specific grant to support LEA expenditure on most aspects of in-service training. It is envisaged that the grant will fall into two parts; grants for national priority areas of training and a general grant for a locally determined programme. The conditions of the grant are specified in regulations made by the Secretary of State for Education and Science which include that each LEA submits plans for in-service training for central approval.

Interim Conclusions

In this description of the several aspects of TVEI in Northamptonshire, a number of interim conclusions have been implicitly stated. First, added impetus has been given to a considerable number of developments on which work had been done already but not so systematically or with such good resource support. For example, the conceptual framework for experience of work as part of a broad and balanced curriculum for older secondary students has been substantially strengthened. Second, generally there is greater recognition of the importance that adults other than teachers (AOTs) have for the education process than before TVEI was introduced. (As it happens in Northamptonshire the beneficial outcomes here are replicated in several other projects also currently in progress.) Third, the necessity for staff development programmes to support projects designed to achieve school improvement has been accepted as an integral component of TVEI. Indeed, TRIST offers a model for generating curriculum change through staff development. Fourth, the value of coordinators has been enhanced by the project. Fifth, the importance of the contractual relationship between schools and LEAs with the MSC is not yet fully understood. The nature of the various accountabilities are being brought out as the life of the project continues. The contract has set out methods of delivery for curriculum change in such ways that amount to major innovations in the country's maintained education service. Sixth, despite continued and quite widespread expressions of scepticism about whether the school improvement resulting from TVEI will be real, lasting or great enough to justify the loss of autonomy for schools, colleges and LEAs, the facts of achievement do tend already to diminish the weight of the opinions of the critics of TVEI. In Northamptonshire, the positive side is already very impressive and more than sufficient to justify the county's participation.

The Development and Implementation of School Improvement Policies by Education Authorities: A Reponse from the UK Perspective

Michael Henley

Introduction

The participants in ISIP have defined school improvement as 'a systematic sustained effort aimed at change in learning conditions and other related internal conditions in one or more schools, with the ultimate aim of accomplishing educational goals more effectively'. All the words are intended to have significance. For example, to have a clear concept of an 'aim' is important; so are the implications of the concept in securing a systematic or methodical approach towards the reaching of goals. Adopting an 'aim' means making a plan and also accepting an accountability to show whether the aim has been achieved or not. Each of us has his or her own frame of reference for the concept. Likewise, it is also worthwhile to reflect upon the concept of 'a systematic sustained effort' as I shall indicate later. Within ISIP, considerable time has been spent on clarification of terms and concepts as a necessary stage in the development of understanding of the nature of school improvement.

Partnership and Policy Making

For ISIP, policy making is envisaged as a process of the interplay of partnerships. In all OECD countries, partnership activity is promoted in pursuit of school improvement policies and there is considerable agreement about who are the partners. Parents, teachers, educational administrators, politicians, employers, academics, trade unionists, members of the general public and sometimes students are generally included. These groups interplay in partnerships at various levels of government but the methodology of partnership varies, especially according to the level at which policy making is taking place.

Bearing in mind that educational policy making is a public matter the process is deeply influenced by party political interests. As Hans Tangerud indicates, conflicting needs may arise that cause the separation of the interests of the professional and the politician and indeed the lay person from both. The politician wishes policy to look well or to be high sounding, and vagueness of content or non-specificity is inevitable to the extent that it is necessary to gain the allegiance of the majority of voters at national level. Even in government a political party has difficulty in making statements that, on the one hand, do not alienate its supporters and, on the other, make sense to the persons most directly affected. Professionals may, however, disdain a policy that, in their perception, is not relevant, explicit and practical — unless perhaps they can make their own interpretations which often is the case. This however, often causes conflict, variability of implementation, or just non-events.

Often for policy makers, especially at the school level, the most essential factors determining the situation are beyond their control. Pluralism in many forms need to be taken into account. Individuals may play various roles at different levels. It is commonplace to remark that all organizations at all levels have a vast potential of knowledge, insight, initiative and creativity. In policy making the real task is to ensure that this potential of resources is fully used. Often this is not so and consequently teachers and other professionals are expected to implement policies that have not been developed with due regard to available knowledge and expertise. In other words, the interplay of the partnerships has not been successful and school improvement policies are also unsuccessful.

The Nature of Policy Affecting School Improvement

At an area group 5 seminar in Oslo in 1985, a number of interesting observations were made about the nature of policy in the context of school improvement. We were led to raise fundamental questions about what education is supposed to be. Education is regarded as a service sector and such sectors distinguish themselves from primary and secondary industries by not producing commodities, but by producing some change, often intangible, in the situation of individuals. They are cured, fed, entertained, educated or transported to another location *etc.* And usually, the clients of such services — customers, pupils, passengers *etc.* — are themselves active participants in the productive process, even to the extent that their form of participation is decisive for the final result. Anyone teaching children will know this by heart.

But there is also more to it: in service processes, it is not only the final result that counts. We do not only want to be fed: the circumstances under which it happens may be as important. For children and youngsters attending school for twelve years what happens to them during those years is, in all probability, much more important that the final outcome measured say in terms of examination marks. If you want to evaluate a process of this kind, the process qualities as experienced by the client may be more important than any final 'outcome'. This is reflected in the TVEI learning strategies described in the case study.

As a consequence, we concluded that external 'expertise' has limited validity in relation to such production processes. Experts usually know something about how to arrive at efficient combinations of inputs and outputs in a process. But the real experts on process quality are the clients themselves. They have a legitimate right to participate in decisions about the process, in line with professional experts. Much school improvement policy at secondary level allows for effective student influence over the learning process the student experiences.

A successful enterprise aims to keep close to its clients so that what it does receives a welcome and thus its products or services are wanted and bought. Policy makers in education should keep close to their clients; if not they suffer frustration or disappointment and rejection in some form: politicians may suffer defeat; heads and professionals may suffer loss of authority.

Relevance of Rules of Good Management

For ISIP, the rules of good management applying to organizations outside education should be seen as a reference point for helping with the development and implementation of school improvement policies. I have found the McKinsey *Framework for Organizational Diagnosis* illuminating in this regard (see figure 1) (*vide.* Peters and Waterman, 1983: 10).

Figure 1: McKinsey 7-S Framework for Organizational Diagnosis

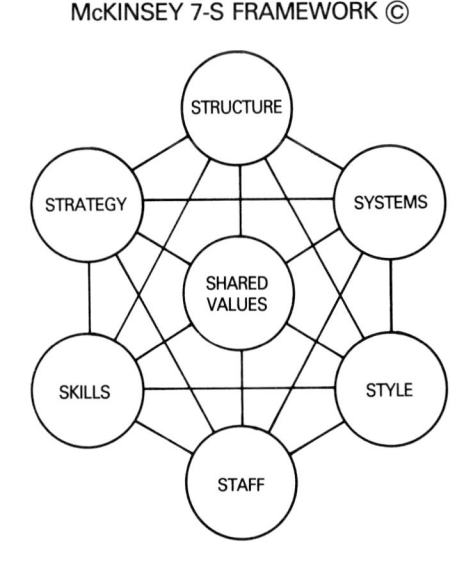

McKINSEY 7-S FRAMEWORK ©

According to McKinsey and others, a successful organization needs to be sound in these various segments. The themes at the conference can be studied in the McKinsey context. Central to success are shared values which secure both the basis of an organization's policies and the commitment of its people. Attempts to introduce change in a situation where values are not shared is fraught with danger for would be policy makers. The passage of proposed policies concerning the use of performance appraisal with teachers as put forward by the Secretary of State demonstrates such danger.

That needs analysis at central government level can, however, lead acceptably to the successful development and implementation of school improvement policies at local and school level is illustrated by the TVEI case study. The TVEI case also illustrates the rule that ambition should be kept in check and that resources should be matched to purpose. The crucial consideration of time, and seeing that sufficient of it is allowed for the change process to flow easily, is well illustrated in both case studies. Another important factor for success in both cases is the extent to which political intervention is controlled. Effective management of the implementation of school improvement means distancing politics and politicians also, except as participants, from the change process.

The focus of all school improvement policies judged successful by the initiators of offering promise of success that have been considered in area five seminars or papers have been directed at specific and relatively limited areas of activity. It is also noteworthy that no particular structure of government or arrangement of the levels between the centre and the schools appears to have special advantage: any can support change and school improvement provided the structure is used intelligently. This means in particular that partnership roles are found to be carefully defined in successfully managed school improvement efforts. And that there has been a realization of ownership of the school improvement amongst the stakeholders from the beginning. Communications have been good and there has been minimum bewilderment as the process has gathered momentum. Parents have also felt at ease.

Importance of Systematic and Comprehensive Programmes of Staff Development

The Pittsburgh public schools case describes an intensive programme of systematic and comprehensive staff development for a whole school system. ISIP has devoted much energy to the study of such activities throughout OECD countries. It should be obvious that school improvement is dependent upon the professional skills of teachers who are the managers of change in the 'learning conditions and other related internal conditions' in their schools and classrooms. The McKinsey framework identifies the staff factor and the skills factor as key segments in the organizational diagnosis necessary to prepare for successful implementation of desired change. The policy maker must take account of the qualifications, experience, attitudes, expectations and so forth of the staff and decide with them their readiness for the tasks to be undertaken. Equally there must have been an analysis of the skills required for these tasks.

ISIP case studies offer no grounds for supposing that all staff in schools are infinitely versatile, any more than the policy makers. Rigorous preparation is required from everyone seeking to develop a school improvement policy or to design and monitor the implementation process. Part of the purpose of such activity is to identify the personal and professional development needs of teachers and their support staff in order to enable them to carry out the policy successfully. The emergence of TRIST as mentioned in the TVEI case and the intended approach to implementing GCSE as mentioned in chapter 5 indicates that staff development is increasingly seen as the key element in certain school improvement policies. This development is theoretically possible, most particularly in cases of school improvement policy where goals are well defined.

Goal Setting and School Climate

Goal setting is at the heart of the school improvement process. The 'accomplishing of educational goals more effectively' has to be achieved. There is a requirement therefore to collect appropriate data. One approach to data collection is given in the Pittsburgh public schools case. Another approach is indicated in the TVEI case. It is evident in the ISIP case studies as presented at this conference and elsewhere that data collection connected with school improvement is becoming more sophisticated. More attention is being given to feedback from students. Their perceptions of their teachers are relevant in terms of maintaining or changing and improving the curriculum offered to them.

The discussion of school-based review in chapter 3 provides a clear view of how data on a school's functioning can be collected and how important such data is in the assessment of the school's potential for any particular school improvement effort or policy implementation. One outcome of a school-based review is a view of the school's climate which needs to be positive if school improvement is to happen. The techniques of evaluation are very important to the development and implementation of school improvement policies. The investment in school improvement has to be justified on the basis of well gathered evidence.

Conclusions

A 'systematic sustained effort' is part of the ISIP definition of school improvement. This means coordination of the several key activities associated with school improvement because these activities have an essential interdependence. There is also an emphasis on the process of successful implementation of school improvement policy. The circumstances under which things happen may be as important as the primary objective. How policy is made is very important if policy is seen as a service, as ISIP suggests it should be.

Given the importance of school climate, the question to answer in any school improvement policy is at what age or ages and to what extent should pupils or students participate in policy making at school level and influence how and what they are taught. The TVEI case offers lessons here and so do the various Low Attainers Projects in West European countries.

There are perhaps some uncertainties about the identities of the partners in the democratic process of school improvement policy making. Not so very long ago, in England and Wales at any rate, central and local government and teachers were seen as major partners. Recently a local authority association presented a document *Education — The Way Ahead* that appeared to supplant teachers by school governors as the third major party. The churches did not figure at all as partners in this document. The Central Advisory Council which used to bring the 'parties' together has not met for many years and is shortly to be finally abolished.

Central government appears to be changing its assessment of who the partners are and, to a degree, so are LEAs in that a number have indicated a wish to see the coopted members on education committees removed or reduced in number. This is a step which, if accomplished, would take away the main outlet of influence for the minor partners, churches, voluntary organizations, institutions of higher education and so on. Effective policy making and implementation cannot happen if those directly affected are not partners in the process at all crucial stages.

This strikes a warning note. In the last analysis improving the quality of schooling is a matter of finding meaning and consensus at national, local, and school classroom level about quality in education. ISIP has found that school improvement happens when systematic efforts take place in a coordinated way across clearly identifiable key areas of influence. Education authorities cannot afford therefore to ignore these areas whether singularly or collectively in any school improvement effort. These areas should be addressed in their totality in any school improvement policy development and at the implementation stage if success is to be achieved.

Reference

PETERS, T and WATERMAN, R (1983) *In Search of Excellence*, New York, Harper and Row.

7 Implications for School Improvement in the United Kingdom

Introduction

*The implications for school improvement in the United Kingdom are consi-
dered from four perspectives in this chapter. The first is that of Philip Halsey
and the Department of Education and Science (DES). In his paper Halsey
describes the various initiatives that the DES has recently taken to contribute
to school improvemet. The list is extensive, which confirms the point made
earlier that there is at present, a great potential for improvement in the
quality of schooling in this country. Halsey confirms this by concluding that
although his paper may appear to be a 'catalogue of the obvious' it is not a
list his predecessors of even ten years ago could have offered.*

*Stuart Maclue, in his witty and perceptive account of the public view of
school improvement, stresses the importance of systematic improvement at the
school and LEA level. He argues that much public sympathy for education
has, for a variety of reasons, been lost over the past decade. Unfortunately
this is not a perception readily changed in the present climate. The public
demand, in his view, is for excellence, in mediocrity as well as everything
else; and for a sustained commitment to systematic self conscious improvement
in the ISIP sense, rather than reactive political posturing.*

*Peter Holly and Michael Henley's account of the views of conference
participants is based on responses to questions such as: what are you (the
participants) taking away with you from this conference? What have you
learnt? What understanding have you gained? On the strength of this
learning experience, what do you intend/resolve to do now? They say that
the vast majority of the responses were positive, supportive and forward
looking. They also claim that a general effect of the conference seems to have
been to encourage many participants to return to their schools/LEA/support
agencies with increased enthusiasm and the determination to promote the
cause of school improvement in their work situations.*

*The fourth perspective is less partisan. It is an attempt by the editor to
summarize the implications of the conference/book for school improvement at*

171

the local level. As such it draws on the major findings of ISIP, relates them to current UK developments and points to certain avenues of development. Although necessarily brief, and despite a number of serious perceptual and systematic barriers to change, the editor remains sanguine about the current potential for improving the quality of schooling in the UK.

School Improvement in the United Kingdom

Philip Halsey

Background

I ought to make it clear at the outset, since this is a United Kingdom conference associated with the OECD/CERI International School Improvement Project, that my contribution relates mainly to England and Wales. Some of my remarks, however, may also apply to other parts of the United Kingdom.

Part of the background to the conference is an OECD report published in 1983, entitled *Compulsory Schooling in a Changing World*. One sentence in that document reads, 'The burden of this report is that the priority for the next ten years will be the improvement of the quality of compulsory schooling'. The present government has issued two white papers on school education in England and Wales. Their titles immediately make it clear that the OECD diagnosis applies here. One, issued in 1983, is called *Teaching Quality* (DES, 1983); the other issued in 1985, is called *Better Schools* (DES, 1985). Improving the quality of schooling is clearly what the government is about.

To proceed from this benevolent generalization of intent to action that yields beneficial change, the government believes it is necessary to: clarify the purposes schools should serve and how they can best serve those purposes; review current performance to identify strengths and weaknesses; concentrate action on remedying weaknesses while maintaining and reinforcing strengths; and then to monitor progress. It is appropriate for government both to lead this work and to undertake part of it. But much of the work necessarily falls — in our system — to the local education authorities, certain voluntary bodies (notably the churches) and the schools themselves.

I can illustrate what I mean by reference to the early pages of *Better Schools*. The White Paper sets out six purposes for school education:

(i)   to help pupils to develop lively, enquiring minds, the ability to question and argue rationally and to apply themselves to tasks, and physical skills;

(ii) to help pupils to acquire understanding, knowledge and skills relevant to adult life and employment in a fast changing world;

(iii) to help pupils to use language and numbers effectively;

(iv) to help pupils to develop personal moral values, respect for religious values, and tolerance of other races, religions and ways of life;

(v) to help pupils to understand the world in which they live, and the inter-dependence of individuals, groups and nations;

(vi) to help pupils to appreciate human achievements and aspirations;

Consultation has suggested that, although almost every word in that list could be endlessly debated, there is very little disagreement in general terms that these are the purposes of school education. These purposes are naturally enough expressed in terms of helping pupils. Action to improve the quality of schooling is therefore effective only if it results in the enhancement of pupils' achievements.

Those purposes have to be given expression in a curriculum providing pupils with a great variety of experiences and covering a wide range of subject matter. *Better Schools* identifies four principles for the construction of that curriculum. It should be broad: it should introduce pupils to a wide range of experience, knowledge and skills; and skills should not be taught in isolation or in a purely theoretical way but in association with a wide range of applications. The curriculum should be balanced, there should be no undue concentration on any particular area. The curriculum should be relevant: all areas should be related to pupil's own experience and taught in such a way as to bring out practical applications and value in adult life. The curriculum should be differentiated: what is taught in each area of the curriculum, and the method of teaching, should be carefully matched to pupils' abilities and aptitudes.

To a large extent the government's review of the current performance of the school system against these purposes and principles has been based on evidence from HM Inspectors' reports on institutions and their national reports prepared in the light of such inspections. Among the government's main conclusions, set out in *Better Schools*, are these:

(i) at their best, the schools in England and Wales grapple with their tasks with a strong sense of purpose, reflecting in all they do the whole hearted enthusiasm and commitment of the staff under the leadership of the headteacher;

(ii) they bring out what the pupils are capable of achieving by setting challenging goals based on high expectations, and by motivating them towards active, well directed enquiry rather than passive learning;

(iii) the best secondary schools turn out young people with self confidence, self respect and respect for others, who are enterprising, adaptable and eager to face the demands of the adult world;

(iv) the present spectrum of quality and the variations between schools are wider than is acceptable in a national system of school education;

(v) the standards now generally attained by our pupils are neither as good as they can be, nor as good as they need to be if young people are to be equipped for the world of the twenty-first century;

(vi) in order to tackle the weaknesses and to improve standards action is necessary:

(a) to secure greater clarity about the objectives and content of the curriculum;

(b) to reform the examinations system and improve assessment so that they promote more effectively the objectives of the curriculum, the achievements of pupils, and the recording of those achievements;

(c) to improve the professional effectiveness of teachers and the mangement of the teaching force;

(d) to reform school government and to harness more fully the contributions which can be made to good school education by parents, employers and others outside the education service.

All these are means towards making the standards achieved by our school pupils both as good as they can be and as good as they need to be for the world in which they will live. The government has set a longer term aim for this purpose: to raise pupil performance at all levels of ability so as to bring 80–90 per cent of all 16-year-old pupils at least to the level of attainment now expected and achieved by pupils of average ability over a broad range of knowledge, understanding and skills in a number of subjects.

Curriculum

The government now intends to carry forward the development of national curricular policy from the generality of *Better Schools* to consider what these general principles mean for the content of the curriculum during the various phases of education and in the various subject areas. It may become more difficult to achieve consensus as the focus of attention narrows but the government is committed to publishing — following wide consultation, and taking into account HMI's own publications — statements of policy on the curriculum in various subject areas. One such statement, on 'Science 5–16', was published at around the same time as *Better Schools*. There is some evidence that it is already making an impact on classroom practice, which indicates that such documents, without prescriptive force but embodying the best of current thinking, can be effective tools for school improvement. The next policy statement, on foreign languages, is well advanced and should be published shortly.

These policy statements are not designed to prevent experiment and diversity at a local level — rather the reverse. It is central to the government's policy for the curriculum that its own activities, as well as developing agreement on national objectives, should stimulate the local education authorities and the schools to consider and develop their own policies for the curriculum, which will bear on their responsibility for what happens in the schools. The Education Bill now before Parliament will make it the duty of local education authorities and schools to consult upon, develop and expose to critical scrutiny (by parents and others) their own curricular policies.

This requirement may be more a formalization of current practice than a major step forward. Responses to Circular 8/83 have shown that the majority of local education authorities already have, or are preparing, comprehensive policies for the curriculum: less than ten years ago a similar exercise showed that such policies were very rare indeed. The new legislation will however, serve to ensure that all authorities can benefit both from the process of forming curricular policies (this requires discussions with teachers, governors and the clients of the education service such as parents and employers) and from using these policies to consider the important management decisions they face and in measuring the effectiveness of their other policies.

Another important development at national level is the Technical and Vocational Education Initiative — TVEI. This has become a fruitful partnership of central funds and local enthusiasm and has allowed all local authorities who wish — and most have done so — to adopt innovative approaches on a pilot basis with a particular technical and vocational relevance across the curriculum for the 14–18 age group. There are lessons to be learnt from the sort of curriculum enhancement, and increased relevance which TVEI has encouraged, which will be applicable to all schools.

Examinations

The government proposes to reform the school examination system, and to improve the assessment and recording of pupils' achievements.

The new GCSE examination has a key role to play in promoting improvements in secondary schools. Examination syllabuses inevitably regulate much of the detail of syllabuses for many older secondary school pupils: it is therefore essential that course and assessment requirements for the new GCSE should be in harmony with the overall objectives for the school curriculum. But the development of national criteria for the GCSE overall, and for the twenty most popular subjects within it, has gone much further than this. The Department has joined with teachers, authorities, higher education and other interests, in constructive debate which has resulted in nationally agreed statements on course objectives, content and assessment methods for the twenty most popular examination subjects. These criteria, and the examination syllabuses which will embody them, are powerful agents for change at school level. Together with the move towards national grade criteria for the GCSE, they will not only encourage but also enable us to measure the success of our aspirations for improving the achievement of all pupils.

Even the GCSE, with its various improvements including school-based assessment of course work and (in due course) grade criteria, will not be able to assess and record all the positive achievements of school pupils. The government has therefore set a further objective: the national introduction by the end of the decade, of arrangements for providing all school leavers with records of achievement. It is intended that these will cover a much wider range of experience and achievements than can be tested in public examinations. Nine pilot schemes, with financial support from the government, are under way and have just completed their first year.

Initial Teacher Training and Career Development

The government believes that the quality of school education depends to a large extent on the quality of the teachers. As *Teaching Quality* said in the first paragraph, 'In the schools the teaching force ... is the major single determinant of the quality of education'. It follows, as *Teaching Quality* immediately pointed out, that the supply, initial training, appointment and subsequent career development and deployment of school teachers are of vital importance. I include headteachers within that, although their importance within our school system — and especially for improving the quality of education — is such that separate mention is essential.

Following consultation conducted through the Advisory Committee on the Supply and Education of Teachers (ACSET) the government has established criteria which initial teacher training courses must satisfy if they are to lead to the recognition of those satisfactorily completing the courses as qualified teachers. The government has set up a Council for the Accreditation of Teacher Education (CATE) to review all initial teacher training courses in the light of these criteria and to recommend for the Secretary of State's approval those found to satisfy the criteria. The criteria bear upon the selection of students, the academic content and standards of the courses, and the practical training provided.

But initial training cannot now, even if it ever could, equip teachers for a complete career. The successful development of a teacher over the years needs progression and a variety of experience with appropriate opportunities for in-service training of various kinds. The successful development of a school needs the right mix of teachers with the necessary range of skills and experience, continually invigorated by good leadership and opportunities for personal development. Those teachers suitable for promotion to posts of higher responsibility, including headteacher posts, need to be identified and helped to develop the additional skills required. It is for reasons of this kind that the government, again after advice from the ACSET, is planning a much more systematic development of in-service training for teachers, supported by a specific grant from the government, and associated with the development of systematic arrangements for the appraisal of teachers' performance. This has substantial implications for the management of both the provision of in-service training and the career development of teachers by local education authorities.

Local education authorities rely on both administrative and professional advisory staff in carrying out their responsibilities. The advisers play a central part in reporting on the quality of the education being provided in an authority's schools; in providing curricular and other developments in primary, secondary and special education; and in providing advice to assist with the formulation of policy (and subsequently in helping schools to put policies into practice). Advisers also have an important role in promoting the professional development of teachers and in advising on the management of the teaching force.

The government has therefore been consulting the local authority associations about the need for guidance on the role of advisory services and on the most effective relationships between their work and that of HMI. Following the completion of the work of a joint working group, a consultative document was issued last September. The responses to this are now being considered in the Department. The outcome of this exercise should enable local education authorities, and those who serve them, to identify ways of making better and more effective use of the valuable resource provided by local advisory services.

School Governors

The goverment believes school governors have an important contribution to make in promoting school improvement. The Education Bill now before Parliament is intended to strengthen the governing body as a powerful force for good in the life of the school. The legislation sets about this in a number of ways:

(i)   it changes the composition of governing bodies of county, controlled and maintained special schools to avoid the domination of any one interest group, giving local authorities and parents equal representation;

(ii)   it makes provision for cooption to such governing bodies to allow a greater representation of relevant community interests, such as employers;

(iii) it gives the governors of these schools the formal duty to establish and publish (after consulting the LEA and headteachers) a statement of curricular aims for the school. The governors will thus have a real opportunity to ensure that the views of parents and the wider community are heard in the debate over curriculum policy — indeed it is a feature of the legislative proposals that no one interest will be able to impose its curricular requirements on the school — but they will have the right to be heard and a constitution which makes theirs an independent and very relevant voice in the debate;

(iv) it requires an annual report to parents of every governing body's activities.

In addition, governors of all schools are to be furnished with annual statements covering the whole of the expenditure of their school, so as to enable them to consider this expenditure in relation to the aims and objectives of the school and form a view as to the efficiency and effectiveness of the allocation of resources. Local education authorities will be required to delegate decisions on some expenditure on books, equipment and stationery, to the governors after consultation with the headteacher. Some authorities are already doing much more than this to involve governors and headteachers in decisions about the use of resources in their schools. Nothing in the legislation prevents such further delegation.

Governments, local authorities, the voluntary bodies and school governors all have responsibilities affecting the quality of schools. But it is the headteachers and teachers in each school on whom falls the heavy responsibility for what actually happens in the classroom. It is the interaction between teacher and pupil that counts.

Monitoring

I have been interested to see the emphasis in some of the papers for this conference on the need for monitoring and review as part of the process of school improvement. *Better Schools* made the same point. Last November the Department held a conference attended by representatives of, I believe, every local education authority in England and Wales as well as teachers and a variety of other interested organizations and institutions. With the assistance of headteachers and chief education officers who wrote papers and discussed experience in their own schools and local authority areas, the conference considered various approaches and techniques for evaluating the performance of schools and appraising the performance of teachers.

These are not easy tasks at any level — national, local authority, school, or even at the level of the individual pupil. A brief glance back at the six purposes of education with which I began makes clear the complexity of the task of evaluating performance. And, perhaps particularly at the level of the school or the teacher, one has to be concerned with the progress of the pupil over a period as well as the standards achieved at the end of that period.

In his concluding remarks at the November conference, the Secretary of State described ways in which the government can lead debate about assessment and monitoring, and make information available to inform that debate and improve practice at the national, local and school level. He called attention to the contribution made at national level by HMI reports, APU reports and public examination results: in combination, they bear upon many of the purposes of education. But he added that, to a very large extent, the place where assessment and appraisal matters most is in the local education authority and in the school. An enormous amount must inevitably depend on the work of the many thousands of teachers, advisers and others engaged in this work. Assessment, evaluation, appraisal and monitoring are not the only activities which improve standards. But they are essential.

I have referred briefly to some of the key activities the government has in hand or is promoting as ways of improving the quality of school education: setting aims and objectives; curriculum review; reform of examinations and assessment procedures; improving training and career development opportunities for teachers; strengthening local management and governing bodies; and monitoring progress. It seems largely, and perhaps inevitably, a catalogue of the obvious. But that may be just because it reflects the needs of the time. It is not a list my predecessors of thirty, twenty or even ten years ago could have offered.

References

DES (1983) *Teaching Quality* (Cmnd 8836), London, HMSO
DES (1985) *Better Schools* (Cmnd 9469), London, HMSO
OECD (1983) *Compulsory Schooling in a Changing World*, Paris, OECD.

Public Perceptions of School Improvement

Stuart Maclure

This is a dissemination conference: dissemination is always the hardest of all the achievements for any kind of development project. So I greatly welcome this conference as an attempt to reap some of the benefits, and spread the message, of ISIP.

This conference has been full of very valuable information. There has been a very great deal of content to it, a great deal to grind on. I am not sure, however, that we all got the full value of the international dimension. I think that is the hardest thing of all to introduce into a discussion of this kind. These cross cultural influences are always particularly difficult to comprehend in this country, where there is a high degree of resistance, particularly at the level of the DES and the government, to any conceivable lessons which might be learned from other countries, particularly countries in Europe which have a lot to teach us.

Perhaps the first conclusion which I have come to about school improvement is that it seems to have been turned into the brand name for a project by ISIP! But, in fact, school improvement is not something new, or something added. It ought to be the regular professional obligation of all educators. I suppose it may well be relevant to question the resources which are available for school improvement at any time, but to think of it as an 'add on' must, in itself, be an error. It ought to be regarded as a first priority, even within existing resources.

That is something which is very easy to say — particularly for someone who never gets much closer to the facts of education than writing leaders every Wednesday morning — but nevertheless the concept of the quest for improvement as something which is an optional extra must be wrong.

If one turns to the 'public perception' of school improvement this has ambiguities woven into it word by word. For example, the word 'public' is a singularly useful compendium of meanings and I have no doubt that I shall use it in many different ways at the same time. The whole idea of 'public opinion' is in itself an interesting and obscure notion. As far as I can see public opinion consists of a set of fairly simple propositions which somehow or other resonate. The ones which resonate most persistently become the backdrop of public opinion. Of course, in a constantly changing world there's no such thing as static public opinion. As far as education is concerned public opinion is what emerges from the bombardment of ideas, in and out of the media, some of which ring bells and others die without trace.

Public perceptions of the school are the next element of this title. They are, in fact, notoriously unreliable. They are based, in part, on the experience of people as children and in part on the experience of parents on behalf of their own children. The public reputation of teachers, for example, is based on personal reminiscence and recollection, and on what people think they know about their children's experience. This, no doubt, is much distorted by the inordinate changes which take place between the door of the school and the door of the home. Teachers in the press, teachers in literature; there is an extraordinary stereotype of the teacher which bears no relation to any particular individual yet which is very powerful in terms of the public mind. Teachers are also reflected in the media through the activities of teachers' unions and what happens in pay disputes. Anyone might assume that a teacher was someone with a low salary, a great deal of anger and long holidays. Those three characteristics are an inadequate description of teachers.

Then if we take the concept of improvement, which is all part of this title, there are all the points which were raised by Philip Halsey in his talk. Improvement suggests that there is some generally understood difference between one state and another, between 'before' and 'after', 'worse' or 'better'. What is an improvement, and what is just a change? How do we recognize improvement? I think back to the 1960s and 1970s when CERI was very much concerned with innovation. Whatever happened to innovation? I ask myself. There was a disposition to equate innovation with improvement. Such optimism is refreshing but not necessarily well founded. The language of advertising equates the word 'new' with 'improved' and everyone knows that this, like matrimony, is often the triumph of hope over experience.

But, if it is assumed that we are concerned with improvement, then presumably, as Philip Halsey said, we have to have some concept of the kind of objectives we are driving at. The technique of support and the processes for the management of change can be systematized but they have to take place within a set of external objectives. Now it seems to me that we are living through a period during which national priorities in education are being spelled out more clearly than at any time since the 1920s or earlier. The political and administrative process is ensuring that this is taking place, but it remains contentious at two levels. First of all about the content and secondly about the very process itself. One of the things which stands out about English education is the tradition of decentralized power. Now this is being challenged — not because anybody really wants central control but because we have discovered our own incapacity to make up our minds collectively in the decentralized system. I think this is one of the problems which has overtaken education in this country over the last thirty-five years. The techniques of decentralization are much better at preventing things from happening than making sure they do happen.

I think these problems have become so great that we have now reached the point where the politicians have contrived a complete change in the approach to the policy making function in education. I do not believe it is a party political issue between the Conservatives and the Labour Party and the Alliance. I think that there is a strong consensus among the politicians and prominent among other things that unite them are their common criticisms and distrust of the educationists.

If we turn away from generalizations about improving 'the system' to think of improvement in terms of an individual school, how does the public react? Let me take the example of school A. School A gets a new head. School A takes off. The public reputation of the school soars; the intake of students 'improves'; the staff gain confidence; there is good leadership which means getting rid of a string of poor teachers (never mind how) and attracting energetic new ones who have the same values and objectives as the head. There is enough agreement on educational aims to provide a coherent background. The school enters an up cycle which lasts till complacency and a hardening of the educational arteries have taken over. Then there is regression to the norm.

The public perception turns on obvious things: examination results; the appearance and behaviour of the students and uniform. Rumours and reports circulate in a most mysterious way in the local saloon bars. The 'bubble, reputation' is what it is all about. The school rises on this bubble and by a series of steps, which no doubt one could examine by the kind of analytical tools which are available in the ISIP project, perception and reality merge.

School B, on the other hand, is going downhill. The head is ill, or tired, or weak. There is dissension and antagonism amongst the staff. Rival philosophies of education contend in the common room. Cliques and cabals form. The trade unions get awkward. Performance deteriorates. Examination results go down. The environment suffers. Graffitt appear on the walls. Behaviour is bad. There is evidence of growing violence. Bad reputations are made worse by evil report and rumour. The school is on a downward path, heading for a loss of pupils, a report by HMI and so on and so forth.

Add in complicating factors about the changing social and ethnic mix and changed political priorities at the local authority level on such matters as equal opportunities or multicultural education, and the despair gets even deeper. But most of the time the public is not looking for miracles but for fairly simple and limited kinds of success. People want stability and dependability and disciplined behaviour. One of the things which we have to learn from the 1960s is that the demands and expectations of the education enterprise can lose touch with those of the public all too easily. There is, of course, good research evidence from the Schools Council *Enquiry Two* which showed the teachers to have one set of values and expectations and the parents and pupils another.

What is clear is that public opinion has enormous difficulty in coming to terms with the meaning of 'secondary education for all'. But that is not really surprising, seeing that the educators and the politicians have not yet managed to come to terms with it either. We are still trying to puzzle out what it means in terms of the curriculum, even if we think we may know what it means in terms of organization.

Excellence and quality remain the two magic words in the educational vocabulary. I remember being told, and I think very wisely, by an Under-Secretary in the DES who was then concerned with the reform of 16+ examinations, that the GCE 'is not about standards, it's about magic'. It became a totem, a symbol, a myth in the sense Hans Tangerud used the phrase. Myths are very important in their way and very dangerous things to tamper with.

The popular idea of high standards is much closer to the absolute and competitive notion of excellence than the sophisticated idea of 'optimum value added', which is really what we all have to strive for if we want to have excellence for everyone in a public education service. The public thinks about excellence in education in the same way as people think of the sprinter's excellence, or the marksman's excellence, or the snooker player's excellence. But we have to be concerned with excellence at every level, including excellent mediocrity. If there is one thing which this country needs it is more really good mediocre people. We have got an awful lot of bad mediocre people, but that is another matter. I think that is a terribly difficult idea for the public to get hold of. And, therefore, it remains really very, very important that in pursuing excellence and quality in education we should keep in mind the fact that whatever else we may offer, the public still needs and demands the concept of pure excellence — the best. I think we know that there are all sorts of confusions at the centre of the notion of criterion referencing in a system which will always be partly norm referenced. As my friend in the DES said, we are dealing with big magic, there is a sense people that are right in demanding excellence which is truly excellent and *non-pareil*.

Well, what about the politics of school improvement, which presumably illuminate an aspect of public perception? In the sixties and the early seventies, the heydey of curriculum development, it was an activity for educators. The setting of the goals was a job for the educators as well as the choosing of the means. And it was 'bottom up', or 'teacher led'; it was inspired by progessive ideals. I remember going to many CERI meetings where the English were always prating on about teacher led development and the values which went with it; the autonomy of the teacher, the teacher controlled curriculum, the teacher led curriculum and so on and so forth. These were all things which in their way had real virtues and values attached to them. But all of them were hostages to fortune, against the time when the politicians would say 'why should we pretend these issues have nothing to do with us and hand them over to teachers when they are issues which concern the national welfare generally?'.

The Great Reaction of the 1970s followed immediately on what you might call the high peak of progressive education which could be discerned in the Plowden Report of 1967. We moved on to Jim Callaghan's Ruskin speech in 1976 and the new era it opened up. The Ruskin speech served all sorts of functions in terms of creating scapegoats, diverting attention from the visit of the International Monetary Fund experts, giving people something else to talk about other than the bad economic news. But at the same time behind the political intervention of the Prime Minister there was the truth of the 'Great Reaction'. A genuine surge of public opinion had taken place and Callaghan's response to it was to point the finger at the teachers for having hijacked the curriculum. If you go back, as Philip Halsey said he did before he came here, and read the Ruskin speech again, it contains a direct accusation that the teachers had preempted the curriculum debate and tried to keep it to themselves. This was quite false, quite untrue. It was the politicians who had connived at the professionalism of the curriculum.

Allowing the curriculum to slip out of the public domain and into the private domain of education was one of the mistakes of the politicians. But it was also the great mistake, as it turned out, for the educators. The teachers got attacked for purloining the curriculum. Standards in the schools were challenged with a version of Morton's fork 'standards are falling or, if standards are not falling, standards are in any case not high enough'. To this there is no answer. Either way the schools, the teachers, the advisers, the administrators have failed and there are various consequences which are thought to follow.

First of all there is the emergence of the centralizing consensus which I have referred to already. We are watching and hearing inside the government, the argument going on between the Department of Education and Science, the Department of the Environment and the Treasury. We see the Prime Minister standing as a hostile umpire on the edge of the field, where the DES is struggling to try and get a more direct control over the money which is spent on education through the local authorities. These arguments are about the extension of specific grants or the introduction of an education block grant or anyway of allowing policy making and the distribution of money to go hand in hand, because for the last twenty-odd years policy making and the distribution of money have been artificially separated. This is a very serious and substantial point in that, given the breakdown of the relationships between central and local government (which I do not think can possibly be reconstructed — Humpty Dumpty has fallen off that wall), the DES, if it wishes to have policies in education, is going to have to have some way of insisting that money voted for education is spent in ways which correspond to the policies of the government.

All this comes after we have had (and this, I think, is the most serious aspect of it all in terms of public perceptions) a ten-year assault on the teachers. For ten years the teachers have been denigrated. We think of this in terms of the present government, and Sir Keith Joseph's clumsy and destructive attempts to focus on the quite genuine problems of a minority of unsatisfactory teachers who are, by the nature of our system, extremely difficult to dislodge. But the attack on teachers goes back, as I have said, to Ruskin and before. Having focussed on what is a perfectly genuine problem, Sir Keith went on to spread a general miasma of criticism across the teachers as a whole. And this has coincided with the devaluation of teachers' pay alongside the pay of other groups. This is not the result, I think, of a deliberate policy aimed at teachers, but a consequence of years of wages policy aimed against the public sector as a whole (apart, that is, for the top people).

Other factors in forming public attitudes towards education include high and rising unemployment, the deterioration of the cities and the multiplication of ethnic issues as education and unemployment become linked in a single equation. The pressure for change has come at a time when the capacity to respond is at its lowest ebb. We talk about a 'teachers' dispute' which has been going on for the best part of three years, one way or another. Wide stretches of the education system have become demoralized. Education seems to the public to be in an awful mess and we now look like compounding that again if the General Certificate of Secondary Education is introduced without adequate preparation.

School improvement depends above all on goodwill. This is especially true in an education system where teachers have been paid for an undefined contract, with no overtime provisions. Goodwill is distinctly strained these days.

So there are really quite straightforward reasons, which are unfortunately not short term, why we are in a mess on these particular issues at the moment. The public perception might well be that for the last ten years, we have had governments pledged to school improvement and what have we got? A situation which is, if anything, worse than it has been at any time in the last ten years. And indeed, if we have had a ten-year period of trying to improve education, why has it got to the state it is?

I think, in fact, these things are hyped up and focussed in a particularly distressing fashion at the moment. But there is no point in hiding the fact there is now a very grave situation in the schools, but suggestions of nationalization or central control are no answer to these problems.

In conclusion, it seems to me that the public demand is for a more systematic management of the education system, a more systematic kind of improvement, the kind of things which we have been talking about here. I doubt if the public is particularly concerned with the issues or the evils of centralization; I do not think the public is particularly committed to local administration of education and I think that we should all be kidding ourselves if we supposed that they are. They difficulty for the education system is to prevent education being dragged down by what amounts to a long drawn out, and as yet, unresolved quarrel between central government and local government, to which there seems no end in sight.

It all comes back to the question of dissemination. The public reaction needs to be stimulated by information, otherwise the politicians and the media form public opinion by their own trial balloons. If we are going to move into a system with a greater degree of parliamentary and political control, then the educators have to become a pressure group among other pressure groups. There is a need to take ideas about school improvement to the public and to make propaganda for them, to generate support for an education party of the kind which was once believed to exist in local government in the days of the percentage grant and the privileged position of the Education Committee. We need to mobilize at the level of the school and, of course, at the level of the local education authority. I suppose, however, that the $64,000 question is 'how can we do this at a time when, for reasons which are perfectly understandable but nevertheless deeply regrettable, the teachers' union are building up their own massive public hostility?'.

The Prospect of School Improvement at the Local Level: The Perceptions of Conference Participants

Peter Holly and Michael Henley

A major component of the conference design were the workshops associated with each presentation. During these workshops discussion centred on the task of finding 'lessons' for educators in the United Kingdom. A number of lessons consistently and strongly came through.

For change to lead successfully to improvement the following criteria were regarded as important:

(i)   there must be careful and accurate situational analysis;
(ii)   needs have to be clearly identified in terms of an agreed methodology;
(iii) the necessity for change must be clearly appreciated by all parties;
(iv) the strategy adopted needs to have been carefully thought through;
(v)   the strategy needs to be communicated clearly to everyone affected;
(vi) the changes must be followed up, reinforced and institutionalized;
(vii) changes in schools should be supported by external agencies and there is also a need for financial support at least in the short term.

The change process in education was recognized at the conference as a collaborative venture requiring all the skills of good management. The school comprises a team and improvement is a team effort. Key members of the team are pupils and parents, teachers, senior management in school and LEA, and the school governors. Good management requires adequate role definition for the team members and active participation of them all in accordance with their roles.

There was great interest in the concept of school-based review (SBR) which was regarded by virtually everyone in a very positive way. It was seen as an instrument of school improvement that all schools should adopt in principle and develop individually. SBR provides a methodology for effective dialogue on the needs of a school as an organization committed to innovation and renewal. Likewise the needs of the school staff as a whole and, to an extent, as individuals should find expression through SBR in a dialogue suited to INSET assessment. Participants in these dialogues were seen to include advisers and education officers whose opportunity to facilitate support activity for school improvement was bound to be enhanced by this means. Frequent reference was made to relevant current good practice in the UK and a valuable exchange of information took place.

Undoubtedly, judging by the sheer volume of the responses of participants, SBR is important for school improvement. Within an integrated approach to school improvement, *ie*, the ISIP approach, SBR has a pivotal role to play. One workshop concluded that the conference helped to 'put the various initiatives that are current in SBR into some sensible whole'. Another workshop, having welcomed 'the message of hope' arising 'from the international experience — that all schools can be improved' observed that 'SBR is compatible both with a national curriculum and a structured framework' on the one hand and with 'an LEA and its schools striving for their own understandings' on the other. The two propositions were seen as complementary as well as expressive of 'counter cultures'; SBR may be used in different ways according to the surrounding culture.

Typifying the intentions of participants was the plan described by one of them 'to discuss with colleagues — teachers' centre wardens and heads and deputies — within the professional association concerned, both GRIDS and the local school review programme'. This participant said he had acquired more confidence in his own perception of school review and the view that it can be effective only when the processes impinge on the consciousness and the practices of people in the school. External agents and perceptions were seen as an essential part of the process.

SBR was also connected in discussion with the concept of a school as a 'society' in which the individual's effectiveness is determined by its 'climate'. A view was expressed that 'the "chosen people" strategy of school improvement (for example TVEI and ESG) with its vocabulary of replication and dissemination, seems very optimistic and affords an interesting comparison with the Pittsburgh "PRISM" approach. (A knowledge of the Old Testament is neccessary to understand this point!)'

Throughout the conference a recurrent theme was the overriding importance of establishing, at school level, a momentum for change developed from within, through the force of a school staff's own perceptions. The strength and, indeed, the persistence of the momentum was seen as dependent on staff morale which the actions of central and local government clearly affect for better or worse. Use of a more positive policy to actively promote a climate of good morale, in which schools can work, was seen as necessary particularly on the part of central government; and also in many areas of local government. A typical conclusion drawn in the workshops was that to achieve school improvement on a widespread basis, the central government and the LEAs have to help create the right working conditions.

There were some doubts expressed about whether grassroots initiatives can ever achieve widespread school improvement without top-down help and ongoing support. Wild flowers need care and cultivation before they are accepted in the window box.

One of the teacher association representatives indicated that he intended to report back to his executive on his perceptions of a growing awareness that the democratic involvement of all teachers in the management of change is the key to future success. He recalled that partnership had recently 'taken a hammering' but concluded all the same that a collegial approach must be seen as a prerequisite in facilitating school improvement. Given trust the representative had no doubt that the vast majority of teachers will 'respond positively'. He saw the promise of a disappearance of the conflict of voluntaryism and compulsion, and thus the release of the most important resource for change, the human resource, since the hindrance to such release is low morale. What was vital in this context was the restoration and nurturing of the self confidence of teachers as professionals.

The workshops had a mixed membership and this was appreciated since the discussions were informed by a wide range of perceptions and experience. As a conference model this mixed membership was commended, the suggestion often being added that an even richer mix would have been an advantage. This would have included more representatives of HMI, administrative staff from the Department of Education and Science, teacher trainers, classroom teachers and elected members of Education committees.

Perhaps, because of the mixed membership of the workshops, many aspects of school management came under scrutiny in the course of deliberations on the case studies. Much emphasis was placed on the importance for school improvement to be systematic, in the ISIP sense, at both school and LEA level. Particular reference was often made to the issue of systematic management behaviour and the inter level components of consistency and coherence in the context of the changing future orientation of INSET from LEA/higher education identified needs to LEA/higher education support for the school in its endeavours to identify its own needs as part of an improvement programme. This theme raised further issues concerning the roles of heads, advisers and education officers. It was suggested that national initiatives, in the action research mode, be taken on: LEA support services; the work of advisory teachers; educational consultancy; and 'action learning' approaches for heads and other managers.

The material in the case studies stimulated not only many reflections about roles and functions, but also provided insights regarded by conference participants as highly valuable into the ways that OECD members' countries are tackling the social/educational problems of our time. Particular participants indicated intentions to follow up OECD country contacts introduced at Nene College. It was evident that the information provided by ISIP in terms of both the case studies and presentation was useful in shaping ideas amongst a number of participants about current and future research in the area of school improvement. Participants from higher education indicated that they had gained a greater awareness of the influence on classsroom activity of politics, organizational structure, evaluation procedures and liaison skills. There was general agreement that the UK has much to learn from 'the OECD experiences'. ISIP was seen to have achieved a model for international debate and exchange of ideas. The evidence at this conference of outcomes from ISIP was seen as impressive. As one participant said: 'Although educational systems in different coutries vary considerably, many joint lessons can be learned. The process of reinventing the wheel is a pointless one. The conference has opened up previously unconsidered avenues of information'.

One of the three aims of the conference was to relate ISIP outcomes to current UK policy concerns and consider their implications. Direct connections were seen between the central government concern to secure greater clarity about the objectives and content of the school curriculum and the reference in the ISIP definition of school improvement to 'the ultimate aim of accomplishing educational goals more effectively'. Consideration of SBR meant giving attention to the goal setting process and relating this to training needs. Further connections were noted in the lessons of ISIP and the central government concern to improve the professional effectiveness of teachers and the management of the teaching force. ISIP was seen to provide a framework for good management practice at LEA and school level where the promotion of student learning is kept as the central purpose in a working environment also committed to professional and institutional autonomy.

Another central government concern is to reform school government and to harness more fully the contribution which can be made to quality school education by parents, employees and others outside the education service. ISIP area 5 was devoted to all aspects of policy making, and the presentation and case studies at the conference focussed attention on many of the issues of school management that go beyond the conventional boundaries of the school as an organization. The need to consider issues of pluralism and of shared values in this regard was recognised by participants, who welcomed the insights presented by the introduction of international perspectives on partnership concerns and the shared governance of schools.

Awareness of ISIP was greatly extended in the UK as a result of the conference. There remains, however, the task to develop UK models of school improvement. There is also a need to follow up the conference and, while the ISIP publications were seen as plainly going to be of great practical benefit, the conclusion reached at the conference was that school improvement as a concept is not yet deeply enough understood in the UK. The dissemination process of the outcomes of ISIP requires more time and reflection, research, and above all, action. The hope was expressed by participants that proactive school improvement networks in the ISIP style will be established in the UK.

Implications for School Improvement at the Local Level

David Hopkins

In contrast to the other contributions to this chapter, the perspectives on school improvement of the DES, the public, and the conference participants, I intend in this concluding section to draw on some of the lessons from ISIP and examine their implications for school improvement at the local level. By the local level, I mean the school and sometimes the LEA. I am less concerned here with national authorities, that brief having already been covered. Neither do I intend to give specific advice in such a brief discussion; it so often turns out to be 'tips for changing schools' and if ISIP has taught us anything it is that school improvement cannot be achieved so easily. In any case the select bibliography contains a number of references of excellent work that offers more specific and detailed advice than can be given here. All I can do in the space available is to raise some general issues and point to some directions.

Perhaps the two most important features of the ISIP work taken as a whole are the emphasis on the school as the prime unit of change and on the qualitative factors comprising the internal conditions of the school. Let me briefly discuss these features in turn.

By referring to the school as the prime unit of change, I am not intending to imply that the school is, or should be, autonomous; the vision, however, is of the 'relatively autonomous school' which exists within a supportive educational environment sustained by the local education authority. The relationship that I envisage between school and LEA is symbiotic with a clear perception of role and expectation. This emphasis on the 'relatively autonomous' school within a supportive LEA needs to be reflected in policy, both local and national. It also assumes that the school itself is 'self conscious' and adopts a school-wide focus towards improvement efforts. This means that the process of change is as important as its substance: for example, that by introducing profiling and records of achievement into a number of subject areas in a secondary school in a systematic way as part of a deliberate policy, the school is also learning about how to change and increasing its capacity to change.

The emphasis on qualitative factors is equally important: here I am referring to internal features such as an emphasis on the teaching/learning process, an agreement on goals, a supportive learning climate, high expectations and so on. Quality schooling occurs when these and similar features are embedded within the fabric of the school. It is these internal factors that make up the climate or culture of the school and give it a unique character. ISIP and related research suggest (*vide* Rutter *et al*, 1979; Mortimore *et al*, 1986) that it is these qualitative factors that result in enhanced student outcomes. These features, which are related to the school as a social system, although somewhat intangible, can be changed, as I noted in chapter 1, by the concerted effort of a school staff. This is no easy task but at least there is the potential for enhancing the quality of schooling residing within the school itself. (It must be admitted, however, that the quantitative factors such as facilities, finance and personnel are also important as HMI reports continue to stress, but they are inevitably less easy for the school to control.)

Taken together these two points, the focus on the school and its culture — the qualitative internal factors — provide us with an optimistic if somewhat daunting prospect for school improvement at the local level.

This potential must be set against the background of what is occurring in education in the UK at the present time. I mentioned in chapter 1 the plethora of recent developments, particularly in secondary education, that, when taken together, constitute a fairly radical programme for change; comparable, in my opinion, to the advent of the comprehensive school (Hopkins, 1986). Many of these changes, as was seen from Philip Halsey's paper, can be conceptualized within a school improvement framework: the emphasis on teaching/learning style in many of the curriculum innovations, specific grant related support, the GRIST arrangements, schemes for teacher appraisal, student profiling and school evaluation are some examples. But it needs to be said that these initiatives do not of themselves necessarily contribute to school improvement. At best they contain the potential for so doing but only if they are implemented within a school improvement strategy. School evaluation, for example, when practised within the GRIDS framework becomes a powerful tool for school improvement. However, when school evaluation is conceptualized within an accountability framework it produces little evidence of school improvement and indeed tends to inhibit it. The same argument applies to teacher appraisal. It is the values underpinning the change and the perspective adopted by the policy and the initiators of the change that are so crucial; and I have already remarked on the somewhat instrumental orientation of *Better Schools*. With this thought in mind let us look more specifically at some of the lessons emerging from the ISIP themes discussed at the conference and in this book.

The first theme, school-based review, is an area where ISIP has made a significant theoretical and developmental contribution. By taking GRIDS as their starting point, the members of this working group developed and adapted procedures for review in schools; for example, the development of the SBR matrix and the adaption of GRIDS to the Belgian situation. The work of the group also emphasized the linking of review to development, so much so, that both GRIDS and the matrix not only provide guidelines for review but also consist of a school improvement process in themselves. So what lessons can we learn from this experience? The first is that review needs to precede development; to know one's situation before one attempts to improve. The second is the attention it gives to organizational processes as well as curriculum substance. The ability to learn how to change is arguably more important than the change itself. GRIDS and the matrix provide a model for problem solving and action that can be used again and again with a range of substantive innovations and by so doing the school itself develops a capacity for handling change. The third is that both approaches provide a basis for systematic planning. Planning is fundamental to effective change despite the fact that the actual change process is never as linear as one intends, being usually much more capricious. Planning is necessary, but the 'fallacy of rationalism' must also be accepted. The fourth lesson is the differentiation of role as detailed in the matrix. This aids planning, points out the problems of control and, it is hoped, assists in making the whole process more democratic and collaborative. Finally, when taken together, these characteristics of school-based review can affect the climate or culture of the school by making it ultimately more conducive to improvement and enhancing quality. The discussion by conference participants seems to support these ideas; there was a widespread acceptance of and interest in GRIDS at the conference.

The second theme was the role of the school leader. The truism that the head is the gatekeeper of change is scattered in various guises throughout the ISIP literature. That important if evident point apart, what else can be learnt? First is the need for preparation for leadership. The papers give a good indication of the various training components necessary for effective leadership in schools. What is of particular interest in these discussions is the emphasis on development rather than training, a sharing or delegation of leadership roles throughout the school, the collaboration between the LEA and the school on development programmes and the 'embeddedness' of such programmes within the school. Second, and despite the somewhat instrumental emphasis associated with training, are the personal qualities that contribute to effective leadership. The case studies illustrated quite clearly that effective leadership is predicated on a range of democratic and humanitarian principles: it is crucial to appreciate those with whom one works. Another aspect of this is the necessary involvement of the school leader in the range of activities required by a particular improvement effort. It is not sufficient to sit in one's office and plan; one also has to get out and become involved. Third, the school leader needs to plan and act within the context of policy. Long-term planning and the creation of policy at the school and local level are important activities for the school leader. Having said that, the role of the school leader is not as instrumental as this point suggests. Policy and planning provide a context and direction within which the school leader expresses his or her creativity and intuition and through which s/he develops, to use Michael Fullan's felicitous phrase, 'a feel for the process of leadership'.

The third theme, external support, introduces a relatively new concept to schooling in the UK. There has always been a support system, of course, but it has not been regarded as such. The advisory/inspection service, teacher centres, the institutes of education and the university and college departments amongst others have not until recently (and some still have not) conceptualized their role within a framework of external support. More significantly, neither had their supposed clients — the schools and this, of course, is the problem. The first lesson to be drawn from the presentations is the need for adequate conceptualization of external support. The contribution of external support to school improvement has to be recognized and the role that the various agencies can provide redefined. The analysis of the US system undertaken by David Crandall for this book needs to be replicated in the UK. The second lesson is that schools also have to reconceptualize external support. They have to begin to think of school improvement as a collaborative effort, to define their needs more clearly and become more proactive in the use of outside assistance. It is, of course, the operationalization and subsequent marrying of these lessons that creates the third: it is that the external support has to match the needs of the school. So often, it is either the wrong type of support that is offered or inappropriate assistance that is requested. The 'problem of the match' needs to recognized and collaboratively worked on.

The fourth theme, policy, is a tricky one. Hans Tangerud quite appropriately pointed to the problems inherent in creating effective policy in pluralistic systems. The other problem is that, irrespective of the quality of the policy, teachers and school people are usually suspicious of it, in whatever form. Policy is often regarded as something handed down from on high, and seen within a 'top bottom' orientation. The first two lessons are then to heed Tangerud's advice on policy formation in pluralistic systems and to educate practitioners as to the utility of policy and encourage policy formation at the local level, as seen in the Pittsburgh case study. When all is said and done, policy is merely a plan, an agreement on action. The third lesson relates to the implementation of policy. Rarely does policy take cognizance of implementation: there is an implicit assumption that implementation is an event, that change occurs next Tuesday or in September, rather than it being a process that extends over a period of years. That recognition needs to be built into policy. The TVEI case study illustrates this point. Awareness of implementation was not satisfactorily built into the central government's TVEI policy; witness the speed with which submissions had to be prepared and executed. In Northamptonshire an implementation policy was worked out at the local level. Often it is not and the innovation is consequently less effective. Incidentally, TVEI is a good example of a centralized policy direction that has to be reinterpreted and assimilated at the local level.

These four themes cover the territory of school improvement fairly comprehensively. The exception, of course, is in-service or professional development, although it has been dealt with implicity in each of the themes. Any change or improvement requires that individuals learn how to do something new. Acquiring new skills and understandings is a difficult enterprise and one at which most in-service programmes have been singularly unsuccessful. Although workshops, lectures and pre-implementation activities all have their place in INSET the implementation of school improvement also requires ongoing professional development activity within the school. It appears that to be really successful, this activity needs to involve 'coaching' of teachers by teachers; or in other words teachers teaching each other the art of teaching. This again is no easy task and one that is most probably different from most teachers' experience. Yet it is becoming increasingly apparent that traditional forms of in-service are inappropriate for the type of school improvement envisaged in this book: and despite the recent enhanced levels of funding for in-service in the UK, it is the quality rather than the quantity of in-service that counts. I can do no better here than to quote Fullan (1986, p. 76):

> The evidence continues to accumulate, and is as convincing as any we need, to make the general point that a new task focussed, continuous professional development, combining a variety of learning formats, and a variety of trainers and other support personnel, is evolving and is effective in bringing about change in practice. While these examples are based on much more intensive and systematic interaction than are traditional forms of in-service, there is some evidence to show that a small amount of time, used under the right conditions over a period of several months alternating between practice and training, can go a long way. Still, there are many unresolved issues, most of which pertain to management questions of how to initiate, design and follow through on what amounts to a sophisticated, highly integrated approach to professional development.

So in such a brief review of 'Implications for School Improvement at the Local Level' what else is there to be said? Just this: Rene Daumal in another context once remarked that 'art is knowledge realized in action'. Daumal was talking about climbing mountains, but the same applies to improving schools and enhancing the quality of education. ISIP has taught us many things, so too has the effective schools/in-service literature; and also our own inner-self retain, when we allow it to speak, is often endowed with wisdom. Yet all too often, we act without reference to what we intuitively know is right and in compliance to arbitary external factors. If we are to make school improvement work for us in our school, our college or jurisdiction, we must engage ourselves and others, systematically in a dialectic between the knowledge base, the local situation and our own experience. Ultimately that is what school improvement is about: it is a group of individuals using what they know intelligently, taking responsibility for their actions within a collective enterprise and working hard, very hard, together towards a common goal. But despite the necessity for collaboration and collective ownership, change that means anything at all stems from individual commitment and understanding. It is at this point that the success of any school improvement effort is determined. Referring to the dialectical nature of human experience — but he could equally have been talking about the lessons to be gleaned from ISIP, Walt Whitman says this:

> You shall no longer take things at second or third hand ... nor look through the eyes of the dead ... nor feed on the spectres in books,
> You shall not look through my eyes either, nor take things from me,
> You shall listen to all sides and filter them from yourself.

References

FULLAN, M (1986) 'The management of change' in HOYLE, E and McMAHON, A (Eds) *The Management of Schools*, London, Kogan Page.

HOPKINS, D (1986) 'Recent developments in secondary education: Some premature reflections' *Cambridge Journal of Education*, 16, 3, autumn pp. 195–210.

MORTIMORE, P *et al* (1986) *The ILEA Junior School Project: Summary of the Main Report*, London, Research and Statistics Branch, ILEA.

RUTTER, M *et al* (1979) *Fifteen Thousand Hours*, London, Open Books.

A Select Bibliography on School Improvement

BENNIS, W et al (1969) The Planning of Change, New York, Holt, Rinehart and Winston.
The original and still classic text on change.

BOLAM, R (1975) 'The management of educational change' in HOUGHTON, V et al (Eds.), Management in Education, London, Ward Lock.
An early review of the literature that contains some important conceptual analysis.

BOLAM, R (1982) School-Focussed In-service Training, London, Heinemann Educational Books.
Perhaps the most important book on INSET in the UK: a useful combination of analysis and case study.

BOLAM, R (1986) 'The National Development Centre for School Management' in HOYLE, E. and McMAHON, A (Eds) The Management of Schools, London, Kogan Page
A contemporary account of the work of the NDC and its emphasis on management development.

BOLLEN, R and HOPKINS, D (1987) School Based Review: Towards a Praxis, Leuven, Belgium, ACCO.
Probably the only book on school based review: a blend of theory, case study, analysis and guidelines for action.

CLARK, D et al (1984) 'Effective schools and school improvement', Educational Administration Quarterly, 20, 3, summer, pp41–68.
An intelligent and practical synthesis of these two important lines of enquiry.

CRANDALL, D and LOUCKS, S (1983) A Roadmap for School Improvement, Andover, MA, The Network Inc.
A summary of the DESSI study that reviewed all the major initiatives in

school improvement in the United States during the previous decade and initiated a more sophisticated level of analysis.

DALIN P and RUST, V (1983) *Can School Learn?*, Windsor, NFER-Nelson.
A description of the ubiquitous and successful IMTEC method of improving schools.

EVERARD, K and MORRIS, G (1985) *Effective School Management*, London, Harper and Row.
A recent UK contribution to the management/change literature that contains much useful material.

FULLAN, M (1982) *The Meaning of Educational Change*, Toronto, OISE Press.
A seminal book; provides essential and intelligent analysis and a comprehensive review of the literature.

FULLAN, M (1985) 'Change processes and strategies at the local level', *Elementary School Journal*, 85, 3, pp391-421.
An important and reasonably practical review of change strategies at the school/LEA Level.

FULLAN, M (1986) 'The management of change' in HOYLE, E and McMAHON, A (Eds) *The Management of Schools*, London, Kogan Page.
A more recent update of his previous publications.

FULLAN, M et al (1980) 'Organization development in schools', *Review of Educational Research*, 50, 1, pp212–83.
A comprehensive and authoritative review of organization development undertaken at a time when the movement was at its zenith.

FULLAN, M and PARK, P (1981) *Curriculum Implementation*, Toronto, Ontario, Ministry of Education.
An extremely useful guide to curriculum implementation for all those concerned with change at the local level.

GOODLAD, J (1984) *A Place Called School*, New York, McGraw-Hill.
The 'state of the art' of education in the US: a readable account of a major, if pessimistic research effort.

GLATTER, R (1986) 'The management of school improvement' in HOYLE, E and McMAHON, A (Eds) *The Management of Schools*, London, Kogan Page
An overview of the work of ISIP together with some of its implications for the management of schools.

HOPKINS, D and WIDEEN, M (1984) *Alternative Perspectives on School Improvement*, Lewes, Falmer Press.
An early attempt to make sense of the complexity of school improvement from a predominantly UK perspective.

HOYLE, E (1976) *Strategies of Curriculum Change*, Unit 23, Open University Course E203: Curriculum Design and Development, Milton Keynes, Open University Press.
A compendium of the conventional wisdom on educational change to that date in a very accessible format.

HOYLE, E (1986) *The Politics of School Management*, London, Hodder and Stoughton.
A sophisticated yet understandable account of management and change in schools from a social science perspective.

HOYLE, E and MCMAHON, A (Eds) (1986) *The Management of Schools*, London, Kogan Page.
Contains the most comprehensive and relevant collection of papers on management and change in education to date: essential reading.

HUBERMAN, M and MILES, M (1984) *Innovation Up Close*, New York, Plenum Press.
A very detailed and illuminating account of the process of school improvement in twelve American schools.

JOYCE, B and SHOWERS, B (1980) 'Improving in-service training: The messages of research', *Educational Leadership*, 37, 5, February, pp379–85.
The paper on in-service; all you need to know about the design of in-service programmes in six pages.

JOYCE, B et al (1983) *The Structure of School Improvement*, New York, Longman.
A highly readable yet sophisticated account of the process of school improvement from the perspective of the school. It is American in origin and orientation: its message, however, travels well.

KYLE, R (1985) *Reaching for Excellence: An Effective Schools Sourcebook*, Washington, DC, US Government Printing Office.
A comprehensive compendium of materials, practices and programs for effective schools: although based on the US experience it is also applicable to other school systems.

LEHMING, R and KANE, M (1981) *Improving Schools*, Beverly Hills, Sage.
A collection of commissioned review articles that provided the foundation for the recent US work on the topic.

LOUCKS, S (Ed) (1983) 'Ensuring success' (Special Edition), *Educational Leadership*, 41, 3, November.
The outcomes of the DESSI study in six brief and accessible articles.

LOUCKS, S and HERGERT, L (1985) *An Action Guide to School Improvement*, Andover, MA, ASCD/Network.
A prescriptive yet quite profound 'DIY' kit for school improvement.

McMahon, A *et al* (1984) *Guidelines for Review and Internal Development in Schools*, York, Schools Council/Longmans.
The guidelines for schools who wish to undertake self evaluation and review for themselves.

Mortimore, P *et al* (1986) *The ILEA Junior School Project: Summary of the Main Report*, London, Research and Statistics Branch, ILEA.
A longitudinal study of the progress and attainment of 2000 junior school pupils that extends the Rutter research and confirms many of its findings.

Nuttall, D *et al* (1987) *Studies in School Self Evaluation*, Lewes, Falmer Press.
Presents an up-to-date theoretical and empirical view of school self-evaluation in England and Wales. It is the outcome of six years of research, undertaken in the School of Education at the Open University.

Peters, T and Waterman, R (1982) *In Search of Excellence*, London, Harper and Row.
An American bestseller on successful corporate organizations that has had an unprecedented impact on educational thinking.

Purkey, S and Smith, M (1983) 'Effective schools: A review', *Elementary School Journal*, 83, pp427–52.
The original review of the effective schools literature.

Purkey, S and Smith, M (1985) 'School reform: The district policy implications of the effective schools literature', *Elementary School Journal*, 85, pp353–90.
Takes an LEA perspective on the effective schools literature with a view to developing policy at the local level.

Reynolds, D (Ed) (1985) *Studying School Effectiveness*, Lewes, Falmer Press.
A compendium of British accounts on school effectiveness; useful, but less sophisticated than its US counterparts.

Runkel, P *et al* (1979) *Transforming the Schools Capacity for Problem Solving*, Eugene, OR, GEPM, University of Oregon.
An important and serious effort to understand the process of change in schools.

Rutter, M *et al* (1979) *Fifteen Thousand Hours*, London, Open Books.
A major British study on school effectiveness that clearly demonstrated that individual schools can made a difference.

Sarason, S (1982) *The Culture of the School and the Problem of Change*, 2nd edn, Boston, MA, Allyn and Boston.
A seminal and classic book that squarely confronted and highlighted the concept of the culture of the school.

SCHMUCK, R and RUNKEL, P (1985) *The Handbook of Organizational Development in Schools*, 3rd edn, Palo Alto, CA, Mayfield.
An authoritative and comprehensive guide to the strategies and activities that can assist in achieving effective change at the school level.

SHOWERS, B (1985) 'Teachers coaching teachers', *Educational Leadership*, 42, 7, April, pp43–8.
Documents the contribution of coaching to the range of strategies for inservice at the school level.

VAN VELZEN, W *et al* (1985) *Making School Improvement Work*, Leuven, Belgium, ACCO.
The book on ISIP: discusses analytically the initial concepts, strategies and cases emanating from the project.

Publications from the International School Improvement Project

Published

Hopes, C (Ed) (1986) *The School Leader and School Improvement.*
Case studies from ten OECD countries, 432 pages. (ISIP Technical Report).

Hopkins, D (1985) *School Based Review for School Improvement.*
A preliminary state of the art, 95 pages. (ISIP Technical Report).

Loucks-Horsley, S and Crandall, D (1986) *The External Support System Profile.*
An instrument for analyzing external support for school improvement, 80 pages.
(ISIP Technical Report).

van Velzen, WG, Miles, MB, Ekholm, M, Hameyer, U and Robin, D (1985)
Making School Improvement Work.
A conceptual guide to practice, 315 pages. (ISIP book).

In Press

Blum, R and Butler, J (Eds) *School Leader Development for School Improvement.*
Bollen, R and Hopkins, D *School-Based Review: Towards a Praxis.*
Hopkins, D (Ed) *Doing School-Based Review: Instruments and Guidelines.*
Louis, K *et al* (Eds) *Supporting School Improvement: Structures, Policies and Strategies.*
Louis, K and van Velzen, W (Eds) *Key Issues in School Improvement Policy Making.*
Miles, M *et al* (Eds) *Lasting School Improvement: Exploring the Process of Institutionalization.*
Petri, M *et al* *School Development: Organizational and Educational Models.*
Robin, D *Evaluation with Weak Data.*
Stego, E *et al* (Eds) *The Role of School Leaders in School Improvement.*
Van den Berg, R and Vandenberghe, R *Strategies for Large-scale Change in Education: Dilemmas and Solutions.*
Van den Berg, R and Hameyer, U (Eds) *Dissemination of Innovations from an Implementation Perspective.*
All these books are or will be published by ACCO Publishing Co., Tiensestraat
134–136, 3000 Leuven, Belgium and are obtainable from that address.

Improving the Quality of Schooling: UK Conference. List of Participants

Miss R Abbot	Education Officer, London Borough of Ealing, Education Offices, Hadley House, 79/81 Uxbridge Road, London, W5 5SU
R Abbott	School Curriculum Development Committee, Newcombe House, 45 Notting Hill Gate, London, W11 3JB
B Arthur	Her Majesty's Chief Inspector, Department of Education and Science, Elizabeth House, York Road, London, SE1 7PH
M Ash	Senior General Adviser, Southern Area Education Office, St Helen Court, County Hall, Bond Street, Ipswich, 1P4 2JR
Ms A Baker	Warden, Haringey Teachers' Centre, 336 Philip Lane, Tottenham, N15 4AB
K Baker	Senior Adviser, Avon Education Department, PO Box 57, Avon House North, St James Barton, Bristol, ES99 7EB
M Baxter	Senior Adviser, Buckinghamshire Education Department, County Hall, Aylesbury, Buckinghamshire
PJ Bibb	Education Officer, Haringey Education Service, 48–62 Station Road, Wood Green, London
R Blackwell	Education Officer (Secondary), London Borough of Waltham Forest, Municipal Offices, High Road, Leyton, London, E10 5QJ
R Bolam	Director, National Development Centre for School Management Training, 35 Berkeley Square, Bristol, BS8 1JA
R Bollen	General Pedagogic Study Centre (APS), Buitenveldertselaan 106, Postbus 7888. 1008 AB Amsterdam

P Bowden	Chief Inspector (Schools), City of Newcastle Upon Tyne, Civic Centre, Newcastle Upon Tyne, NE1 8PU
Miss P Brain	Headteacher, Southfield School, Kettering, Northamptonshire
A Breed	Headteacher, Higham Lane School, Nuneaton, Warwickshire, CV10 0BJ
J Burchill	Inspector of Schools, London Borough of Croydon, Education Department, Taberner House, Park Lane, Croydon, Surrey, CR9 1TP
JW Carnall	Principal Education Officer, Southern Area Education Office, St Helen Court, County Hall, Bond Street, Ipswich
P Cates	Assistant County Education Officer, Shropshire County Council, Education Department, Shire Hall, Shrewsbury, Shropshire
HR Cathcart	Head of Department, Further Professional Studies in Education, The Queen's University of Belfast
WH Cavill	Senior Adviser, Rotherham Education Department, Norfolk House, Walker Place, Rotherham S65 1ES
EL Clark	Senior Adviser, Devon County Council, County Hall, Exeter, Devon
C Clerkin	Headteacher, Manor JM and I School, Richardson Road, London, E15 3BA
P Clift	Educational Researcher, Open University, Walton Hall, Milton Keynes, Bucks, MK7 6AA
D Cloke	Warden, West Devon Teachers' Centre, Ernesettle, Plymouth, Devon, PL5 2PY
NA Coates	Chief Inspector, Wolverhampton Education Authority, Civic Centre, St Peter's Square, Wolverhampton, WV1 1RR
D Cooper	Education Consultant, 48 West End, March, Cambridgeshire, PE 15 8D1
Mrs J Cottee	Headteacher, Didcot Girls' School, Sherwood Road, Didcot, Oxon, OX11 0DA
D Cracknell	Deputy County Education Officer, East Sussex County Council, Education Offices, PO Box 4, County Hall, St Anne's Crescent, Lewes, East Sussex, BN7 1SG

D Crandall	Executive Director, The Network Inc, 290 South Main Street, Andover, Massachusetts 01810, USA
GJ Crompton	Deputy Director of Education Services, Doncaster Education Department, Princegate, Doncaster, DN1 3EP
L Dale	Headteacher, Montsaye School, Greening Road, Rothwell, Kettering, Northants
Ms C Davies	Adviser, Shropshire County Council, Education Department, Shire Hall, Shrewsbury, Shropshire
Mrs E Davies	Headteacher, Whitehall School, Cowley Road, Uxbridge, Middlesex
KP Davies	Chief Adviser, Mid Glamorgan County Council, County Hall, Cathays Park, Cardiff
PN Davies	Inspector of Schools, Wolverhampton Education Department, Civic Centre, St Peter's Square, Wolverhampton, WV1 1RR
CW Day	School of Education, University of Nottingham, University Park, Nottingham, Notts, NG7 2RD
J Dewy	Deputy Director of Education, Education Offices, Gateway House, Standishgate, Wigan WN1 1XL
RH Duckworth	Principal Education Officer, County Offices, Newland, Lincoln
MH Edwards	County Education Officer, Norfolk County Council, Education Department, County Hall, Martineau Lane, Norwich
DG Esp	Director of Education, County Offices, Newland, Lincolnshire
FB Fidler	Lecturer in School Management, Bulmershe College of Higher Education, Earley, Reading, Berkshire
JS Fitzpatrick	Assistant County Education Officer, Northamptonshire Education Department, Northampton House, Northampton, Northamptonshire
Mrs J Fogg	Headteacher, Longford School, Tachbrook Road, Feltham, Middlesex, TW13 6RE
D Fone	Headteacher, Northfields Upper School, Houghton Road, Dunstable, LU5 5AB
J Fox-Russell	Deputy Headteacher, 1 The Priory, Sedgeley, West Midlands, DY3 3UB

J Francombe	Headteacher, Sandy Upper School, Engayne Avenue, Sandy, SG19 1B2
R Glatter	Professor of Educational Administration, School of Education, Open University, Walton Hall, Milton Keynes, Buckinghamshire
J Glazier	Principal, SE Essex Sixth Form College, Runnymede Chase, Benfleet, Essex, SS7 1TW
D Goddard	Advisory Officer, Education Department, London Borough of Enfield, PO Box 56, Civic Centre, Silver Street, Enfield, EN1 3XQ
B Griffiths	Director of Education, Tameside Metropolitan Borough Education Department, Council Offices, Wellington Road, Ashton-Under-Lyne, Tameside, 026 6DL
G Gyte	Senior Inspector, Northamptonshire Education Department, Northampton House, Northampton, Northamptonshire
P Halsey	Deputy Secretary, Department of Education and Science, Elizabeth House, York Road, London, SE1 7PH
JR Hanson	Director, North-West Educational Management Centre, Montpelier, Spring Hall Lane, Halifax, West Yorkshire
AN Harris	Senior Inspector, Department of Education for Northern Ireland, Rathgael House, Balloo Road, Bangor, County Down, BT19 2PR
M Henley	Northamptonshire Education Department, Northampton House, Northampton, Northamptonshire
P Holly	Lecturer, Cambridge Institute of Education, Shaftesbury Road, Cambridge CB2 2BX
J Hood	Senior Education Adviser, Darlington Education Office, 'Craig Lea', Uplands Road, Darlington, County Durham
J Howard	Headteacher, Henry Gotch School, Kettering, Northamptonshire
DM Howe	Area Inspector, Education Department, 22 Northgate Street, Warwick, CV34 4SR
J Howells	Acting Headteacher, The Buckpool School, Brierley Hill Road, Wordsley, Stourbridge, West Midlands
Miss L Hubah	BEMAS, 8 Worcester Road, Walthamstow, London, E1T 5QR

G Hutchinson	Director of Education, Enfield Education Department, PO Box 56, The Civic Centre, Silver Street, Enfield, EN1 3XQ
DG Hutt	District Inspector, Education Offices, Tipping Street Stafford, ST16 2DH
M Inman	President, NAS/UWT, The Grove Farm, Waterfall, Waterhouses, Stoke on Trent, Staffordshire
QJ Johnston	Lecturer in Education, Queen's University of Belfast, University Road, Belfast, BT7 1NN
D Jones	Headteacher, Sir Christopher Hatton School, Wellingborough, Northamptonshire
Miss G Jones	Adviser, Education Department, London Borough of Enfield, PO Box 56, Civic Centre, Silver Street, Enfield, EN1 3XQ
RG Jones	Area Education Officer, Arundel Towers, Portland Terrace, Southampton.
Mrs O Kanu	Student, Department of International and Comparative Education, London Institute of Education, 20 Bedford Way, London, WC1H 0AL
D Keith	Organization Development Consultant, The OD Unit, Tapton Campus, Darwin Lane, Sheffield
Miss E Keville	Southern Education and Libraries Board, 3 Charlemont Place, The Mall, Armagh, Northern Ireland
P Laderriere	Principal Administrator, OECD/CERI, 2 Rue Andre Pacal, 75775 Paris, Cedix 16, France
Mrs J Lamb	Chairman, Education Committee, City of Newcastle Upon Tyne, Civic Centre, Newcastle Upon Tyne, NE1 8PU
M Lavelle	Organization Development Consultant, The OD Unit, Tapton Campus, Darwin Lane, Sheffield
R Lavender	Senior Inspector, Essex Education Department, PO Box 47, Threadneedle House, Market Road, Chelmsford, CM1 1LD
D Lawton	Director, London Institute of Education, 20 Bedford Way, London WC1H 0AL
TG Ledgard	Headteacher, Atherstone School, Long Street, Atherstone, Warwickshire, CV9 1AE

BN Lee	Chief Adviser, Rotherham Education Department, Norfolk House, Walker Place, Rotherham, 56S 1ES
L Lewis	14–16 Project Coordinator for Northamptonshire, 17 St John's Way, Piddington, Northamptonshire
M Lovett	General Inspector, Northamptonshire Education Department, Northampton House, Northampton, Northamptonshire
JWG MacGregor	Senior Assistant Director of Education, Education Department, Regional Headquarters, Fife House, North Street, Glenrothes, Fife
Mrs H McClenaghan	Senior Education Officer, Southern Education and Libraries Board, 3 Charlemont Place, The Mall, Armagh, Northern Ireland
JT McLoughlin	Assistant Director of Education, City of Newcastle Upon Tyne, Civic Centre, Newcastle Upon Tyne, NE1 8PU
JS Maclure	Editor, Times Educational Supplement, Priory House, St John's Lane, London, EC1M 4BX
R McMullen	Senior County Adviser, Lancashire Education Committee, PO Box 61, Preston
DA McNeill	Senior Depute Director of Education, Fife Regional Council, Education Department, Regional Headquarters, Fife House, North Street, Glenrothes, Fife, KY7 SLT
K McWilliams	Chief Executive, School Curriculum Development Committee, Newcombe House, 45 Notting Hill Gate, London, W11 3JB
Mrs P Marino	Reorganization Centre, Fleeming Road, Walthamstow, London
Ms S Markless	NFER, The Mere, Upton Park, Slough, Berkshire, SL1 2DQ
D Martin	Headteacher, Chenderit School, Archery Road, Middleton Cheney, Banbury, Oxon, OX17 2QR
E Marx	Rijksuniversiteit Leiden, Subfaculteit der Sociologie, Postbus 9508, 2300 RA Leiden, Netherlands
MJ Mason	Director of Education, Tameside Metropolitan Borough Education Department, Council Offices, Wellington Road, Ashton-Under-Lyne, Tameside, 026 6DL

C Metcalf	NUT Representative, 23 Broomfield Road, Tilehurst, Reading, Berks, RG3 6AJ
Ms R Micklem	Professional Assistant, Northamptonshire Education Department, Northampton House, Northampton, Northamptonshire
IC Middlebrough	General Adviser, Teachers' Centre, Royton Town Hall, Rochdale Road, Oldham
Miss D Moir	Headteacher, Cowes High School, Crossfield Avenue, Cowes, Isle of Wight
Mrs J Mundy	Sheffield City Polytechnic, Pond Street, Sheffield, S1 1WB
G Newman	Coventry Education Department, New Council Offices, Earl Street, Coventry, CV1 5RS
T Nolan	Chief Officer, South Eastern Education and Libraries Board, 18 Windsor Avenue, Belfast, BT9 6EP
Sister J O'Reilly	Headteacher, St Dominics High School, Falls Road, Belfast, BT1Z 6AE
Sister A O'Shea	11–16 Programme, Stranmillis College, Belfast, BT9 5DU
Mrs G Ogden	Chairman, Education Committee, Northamptonshire LEA, Northampton House, Northampton, Northamptonshire
D Oliver	Headteacher, Eaglescliffe Comprehensive School, Urlay Nook Road, Eaglescliffe, Cleveland, TS16 0LA
GL Otley	Nene College, Moulton Park Campus, Boughton Green Road, Northampton
G Papadopoulos	Deputy Director for Education, OECD, 2 rue Andre Pascal, 75775 Paris, Cedex 16, France
IT Parry	Chief Adviser, West Glamorgan County Council, Education Department
Islwyn Parry	TRIST Coordinator, Technical and Vocational Education Centre, Bridge Street, Llangefny, Gwynedd
AJ Parsons	Director of Education, London Borough of Brent, Chesterfield House, 9 Park Lane, Wembley, Middlesex, HA9 7RW
NA Paterson	Assistant Deputy Director of Education, Education Department, County Hall, Glenfield, Leicestershire

AC Perry   Principal Education Adviser, Newham Education Dept, 379/383 High Street, Stratford, London, E15 4RD

M Petri: Algemeen Pedagogisch Studiecentrum, Buitenveldertselaan 106, 1008 AB Amsterdam, Netherlands

Miss A Reilly   Education Adviser, Berkshire Education Department, Shinfield Park, Reading, RG2 9XE

Mrs E Ricatti   Ispettrice Tecnica per la Lombardia, Via Tintoretto 8, 20145 Milano, Italy

R Richardson   Principal Adviser, Brent Education Dept, Chesterfield House, Park Lane, Wembley, HA4 7RW

P Robertshaw   General Adviser, Derbyshire Education Department, County Offices, Matlock, Derbyshire, DE4 3AG

Theodora Samuel   BEMAS, 68 Glebelands Avenue, Newbury Park, Ilford, Essex, IG2 7DL

T Scholey   Chief Inspector, Northamptonshire Education Department, Northampton House, Northampton, Northamptonshire

J Scott   Principal, Ballee High School, Ballee Road, Ballymena, County Antrim

R Selby   Chief Adviser, Education Offices, County Hall, Northallerton, North Yorkshire

M Shorney   Chief Inspector/Adviser, Clwyd Education Department, Shire Hall, Mold, Clwyd

KF Skelton   Senior Education Officer, Doncaster Education Department, Princegate, Doncaster, DN1 3EP

M Smith   Senior Adviser (Secondary Education), Sheffield Education Authority, PO Box 67, Leopold Street, Sheffield

P Smith   TVEI Office, Cliftonville Middle School, Cliftonville Road, Northampton, NN1 5BW

T Smith   Chief Inspector of Schools, Room 281, County Hall, London, SE1 7PB

PJ Snell   Headteacher, Preston Manor School, Carlton Avenue East, Wembley, Middlesex, HA9 8NA

N Speers   Stranmillis College, Stranmillis Road, Belfast, BT9 5DY

CJ Spivey   Director, Centre for the Study of Comprehensive

	Schools, Wentworth College, University of York, York, YO1 5DD.
SD Steadman	School Curriculum Development Committee, Newcombe House, 45 Notting Hill Gate, London, W11 3JB
E Stego	Director, School Leader Education, Box 249, 5-581 02 Linkoping, Sweden
Mrs M Stephenson	Headteacher, Brudenell County Secondary School for Girls, Stanley Hill, Amersham, HP7 9HH
Ms J Stocks	Cambridge Institute of Education, Shaftesbury Road, Cambridge CB2 2BX
H Tangerud	Research Consultant, Valdresgt 1B, 0557, Oslo 5, Norway
FW Taylor	Senior Adviser, Metropolitan Borough of Knowsley Education Office, Huyton Hey Road, Huyton, Merseyside, L36 5YH
AM Thomson	Depute Director of Education, Tayside House, 28 Crichton Street, Dundee
CC Tipple	Director of Education, Education Department, County Hall, Morpeth, Northumberland
H Tomlinson	Headteacher, Manor School, Northdowns Road, Cheadle Hulme, Cheadle, Cheshire
E Tweddle	Deputy County Education Officer, Surrey Education Department, County Hall, Penrhyn Road, Kingston upon Thames, KT1 2DJ
RG Wallace	Chief Adviser, Education Department, County Hall, Hertford SG13 8DF
WS Walton	Chief Education Officer, Sheffield Education Authority, PO Box 67, Leopold Street, Sheffield, S1 1RJ
CG Way	Chief Inspector of Schools, Norfolk County Council, Education Department, County Hall, Martineau Lane, Norwich
R Weindling	Head of Educational Management Department, National Foundation for Educational Research, The Mere, Upton Park, Slough, Berkshire, SL1 2DQ
RO Williams	Principal Adviser (Secondary Education), Dean Education Centre, Belford Road, Edinburgh, EH4 3DS

NE Willis	Assistant Director, Council for Educational Technology, 3 Devonshire Street, London W1N 2BA
P Wingfield	Headteacher, Manor School, Mountbatten Way, Raunds, Wellingborough, NN9 6ND
P Worrall	Principal, Moat Community College, Maidstone Road, Leicester, LE2 OTU

Notes on the Contributors

Ray Bolam is Director of the National Development Centre and Director of Further Professional Studies in the School of Education, University of Bristol. He is also a member of the UK ISIP Steering Group.

Robert Bollen is a staff member at the General Pedagogic Centre in the Netherlands. In ISIP he acted as Coordinator of Area One and is now Chair of the ISIP Foundation.

Phil Clift is a lecturer in education at the Open University and a member of the UK ISIP Steering Group.

Don Cooper is an educational consultant associated with the School Curriculum Development Committee.

David Crandall is Executive Director of the NETWORK Inc., an educational research and development centre and regional laboratory in Massachusetts, USA.

Jan Depoortere is an external change agent (representing the Catholic schools) responsible for the organization and guidance of the RPS project in the Flemish speaking part of Belgium.

Peter Earley is a research officer at the National Foundation for Educational Research.

Ron Glatter is Professor of educational administration and management at the Open University and a member of the UK ISIP steering group.

Philip Halsey is a Deputy Secretary at the Department of Education and Science.

Johan Hellyn is an external change agent (representing the state schools) responsible for the organization and guidance of the RPS project in the Flemish speaking part of Belgium.

Michael Henley is County Education Officer for Northamptonshire and Chair of the UK ISIP Steering Group.

Peter Holly is a tutor at the Cambridge Institute of Education.

David Hopkins is a tutor at the Cambridge Institute of Education.

Keith McWilliams is Chief Executive of the School Curriculum Development Committee and a member of the UK ISIP Steering Group.

Stuart Maclure is Editor of the *Times Educational Supplement*.

George Papadopoulos is Deputy Director for Education, Organization for Economic Cooperation and Development.

Eloisa Ricatti is a school inspector in the province of Lombardy, Italy.

Peter Smith is Coordinator of the TVEI project in Northamptonshire.

Marc de Soete is an external change agent (representing the municipal schools) responsible for the organization and guidance of the RPS project in the Flemish speaking part of Belgium.

Eskil Stego is Co-Director of the School Leader Education Progamme in Sweden.

Hans Tangerud is a research consultant at the Ministry of Education, Norway.

Wim van Velzen is the Deputy Director General for Secondary and Further Education in the Netherlands and one of the originators of ISIP.

Richard Wallace is the Superintendent of Schools in Pittsburgh, USA.

Dick Wiendling is Head of the Educational Management Department at the National Foundation for Educational Research.

Index

Pages numbers in *italics* refer to tables and figures, those followed by 'n' refer to notes, and those followed by 'r' refer to references.